PHILOSOPHIC
PERSPECTIVE
FASHION

PHILOSOPHICAL PERSPECTIVES ON FASHION

Edited by Giovanni Matteucci and Stefano Marino

Bloomsbury Academic
An imprint of Bloomsbury Publishing Plc

B L O O M S B U R Y
LONDON • OXFORD • NEW YORK • NEW DELHI • SYDNEY

Bloomsbury Academic
An imprint of Bloomsbury Publishing Plc

50 Bedford Square
London
WC1B 3DP
UK

1385 Broadway
New York
NY 10018
USA

www.bloomsbury.com

BLOOMSBURY and the Diana logo are trademarks of Bloomsbury Publishing Plc

First published 2017

British Library Cataloguing-in-Publication Data
A catalogue record for this book is available from the British Library.

ISBN: HB: 978-1-4742-3747-5
PB: 978-1-4742-3746-8
ePDF: 978-1-4742-3749-9
ePub: 978-1-4742-3748-2

Library of Congress Cataloging-in-Publication Data
Names: Matteucci, Giovanni. | Marino, Stefano, 1936–
Title: Philosophical perspectives on fashion / edited by Giovanni Matteucci and Stefano Marino, University of Bologna, Italy.
Description: London ; New York : Bloomsbury Academic, an imprint of Bloomsbury Publishing Plc, 2017.
Identifiers: LCCN 2016025272 | ISBN 9781474237475 (hardback) | ISBN 9781474237468 (paperback) | ISBN 9781474237482 (epub) | ISBN 9781474237499 (epdf)
Subjects: LCSH: Fashion--Social aspects. | Aesthetics--Social aspects. | Fashion--Philosophy. | Clothing and dress--Philosophy. | BISAC: DESIGN / Fashion. | PHILOSOPHY / General. | ART / Criticism & Theory. | PHILOSOPHY / Aesthetics.
Classification: LCC GT525 .P47 2017 | DDC 391–dc23 LC record available at https://lccn.loc.gov/2016025272

Cover design: Sharon Mah

Typeset by RefineCatch Limited, Bungay, Suffolk
Printed and bound in India

CONTENTS

List of Illustrations vii

INTRODUCTION: PHILOSOPHICAL PERSPECTIVES ON FASHION 1

Giovanni Matteucci and Stefano Marino, University of Bologna, Italy

1 **PHILOSOPHICAL ACCOUNTS OF FASHION IN THE NINETEENTH AND TWENTIETH CENTURY: A HISTORICAL RECONSTRUCTION** 11

Stefano Marino, University of Bologna, Italy

2 **FASHION: A CONCEPTUAL CONSTELLATION** 47

Giovanni Matteucci, University of Bologna, Italy

3 **ANTI-FASHION: IF NOT FASHION, THEN WHAT?** 73

Nickolas Pappas, The Graduate Center, CUNY, United States

4 **FITS OF FASHION: THE SOMAESTHETICS OF STYLE** 91

Richard Shusterman, Florida Atlantic University, United States

5 **ON FASHION CRITICISM** 107

Lars Svendsen, University of Bergen, Norway

6 **THOUGHT WITHOUT CONCEPT: CAROL CHRISTIAN POELL'S PARADOXICAL AESTHETICS** 119

Christian Michel, Université de Picardie Jules-Verne (Amiens), France

7 **CAPRICES OF FASHION IN CULTURE AND BIOLOGY: CHARLES DARWIN'S AESTHETICS OF "ORNAMENT"** 137

Winfried Menninghaus, Max Planck Institute for Empirical Aesthetics (Frankfurt am Main), Germany

8 **FASHIONABLE PROTEUS: ESSAY ON THE EUPHORIA OF FASHION FOR FASHION'S SAKE IN AN AGE OF SHALLOWNESS** 151

César Moreno-Márquez, University of Seville, Spain

9 **THE FASCINATION OF CONTINGENCY: FASHION AND MODERN SOCIETY** 175

Elena Esposito, University of Modena and Reggio Emilia, Italy

Index of Names 191
Index of Subjects 195

LIST OF ILLUSTRATIONS

1.1. Oscar Wilde, portrait, 1890. Photo by Universal History Archive/UIG via Getty Images. 17

1.2. A woman being dressed with the aid of long poles to lift her crinoline dress over the hoops. Photo by London Stereoscopic Company/Getty Images. 27

2.1. The fashion designer Paul Poiret as a painter, 1933. Photo by Unionbild/ullstein bild via Getty Images. 49

2.2. Different kinds of experience of beauty. © Giovanni Matteucci. 70

3.1. Ms. 9243 Chroniques de Hainault, Dedication page: Filippo III il Buono di Borgogna riceve un manoscritto. Bibliotheque Royale Albert I, Bruxelles. © 2016. Photo Art Resource/Scala, Florence. 77

3.2. Panathenaic prize amphora (*c.* 530 BC), attributed to the Euphiletos Painter. The Metropolitan Museum of Art, New York. 84

4.1. Different branches and dimensions of somaesthetics and of their interrelations. © Richard Shusterman. 104

6.1. Overlock-seam. Photographer: Christian Michel. 122

6.2. Chain-seam. Photographer: Christian Michel. 123

6.3. Invisible-seam. Photographer: Deepti Barth. © 2015 C.C.P. Srl Italy. 125

6.4. Dead-end scar. Photographer: Deepti Barth. © 2015 C.C.P. Srl Italy 129

7.1. J. de Lajoüe Jn. and G. Huquier (1735). La Fontaine—A Paris chez Huquier vis a vis le Grand Chatelet avec privilege du Roy. © Staatliche Museen zu Berlin, Kunstbibliothek. 141

7.2. Johann Baptist Sonderland (1805–78). Stock Certificate Harpener Bergbau AG. © Museum Wertpapierwelt/Stiftung Sammlung historischer Wertpapiere (Museum for Historical Stock Certificates), Olten, Switzerland. 143

8.1. Paris Fashion Week Haute Couture S/S 2010—Givenchy. Photo by Dominique Charriau/WireImage/Getty Images. 158

8.2. Lindsay Lohan shopping in Milan. Photo by Robino Salvatore/GC Images/Getty Images. 161
9.1. Jean de la Bruyère, *c.* 1670–96. Photo by Kean Collection/Archive Photos/Getty Images. 177
9.2. Coco Chanel, 1929. Photo by ullstein bild/ullstein bild via Getty Images. 183

INTRODUCTION: PHILOSOPHICAL PERSPECTIVES ON FASHION

Giovanni Matteucci and Stefano Marino

Fashion represents one of the most relevant, fascinating, and, to some extent, also difficult to comprehend, phenomena of the modern age, if not a phenomenon characterizing in various ways the entire history of the human species. In this respect the theorists' views largely differ, opposing those who see an intrinsic connection between the essence of fashion and the spirit of modernity to those who, vice versa, have a "universalistic" approach and thus understand fashion as something whose roots lie in the very nature of the human being as such, and not in the spirit of a particular epoch in the history of mankind.[1] In any case, it is out of doubt that fashion represents one of the cultural forms that perfectly embody the heterogeneous, multiform, contradictory, to some extent perhaps superficial but also exciting tendencies of the present age. From this point of view, fashion can be assumed as a mirror of the contemporary age and appears then of decisive importance in order to gain insight into ourselves and the world we live in.

Although often criticized because of its frivolous character and put aside until recent times as a topic considered not being worthy of broadly speaking intellectual consideration, for the past few decades now fashion apparently seems to have been recognized in its significance by a growing public of both common people and academic scholars. Gradually it has thus acquired the status of a subject worthy of scientific inquiry, notwithstanding the persistence of some resistances to this kind of recognition that must not be withheld. More precisely, it is apparent that since the early 1980s there has been a real "explosion" of fashion studies and theories that may be understood, among other things, as a consequence of a wide movement of redefinition, rethinking, and, so to speak, reweighting (or leveling, from the point of view of various critics of such tendencies) of cultural spheres and hierarchies that can be associated, in turn, to the advent of the so-called "postmodern condition" (Lyotard 1999). It is thus not by accident that several distinguished fashion theorists have established an essential, intrinsic connection between the rise of fashion as a decisively influencing factor on our lives and also as a subject of scientific inquiry, on the one hand, and the entrance in the postmodern age, on the other hand. At the same time, the fashion/postmodernity relationship should not be overemphasized, inasmuch as the relative crisis that seems to affect to some extent postmodern thought today—and that is perhaps testified, in the specific field of philosophy, by the gradual weakening of hermeneutics and postmodernism as leading philosophical paradigms—does not imply in any way, in our view, a parallel crisis in the field of fashion studies and theories.

Quite the contrary, even a brief survey of the field reveals that, if until very recent times fashion could not "at any rate be said to be a fashionable theme in philosophy" (given that, notwithstanding the 1980s–1990s "stream of academic publications on fashion," with a few exceptions "these have not been written by philosophers" (Svendsen 2006: 17)), at least to some extent the situation has changed and so today it is also possible to find philosophical entries in the main bibliographies of fashion studies. It is precisely within this general trend, as we will further explain, that the present collection also aims to place itself and should therefore be contextualized. What has been just said, however, does not exclude that philosophical works still remain a minority in the field of fashion studies. In other words, and plainly speaking, although philosophical research on fashion cannot be said to be entirely missing, it is nevertheless true that the major part of scientific inquiries into fashion have been and are conducted with sociological, psychological, anthropological or cultural studies-influenced approaches.

This has perhaps to do with the very nature of philosophy as it has been conceived in the Western tradition from Plato onwards, namely as a theoretical activity concentrated on the non-transient and profound essence of things. Conversely fashion has rather and always to do, because of its very nature, with surfaces, appearances, transience, and mere play of forms. So, although the history of nineteenth- and twentieth-century philosophy shows that a heterogeneous group of thinkers expressed a genuine curiosity and interest about clothing and fashion, and although various authors have recently attempted at developing philosophical (and, in particular, aesthetic) inquiries into fashion,[2] it still remains true that there is a gap on this point, namely on the fashion/philosophy relationship, that needs to be filled. Our present goal lies precisely in the attempt to contribute to the filling of this gap by calling for a specifically philosophical in-depth analysis of fashion, where "specifically philosophical" is referred here to interpretations and perspectives basically based on a conceptual approach (rather than on empirical research, mathematical-experimental method or other approaches otherwise characterizing the field of science). A conceptual approach that we assume to be the characteristic approach of strictly speaking philosophical work, also following an insight provided by Ernst Cassirer who once defined Socrates' so-called discovery of concept and its further developments as the fundamental event of the entire history of Western thought (see Cassirer 1981: 275–87).

As Herbert Spencer once noted, fashion is a phenomenon that "is difficult to deal with in a systematic way" (Spencer 1966: 205). In our view, this is due to the nature of both fashion and philosophy. On the one hand, the topic "Fashion" may be inquired into from different points of view, because of the well-known protean and ultimately ambiguous nature of fashion itself. On the other hand, the existence of different philosophical ways of approaching the same subjects or contents by means of conceptual analysis testifies the constitutively multiform nature of philosophy as such and, in particular, of contemporary philosophy. Given all this, it is appropriate to speak here of "interpretations" and "perspectives" in the plural form. The present book consists of nine chapters, each autonomous from the other, but at the same time all united both by a common subject, namely fashion, and a common general framework, represented by the abovementioned conceptual approach. In conceiving and structuring our volume this way we have been guided by the conviction that a collection of different contributions from various authors, although probably lacking the systematic consistency of a monograph (which, however, is sometimes obtained at the price of a lack, in turn, of variety and pluralism), would be more coherent and fitting with the variety, the unending dynamism, and the pluralist character of the matter itself at issue, namely fashion. The nine chapters of the book address different aspects of this complex and fascinating phenomenon, mostly focusing on fashion as referred to the experience of clothing but at the same time highlighting the way in which fashion, understood in its essence or concept, may apply to many other domains of the human experience, virtually to the human experience in its entirety.

Our proposed selection and organization of the materials, our approach, and our treatment of the subject, are aimed at providing a somehow unique combination of methodological accuracy and argumentative rigorousness applied to such a popular and (seemingly . . .) light or simple subject. It is our hope that this will encourage a broad audience—potentially ranging from philosophers to academics and students of various disciplines (fashion studies, art history, sociology, psychology, philosophy, cultural studies, humanities) to a wider public of common people theoretically or even practically, i.e., in their everyday-life experience, attracted by fashion—to read the book and discover in, through, and beyond it innovative ways of dealing with things that everyone of us consciously or unconsciously has to do with most every day. It is our basic conviction that such publications as the proposed one are actually much needed in the field of *philosophy*, in order to contribute to bridging the gap between a certain tendency to excessive abstraction and even asceticism that has sometimes characterized philosophical reflection, on the one hand, and the attention to the manifestations and even appearances of the "real world" that is nevertheless required from all of us, on the other hand. But the same need goes for the field of *fashion studies*. As a matter of fact, it is probably true that:

> There is no one set of ideas or no single conceptual framework with which fashion might be defined, analysed and critically explained. [...] Rather, there are theories about fashion or, to put it another way, there are fashion theories. What one finds is that various and diverse academic disciplines apply themselves or are applied to the practices, institutions, personnel and objects that constitute fashion. [...] There are many academic disciplines, then, that take an interest in the history, analysis, and critical explanation of fashion. Each discipline will have its own idea, or theory, of what fashion is and of what sorts of activities count as analysis and explanation.
>
> **BARNARD** 2007: 7–8

It is precisely the aim of this book to try to show that also philosophical approaches, beside those of other abovementioned disciplines, can prove to be useful in order to gain a better understanding of such a complex and elusive expression of the human culture as fashion.

Having taught and lectured in Philosophical Aesthetics at the Degree Course in "Fashion Cultures and Techniques" at the University of Bologna for many years now, and having confronted our opinions with colleagues and also students, we have understood that the world of fashion studies is precisely in need of works that may open new horizons and directions in the interpretation of fashion, as we assume a philosophical account of it will do. This is why we felt so motivated to publish a book on this subject now, hoping that our proposal may be welcomed as a source of ideas, insight, and information: more precisely, as a valuable contribution to contemporary fashion theory, one that enriches the way one looks at the form, purpose, and meaning of fashion.

Both the two first contributions, written by the book editors, have to some extent the character of a reconstruction: a historical-philosophical reconstruction, the former, and a conceptual reconstruction also containing a specific theoretical proposal, the latter. In his essay, Stefano Marino moves from the assumption that, notwithstanding the great importance of clothing and fashion for the human being, there has been until recent times a general intellectual tendency to ignore them. Now, if this is true for the field of the social sciences, as various scholars have argued, it is even more valid and appropriate for philosophy. At the same time, however, a survey of the field shows that various philosophers expressed a genuine interest in fashion, sometimes only in a cursory way, but at other times in a more systematic way. The aim of the author is thus to provide a historical reconstruction of some stages in the development of a philosophical discourse on fashion during the nineteenth and twentieth centuries, and also to show that fashion, should one want to assign it to a particular domain within the great field of philosophical disciplines, would definitely need to be assigned to the field of aesthetics and thus considered as an aesthetic problem. Giovanni Matteucci's contribution, for his part, highlights, by means of a survey of the main philosophical implications of fashion, how the latter may lead to a general rethinking of the aesthetic phenomenon. This essay is systematically divided into four parts, the first of which deals with the question concerning the place of fashion within the existing cultural system and is meant to rehabilitate the nature of the aesthetic as everyday practice, thus criticizing the traditional ideology of the fine arts. The second part discusses the categorial structure of fashion, by virtue of which the aesthetic appears as a dynamic field exceeding one-sided definitions, while the third part is dedicated to an understanding of fashion as an anthropological problem and especially deals with aesthetic factors participating to the constitution of our identity. A crucial aspect of this analysis is the concept of the aesthetic as a "form of life," i.e., as the space in which "institutionalizing" but not "institutionalized" practices arise: practices that possess a normative, binding, and distinctive character without being prescriptive or discriminating, and therefore rooted in the everydayness. Finally, the fourth part dwells on the specific ("Adonic") experience of beauty that is characteristic of fashion, where the aesthetic corresponds to an ephemeral but original kind of appearance. According to the author, fashion thus proves to be a constellation, a field rich in relations and tensions between mutually irreducible poles, that finds its fulfillment in the moment of its manifestation, thus amounting to an essential source of meaningfulness that appears particularly efficient today.

The next three contributions, by Nickolas Pappas, Richard Shusterman, and Lars Svendsen, display particular philosophical perspectives by focusing on crucial issues. In his essay, Nickolas Pappas starts with the observation that one way that philosophers understand an object is by understanding what it is not. But approaching fashion this way, as Pappas explains, yields several opposites: the unfashionable, or dress before fashion, etc. By another route we find the specific kind of rejection of fashion known as "anti-fashion." According to Pappas, if fashion rests on the mechanism of social imitativeness, anti-fashion represents instead the attempt to justify social presentation without reference to social forces. In antiquity, Greek athletic nudity and black dress in several cultures worked as anti-fashion, whereas today's anti-fashions include jeans, black clothing, tattoos, the shaved head, and the man's suit. Anti-fashions, so Pappas, are typically male, often arise in religious contexts, and tend to abide a long time without changing. To some extent they all bear witness to the (male) body, taking that body as the natural object that determines the appearance, and justifies the social function, of the anti-fashion. Based on his personal experience with the fashion industry, in his essay Richard Shusterman—one of the main representatives today of pragmatist aesthetics and the theorist of a new philosophical orientation known as "somaesthetics"—first explains the crucial but theoretically ignored function of the fit model in the making and marketing of clothes, outlining how the model's defining exemplarity as ideal rests paradoxically on being average in a particular, desirable way. The essay then shows how the paradoxical figure of the fit model is emblematic of other important, paradoxical features of fashion that relate more generally to contrasting ambiguities in the concept of style, such as inclusion and exclusion, novelty and familiarity, group identity and personal distinction, classification and evaluation. Shusterman then explores how fashion can be essentially understood as trying to reconcile such opposites or contrasts by integrating them into a dynamic, changing fit. In doing so, he also considers the views of such important theorists as Georg Simmel and Adolf Loos. The contribution of Lars Svendsen moves from the presupposition that the legitimacy of fashion as an aesthetic practice depends on the existence of genuine fashion criticism. However, with some notable exceptions, for Svendsen such criticism is virtually non-existing in the domain of fashion. There has been little tolerance for negative criticism in the realm of fashion, and this marks it off from all the other arts. Fashion criticism places itself somewhere in the continuum between fashion reportage and fashion theory. In Svendsen's view, proper criticism has five major components: evaluation, description, comparison, contextualization, and interpretation. The key feature of criticism is evaluation. Genuine criticism aims at drawing distinctions, separating what is of higher value from that which is only of lesser. The goal of thinking about fashion is not to produce abstract knowledge, but rather to give us the ability to judge, to make distinctions. Which is what fashion criticism should do.

At this point in the book we encounter an intriguing case-study: Christian Michel's philosophical analysis of what he defines as Carol Christian Poell's "paradoxical aesthetics." Poell is an Austrian designer who holes up in a studio in Milan's Naviglio district where he unperturbedly designs collections that he displays to the public only when he pleases. In Poell's work each and every constituting element of a garment (fabrics, stitches, shapes) is interrogated in its structure, function, and meaning. Poell, however, does not only play with fabrics and shapes, but also interrogates the specific identity of what makes a garment, notably its *catastrophic* points (in the sense established by René Thom), i.e., the points where a sudden change appears on a surface (*kata-strophê* meaning "change of form"), where the stitches play a major role. His thoughts, however, are not conceptual, they are neither worded nor verbalized, but incarnated, embodied in the garment: according to Michel, like any artist or craftsman Poell thinks materially. By remaining silent, his thoughts are nevertheless true thoughts, since his works bear the trace of an investigation that: (1) explores all the logical possibilities of a form or a technique; (2) displays them logically and articulates them together; and (3) gives the form/technique both an aesthetical and ontological meaning. In Michel's interpretation, what Poell proposes is a formal and material transposition of the struggle opposing life and death, which constitutes the main theme of his work, and which is revealed through the tension between continuity and discontinuity. This is what defines the Poell garment as essentially paradoxical and makes it possible to explain the contradictory feelings experienced by wearers of these creations: an impression of confidence and omnipotence, as the garment is a shell, but, at the same time, induces a feeling of fragility and anxiety, for it is constantly menaced by loss.

If Michel's contribution is the only one, in the present collection, that concretely deals with the effective creations of a specific fashion designer, Winfried Menninghaus' essay is the only one, in turn, explicitly interlacing philosophical and scientific (more precisely, Darwinist) perspectives. Menninghaus' contribution traces how Charles Darwin renegotiated the close relationship between aesthetics and biology that already informed late eighteenth-century aesthetics, most notably Kant's *Critique of the Power of Judgment*. Darwin did so by creatively projecting both the aesthetics of capricious ornaments and the modern notion of fashion onto his understanding of the many elaborate sexual body ornaments found throughout the animal kingdom (see also Menninghaus 2007: 66–137). For Menninghaus, Darwin's hypothesis regarding the evolution of human naked skin serves as a key example of the novel perspectives opened up by his transformative use of concepts of cultural aesthetics to highlighting key aspects of his evolutionary theory of sexual selection. The anthropological roots of fashion also represent (though in another way) the core of César Moreno-Márquez's essay that methodologically assumes the point of view of "fashion as such" rather than that of "fashions/styles." In his investigation Moreno-Márquez recovers the figure of Proteus (borrowed from Pico della Mirandola) in order to determine the specific trait of the human being and introduce the semio-sociological aspect of the problem. Such an approach allows us to gain a better understanding of the fashion phenomenon from the reflexive, "specular," and spectacular point of view of the desire of being fashionable. In this context, the author pays attention to "euphoric manifestations" (Roland Barthes) of the fashion phenomenon that become significant because of their high level of reflexivity, that actually take place in at least two showing spaces (the "fashion show" and the "street fashion"), and that are also given in a precise temporal dimension, namely that of the quick-time of "fast fashion." On this basis, the author attempts at explaining the reason why we are witnessing today the explosion of such tendencies as "fashion as such" or "fashion for fashion's sake": a minimum of signified for a maximum of signifier. If Proteus constitutes the pillar of diversity and change, Narcissus represents in turn the *ars combinatoria* in the horizon of possibilities of personalization. From this point of view, it is difficult to interpret fashion today as limited to mere imitation. In our disseminated and fragmented societies the ideal condition to be achieved in the world of fashion is not that embodied by imitation but rather that of the "process of personalization" (Gilles Lipovetsky). The "liquid" relations predominating in the social relations of our time require a sort of liquid fashion and liquid "care-for-oneself" that pay attention to the fragmentary, occasional, superficial appearances recognizable by other people. So "fashion for fashion's sake" perfectly fits with the requirements of today's quick life and its peculiar quick time, at the same time working as an accelerator of this same temporality. The last chapter by Elena Esposito assumes a philosophical-sociological perspective and inquires on this basis, in particular, into the decisive question concerning the relationship between fashion and modernity. According to Esposito, fashion is an inherently paradoxical phenomenon, as it was observed in the seventeenth century, namely at the beginning of its diffusion. Fashion relies on different mechanisms that are intertwined and support each other, implementing a very efficient combination of flexibility and reliability, and allowing for a complex and unlikely form of imitation that seems capable of combining the orientation towards others with individual specificity. In Esposito's view, fashion thus involves crucial aspects of modern semantics, as the forms of individuality and the relationship with time. The key issue of her essay is the concept of contingency, which in modern times acquires an unprecedented significance, illustrated by fashion and its forms. In general, the mechanisms that are at the basis of fashion show the spread of contingency in modern society, which moves from necessary and stable references to transitional and fungible references, that hold just because they could be different and one knows it. The observation of fashion allows us to reflect on these changes and their concrete social impact. Fashion always changes, and thereby its variability becomes a stable reference. Furthermore it allows everyone to express his/her originality, imitating models that are the same for everyone, and in this ambition everyone is like everybody else. The efficacy of fashion relies then on an accumulation of paradoxes, showing how contingency can generate its own flexible and complex form of order.

Considering the mutual relationships between aesthetics, modern society and culture, fashion and the fine arts, and the way these relationships have influenced and shaped our views on identity and taste, the contributions collected in this book explore the various intellectual and cultural movements that inform how people dress. As we have noted, the fashion and philosophy scholars contributing to this volume refer to and apply theories posed by key thinkers of the modern and contemporary age, from Darwin and Wittgenstein to Goodman and Barthes, from Simmel and Husserl to Danto and Baudrillard, in order to answer such questions as: "What is the essence of fashion and what are the reasons behind its fascination?"; "What is anti-fashion?"; "What or who do we imitate when we 'follow' fashion?"; "What is fashion criticism and what should it be?"; "Can philosophy remain unconcerned to fashion or can fashion lead philosophy to rethink itself?" To the extent that *Philosophical Perspectives on Fashion* succeeds in contributing to the clarification and disentanglement of such major questions concerning fashion, the book will lead (we hope) to a better and indeed new understanding of the matter at issue, open new theoretical horizons, and thus make significant advancements within this field.

Notes

1 Among the main representatives of these two different interpretive lines one may mention, respectively, Gilles Lipovetsky and René König.

2 Beside Lars Svendsen's attempt to develop a veritable and, so to speak, systematic philosophy of fashion (see Svendsen 2006), other works on fashion that appear as broadly speaking or strictly speaking *philosophically* interesting include those of Lehmann 2000; Meinhold 2005; Scapp and Seitz 2010; Edwards 2011; Wolfendale and Kennett 2011; Gecky and Karaminas 2012; Rocamora and Smelik 2015. More specifically conceived from an aesthetic point of view, that is, aimed at providing an interpretive framework for those aspects of fashion that are mostly interesting for philosophical aesthetics, are—for example—the works of Eckman and Wagner 1995; DeLong 1998 and 2011; Loschek 2009.

Bibliography

Barnard, M. (2007), "Introduction", in M. Barnard (ed.), *Fashion Theory. A Reader*, 1–10, London-New York: Routledge

Cassirer, E. (1981), *Kant's Life and Thought* (1923), trans. J. Haden, New Haven-London: Yale University Press

DeLong, M.R. (1998), *The Way We Look: Dress and Aesthetics*, New York: Fairchild Publications

DeLong, M.R. (2011), *Aesthetics of Dress*, Oxford-New York: Berg

Eckman, M. and J. Wagner (1995), "Aesthetic Aspects of the Consumption of Fashion Design: The Conceptual and Empirical Challenge", *Advances in Consumer Research*, 22: 646–9

Edwards, T. (2011), *Fashion in Focus: Concepts, Practices and Politics*, London-New York: Routledge

Gecky, A. and V. Karaminas, eds (2012), *Fashion and Art*, London: Bloomsbury

Lehmann, U. (2000), *Tigersprung: Fashion in Modernity*, Cambridge (MA)-London: The MIT Press

Loschek, I. (2009), *When Clothes Become Fashion: Design and Innovation Systems*, Oxford-New York: Berg

Lyotard, J.-F. (1999), *The Postmodern Condition: A Report on Knowledge* (1979), trans. G. Bennington and B. Massumi, Minneapolis: University of Minnesota Press

Meinhold, R. (2005), *Der Mode-Mythos: Lifestyle als Lebenskunst*, Würzburg: Königshausen & Neumann

Menninghaus, W. (2007), *Das Versprechen des Schönheit* (2003), Frankfurt a.M.: Suhrkamp

Rocamora, A. and A. Smelik, eds (2015), *Thinking Through Fashion: A Guide to Key Theorists*, London: I.B. Tauris

Scapp, R. and B. Seitz, eds (2010), *Fashion Statements: On Style, Appearance, and Reality*, New York: Palgrave Macmillan
Spencer, H. (1966), *The Principles of Sociology* (1874–96), 3 vols, Osnabrück: Otto Zeller (reprint of the 1902 edition)
Svendsen, L. (2006), *Fashion: A Philosophy* (2004), trans. J. Iron, London: Reaktion Books
Wolfendale, J. and J. Kennett, eds (2011), *Fashion—Philosophy for Everyone: Thinking with Style*, Malden (MA)-Oxford: Wiley-Blackwell

1 PHILOSOPHICAL ACCOUNTS OF FASHION IN THE NINETEENTH AND TWENTIETH CENTURY: A HISTORICAL RECONSTRUCTION*

Stefano Marino

I am ahead, I am advanced
I am the first mammal to wear pants.

PEARL JAM. *Do the Evolution*

I wore the clothes you wanted
I took your name
If there is some confusion
Who's to blame?

R.E.M. *I Took Your Name*

1. Preliminary remarks: On imitation

In this chapter I will provide an overview, a reconstruction of a certain number of various articulations of philosophical thought about fashion by means of single, specific examples. From this point of view, the aim of this chapter is not strictly speaking *theoretical*, is not to neatly develop a central argument or idea across the philosophers I discuss, but is rather *historical*, reconstructive, and descriptive. This, however, does not exclude applying an *interpretive* and to some extent also *critical* approach to each single philosopher discussed. So, for example, it will be attempted to throw light on the limits and deficiencies of some philosophical approaches to fashion.

This chapter does not claim completeness and thus it is not my goal to reconstruct the whole history of the philosophy of fashion—which would be clearly very difficult to do in the limited space of just one chapter. Rather, I will focus upon a few *key figures* in the history of nineteenth- and twentieth-century philosophy (and sociology) of fashion.[1] In my view, this historical development can be interpreted in a quasi-teleological way—much in the same way in which one, for example, once used to interpret the history of seventeenth- and eighteenth-century philosophy as a quasi-teleological development culminating in Kant's reconciliation and at the same time overcoming of different traditions by means of his new transcendental approach. Namely, I will interpret it as the gradual development of an investigation of fashion mostly centered on the moment of *imitation*, and sometimes on the moment of class or individual *differentiation*, meant as quintessential to the phenomenon of fashion.[2] The development in theories of fashion is gradual, and viewed retrospectively it appears *as if* it were meant, quasi-teleologically, to lead to the overcoming of the "either/or" logic: imitation *or* differentiation, imitation *as opposed to* differentiation. In place of that logic fashion can be seen to move toward a reconciliation of both moments or forces, in a certain, so to speak, richer and more nuanced conception of fashion that contains imitation *and* differentiation, imitation *on the condition of* differentiation. In my view, the first occurrence of such a reconciliation or, as it were, dialectical synthesis is traceable to the conception of fashion of the German theorist Georg Simmel. From this point of view, I will suggest to interpret Simmel's theory as a *turning point* in the historical development of a philosophy of fashion: that is, as the culmination and fulfillment of previous tendencies, and also as the basis for further treatments of this subject.

By choosing to focus on the conceptual pair imitation/differentiation I obviously do not want to deny that also other concepts and dimensions may play an important and sometimes even essential role in defining this phenomenon. As has been noted, fashion represents indeed such a *multifaceted* reality that it is actually possible to understand it as "a process of individualization and socialization," and then, for example, also as "a means of self-presentation and social mobility," or in terms of "relation between production and consumption," or finally as "a means of differentiation with regard to the dimensions of gender and age" (Riello 2012: IX). Far from denying all this, namely the possibility of applying various concepts to the world of fashion in order to try to understand it, in this chapter I will rather try to show that those nineteenth- and twentieth-century philosophers who, unlike other thinkers, paid a non-superficial or not merely occasional attention to fashion, implicitly or explicitly relied on the ideas of imitation and demarcation in the attempt to grasp the *essence* of fashion. However, as I said, it was only with Simmel—at least in the specific field of philosophy and at least in the historical period taken into consideration here—that the complexity of the dialectical relationship between these two moments or aspects of fashion was fully and explicitly understood. From this point of view, namely from the point of view of the attempt to define the *concept* of fashion, I argue that Simmel outdid most of his philosophical predecessors in understanding what we may call the *ambivalent* nature of fashion.

Of course, just saying that in this chapter we will be talking about *imitation* might appear a little bit too general and too abstract. So it is perhaps a good idea to say a little more about what we can observe happening to this concept during the course of modern theorizing about fashion. Did fashion consist entirely in imitation, or did that imitation also have to incorporate elements of differentiation? And what kind of imitation do we find here? Is there actually just one kind of imitation, i.e., just one kind of imitative relationship at the basis of psychological and socio-cultural forms like fashion, or different varieties or typologies?

Some valuable insights into this question have been provided, among others, by Yuniya Kawamura. As she notices, "what earlier sociologists share in the discussion of fashion is the concept of imitation" (Kawamura 2005: 20). According to her, this is the case, for example, of such nineteenth- and twentieth-century sociological works on fashion as those of Veblen, Tarde, Sumner, Tönnies, and later also Bell and König. And this, as I said (and as I will try to show in more detail later), also applies to earlier philosophical surveys of fashion. Now, the classic explanation of the nature of fashion (and, in sociological discussions, of its diffusion) in terms of imitation has been often connected to the so-called *top-down* or *trickle-down* model. As is well known, according to the classic model "new styles are first adopted by upper-class elites and then the working class," so that the imitation process or, as it were, "the direction of flow" is "typically from superior to inferior, which has been called trickle-down" (Kawamura 2005: 78). However, in more recent times doubts have been raised by some theorists about the explanatory power of the classical model (Kawamura mentions the relevant examples of Blumer and Davis), and thus alternative schemes have been elaborated. So, under the label of *bottom-up* or *trickle-up* theories we encounter different explanation models, according to which "new styles emerge in lower-status groups and are later adopted by higher-status groups." In this model, "the innovators generally emerge from communities in urban areas that are seedbeds for other types of innovation, such as popular music and the arts," and they often are "small firms [. . .] created by individuals who belong to the communities in which the innovations originate." However, in order to be "disseminated to a larger audience, innovations have to be discovered and promoted," and thus, according to this explanation scheme, "if the style or fad shows signs of becoming popular, large firms begin to produce their versions of it and to market it aggressively" (Kawamura 2005: 78–9).

Leaving aside those problems, which might lead our discussion astray, we still have to wonder whether the new alternative schemes developed to understand fashion's function in contemporary society can in fact do without the conceptual pair imitation/distinction. Of course, the undeniable (although sometimes only seeming or illusory ...) democratization of society occurred in the twentieth century, and the emergence of new social actors (most noticeably, the class of young people, the social category of youth), require one to overcome the old, one-sided and, so to speak, one-directional idea of mere imitation of superiors by inferiors. However, debunking the so-called trickle-down process does not mean, in itself, that one must play down the importance of imitation as such in psychological and social relationships. Should one understand fashion as guided by trickle-up or even trickle-across processes, this would not imply that imitation (and, conversely, differentiation) plays no role in it: that is, it could be still interpreted, I think, as that "particular instance among the many forms of life by the aid of which we seek to combine in a unified act the tendency towards social equalization with the desire for individual differentiation and variation" (Simmel 1997: 189).

Anyway, what really matters for the specific purposes of the present historical reconstruction is that most (if not all) late nineteenth-century and early twentieth-century philosophers that I will take into examination here relied on what I have previously defined as the classic model. More precisely, some of these thinkers were actually responsible, if not of the original coinage, at least of the systematic definition of the so-called trickle-down model and the idea of fashion as an imitative practice. During the twentieth century, then, the predominance of the classic explanation scheme gradually lost its grip or at least underwent a process of revision. As we will see, also philosophical theorization about fashion became more complex, nuanced, sophisticated, and open to different contributions and intersections with different perspectives. By the way, the unquestioned predominance of the classic model until a certain age, and the subsequent need to revise it or at least rethink it, are easily explained by the changes occurring in the field of concrete fashion practices, including production, consumption, promotion and dissemination, the cultural, economic, and aesthetic shifts from *haute couture* to *prêt-à-porter*, and so on. As has been noted, indeed,

> As the concept of fashion changed historically, so did the phenomenon of fashion. The concept would not exist if the phenomenon did not exist. Fashion in the fifteenth century is something quite different from fashion in the nineteenth and the twentieth centuries. In the fifteenth century, fashion was an indicator of class status, a court privilege, practically monopolised by the aristocracy while the commoners would hardly have dared to call themselves fashionable; in the nineteenth century, social life had changed greatly [...]. No longer did the aristocracy alone lead fashion, but the wealthy who had the

material means were slowly invading into their social place [...]. In the twentieth century, fashion became increasingly democratic, and everyone, regardless of rank or status, had a right to look fashionable.

KAWAMURA 2005: 5

Notwithstanding the somehow abstract nature of theorizing as such (and especially of philosophical theorizing), in inquiring into the history of recent philosophical *concepts* of fashion it is also required to always bear in mind the historical transformations of the real, concrete *phenomenon* of fashion itself. So, in short, anticipating here in a few words what will result from the complex of my examination of several texts on this subject, what we find is a growing complexity among these philosophers in how they presented fashion, in general, and how they thought about fashion imitation, in particular. That is, a progressively higher level of philosophical awareness of the complex and broad-spectrum nature of fashion, as well as of the need to conceive of the latter as a combination of various factors also including imitation and what may appear as its very opposite, namely differentiation or demarcation—that which may explain the way I used before the concept of "dialectical synthesis" in referring to Simmel.

2. Fashion as a philosophical question

Notwithstanding the great importance for the human being of *clothing*, in general, and *fashion*, in particular, there has been until recent times (and, to some extent, still today) a general tendency to ignore them and neglect intellectual and institutional significance to them.[3] As has been noted, "the study of fashion is of recent origin" and it took quite a long time "before fashion became a legitimate research topic for scholars, including social scientists." An "interest in fashion as a topic was aroused as fashion changes were taking place more and more rapidly" throughout the nineteenth century, but even in the twentieth century "fashion and/or clothing as a research topic have never been popular in social science disciplines." So, the scholars involved in the field of so-called fashion studies often had and still have to face "the academic devaluation of fashion as a topic" (Kawamura 2005: 6–8). As a matter of fact, although fashion "is essential to the world of modernity," it is nevertheless apparent that fashion has been "constantly denigrated" and that, therefore, "the serious study of fashion has had repeatedly to justify itself": "all serious books about fashion seem invariably to need to return to first principles and argue anew for the importance of dress" (Wilson 2003: 12, 47, 271).

Now, if this is true for the field of the *social sciences* (see Monneyron 2006: chap. 1), it is even more valid and appropriate for the specific field of *philosophy*. In fact, although it must be surely acknowledged that "before fashion became a legitimate research topic for scholars, including social scientists, it was the topic often taken up by philosophers and moralists" (Kawamura 2005: 6–7), I would also suggest not to take such a reference to "philosophers" too literally, or better to contextualize it and understand it as referring to a very broad concept of "philosophy." Namely, to a concept of philosophy that also includes, beside philosophers strictly speaking, such figures as "philosophical" poets and novelists (i.e., writers whose works are rich in observations and meditations on philosophical questions), intellectuals, artists, or still—as Kawamura herself adds—moralists. In fact, the names most frequently cited when dealing with fashion as a subject of intellectual discussion in the last centuries include such authors and works as the *Theory of Moral Sentiments* (1759) by Adam Smith, *The Book of Fashion* (1821) by George Bryan "Beau" Brummell, the *Dialogue Between Fashion and Death* (1824) by Giacomo Leopardi, the *Treatise on Elegant Living* (1830) by Honoré de Balzac, *Sartor Resartus* (1833–4) by Thomas Carlyle, *Dandyism* (1845) by Jules-Amédée Barbey d'Aurevilly, *The Book of Snobs* (1848) by William Makepeace Thackeray, the pamphlet *On Fashion* (1858) by Pierre Jules Théophile Gautier, the fundamental essay *The Painter of Modern Life* (1863) by Charles Baudelaire, the fashion magazine *La Dernière Mode* (1874) by Stéphane Mallarmé, the recently re-issued *Philosophy of Dress* (1885) by Oscar Wilde (one of the most famous examples of dandyism), the essay *Why A Man Should Be Well-Dressed* (1898) by Adolf Loos, *The Eroticism of Clothes* (1906) by Karl Kraus, and other analogous literary and/or essayistic writings. All works, the latter, that, although surely rich in *broadly speaking* "philosophical" contents, and thus significant for a general overview on the various ideas expressed about fashion in the last centuries, cannot be considered as *strictly speaking* "philosophical."

If we refer to somehow more precise and delimited concepts of "philosophy" and "philosopher," then, it becomes difficult to avoid the impression of a veritable "philosophic fear of fashion" (Hanson 1993), i.e., the impression of a fundamentally problematical relationship between fashion and philosophy.[4] Not by chance, in defining the general horizon of *fashion theory* and its different sources, certain scholars have enlisted among the "academic disciplines engaged in theorizing fashion" such disciplines as the "art and design history," the "social sciences," or "business [. . .] and fashion programs" (Lillethun 2007: 77), but *not* philosophy. Far from being arbitrary or unjustified, this exclusion rather rests on the simple fact that most philosophers—due to fashion's "inextricable association with outside interests and purposes," and also with such aspects of our overall life-experience as sexuality, desire, mortality, the bodily dimension of life, and mere *appearances* dualistically understood as opposed to *what is* (i.e., exists, is real) in an essential, fundamental, or even originary way (see Hanson 1998: 157–9)—have not considered fashion "as a subject worthy of philosophical reflection" (Negrin 2012: 43). On this basis, it is thus difficult to deny that fashion "cannot at any rate be said to be a fashionable theme in philosophy": as has been noted, even in "broadly based philosophical works that deal with the genesis of the modern self" fashion

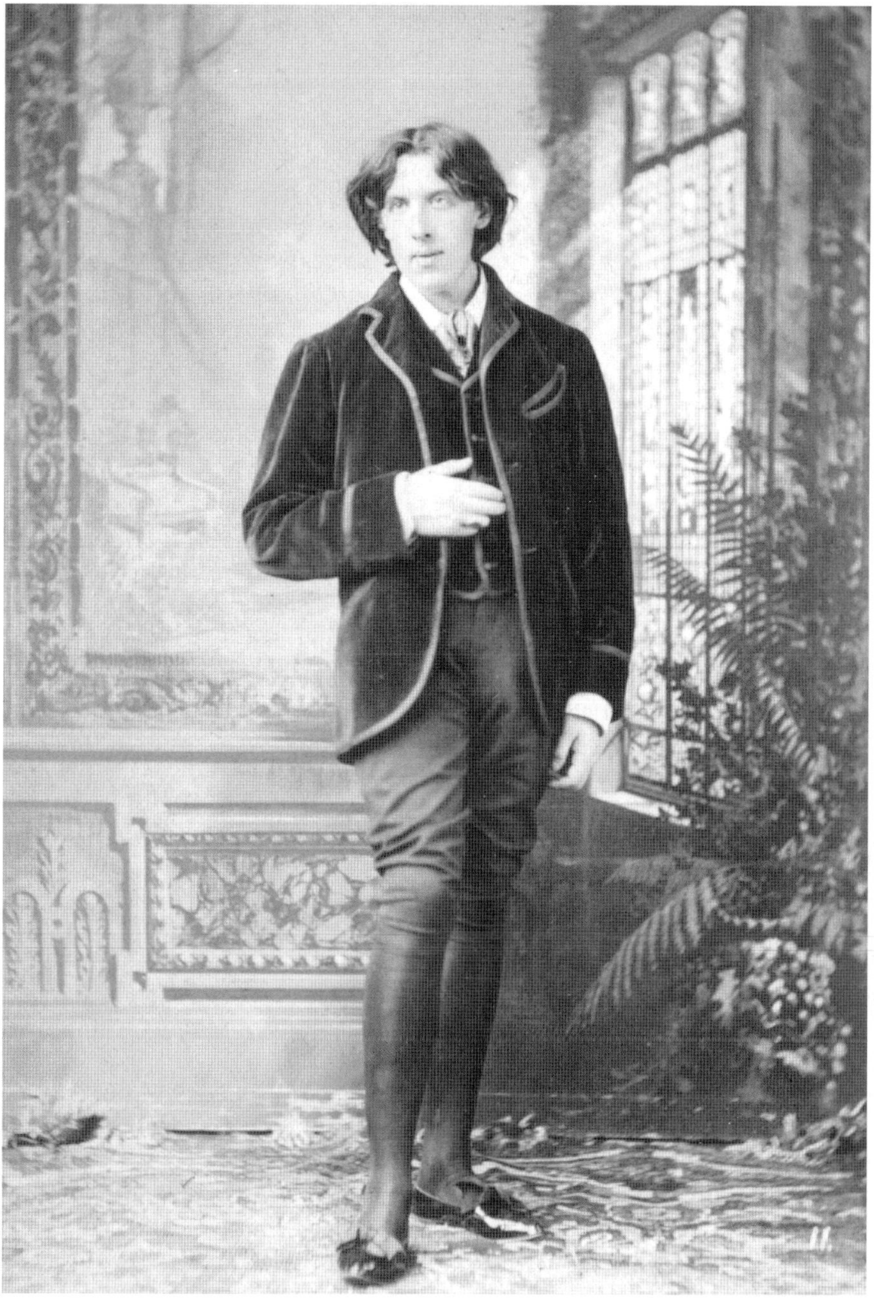

FIGURE 1.1 Oscar Wilde, portrait, 1890.

has been quite incomprehensibly "passed over in silence. [. . .] Traditionally, fashion is not considered a satisfactory object of study," and although "the position has changed to a certain degree in recent years with a stream of academic publications on fashion," with a few exceptions "these have not been written by philosophers" (Svendsen 2006: 17).

However, the undeniable fact that until recent times fashion had received little attention from philosophers strictly speaking[5] does not imply that it received no attention at all, as if the only existing philosophical works on this subject were those of, say, Simmel or Lipovetsky. In fact, if it is true that "if we look back through the history of philosophy" in search of philosophical essays or treatises on fashion "the results are meagre" (Svendsen 2006: 17), it is nevertheless apparent from a survey of the field that several philosophers, especially during the nineteenth and twentieth century, expressed a certain genuine interest in fashion. And although philosophers most often expressed this interest only in a cursory way, at least some of them actually turned it into the subject of more or less extended and systematic works. That which, however, has been seldom recognized by scholars working in the field of fashion studies,[6] so that a rediscovery and, in some cases, also a rehabilitation of some of these figures may appear as much needed.

In the end, it will also become clear from my contribution that *fashion*, should one want to assign it to a particular domain within the great field of philosophical disciplines (including logic, epistemology, ethics, politics, metaphysics, philosophy of language, philosophy of religion, etc.) must be definitely assigned to the field of *aesthetics*, and considered as a fundamental aesthetic problem (Carchia 2005: 185). A question, the latter, which, by the way, will be further investigated and explained in the following chapter by Giovanni Matteucci with a more *theoretical* approach, while the approach adopted in this chapter, as I said, is more *historical* and descriptive.

3. A late eighteenth-century perspective: Christian Garve

Although according to some scholars "theoretical writing on fashion dates at least to 1575" (Lillethun 2007: 77), and although others have also claimed that "it is at the end of the seventeenth century that [. . .] the birth of fashion, including its *conceptual birth*, takes place" (Riello 2012: 27 (my emphasis)), I will focus on the last two centuries. The foundations for a real *philosophical* treatment of this subject were laid in this period. A good starting point for the kind of historical-philosophical reconstruction that I have in mind is represented by Christian Garve, a philosopher who is perhaps best known today as a critical reviewer of Kant's *Critique of Pure Reason* and correspondent with him, but who was also, during his age, one of the most famous thinkers of the late Enlightenment in Germany. More precisely, Garve was a well-known "popular philosopher (*Popularphilosoph*)" and, as such, the author of a work entitled *Versuche über verschiedene Gegenstände aus der Moral, der Literatur und dem gesellschaftlichen Leben* that also included, in its first volume, a quite long essay entitled *Ueber die Moden* (1792).[7]

Garve's writing must be contextualized in an epoch in which fashion designers were still far from being given the attention and interest that we are used to paying to them now. An epoch in which fashion designers, the way we know and understand them today, actually did not exist. An epoch in which Rose Bertin, probably the most famous among the *marchandes de modes* in Paris in the late eighteenth century, the dressmaker of the queen Marie Antoinette, posed for the very first time the question concerning the artistic value of a designer's work (see Morini 2012: 35). A question, the latter, that was later to become a *topos* in the field of fashion, especially after the advent of such great *couturier* as Charles Frederick Worth and Paul Poiret. As I said, it is important to contextualize the various authors' statements in an appropriate way, and thus to always bear in mind also the historical situation of clothing and fashion at a certain age, when reading and interpreting philosophical investigations of fashion (including Garve's, of course).

In his essay *Ueber die Moden* Garve starts with a general observation concerning the relationships between the various members of a certain society, and he claims that, "in addition to the uniformity [. . .] that is produced by nature or derives from the similarity of their positions, the common aspects of their countenances, and the spheres of their activity, there arises among them another uniformity, through *imitation*." Garve explains that "this imitation is in part involuntary," while "another type of imitation is deliberate," and connects this general discourse with the question concerning "the concepts of the beautiful and the ugly [that] are determined by *taste* and *fashion*" (Garve 1985: 119–20). It is already clear from these observations that Garve understands fashion—which he identifies as "the dominant opinion of the beautiful and the proper at any time in [. . .] matters which cannot be regulated with unanimity by the application of the rules of either taste or utility" (Garve 1985: 121–2)—in light of the concept of *Nachahmung*, imitation. According to him, "fashions are a result of man's social nature. People want to be uniform with one another," and "every conspicuous dissimilarity in clothing, accommodation, and lifestyle" originates instead "a distance that hinders affection and obstructs the intimate communication of ideas." From this point of view, Garve also claims that "as long as man has existed there have been fashions" (Garve 1985: 122–3). This claim seems to differentiate his position from that of most fashion theorists, according to whom fashion "does not belong to all ages or to all civilizations," but rather represents something that has "an identifiable starting point in history," something that "sprang up and took hold in the modern West and nowhere else" (Lipovetsky 1994: 15).[8]

Garve also analyzes the fundamental causes and laws that he finds at the root of this peculiar social form (Garve 1985: 127–34, 135–42), and the two main classes of things that stand under the rules of fashion: objects (including *clothes* that actually occupy a special position in this realm) and actions (Garve 1985: 143, 156, 173–9). Beside these aspects, Garve's long essay also includes observations on the temporal variability of changes in fashion that are sometimes slow and sometimes fast (Garve 1985: 192), on whether progress exists or not in this field (Garve 1985: 197), and on whether fashion may have or not any end or final goal (Garve 1985: 291). What matters most for the specific purposes of the present contribution is Garve's firm conviction, restated more than once in his essay, that "the universal principle of fashion" consists in "the drive to imitation (*Nachahmungstrieb*)" and is tied, in turn, to the basic "impulse to sociability" that is common to all humans (Garve 1985: 163, 235).

To be precise, it must be said that Garve, in a single passage of his essay, hints at the fact that, "just as classes separate themselves from one another, and the whole of bourgeois society seems to divide itself into several smaller ones," so fashions may prove to be *both* a means "of unification" *and* "a means of division" (Garve 1985: 123–4). This passage might read as an early and somehow pre-Simmelian intuition of the twofold nature that is characteristic of fashion (unification *and* division; imitation *and* distinction; socialization *and* individualization; etc.). But Garve unfortunately does not seem to develop this intuition in its full range, and throughout his long essay he rather places an almost exclusive emphasis on the "drive to imitation" or "imitative impulse" as the real and indeed unique source from which fashion derives. By doing so, he seems to miss a good chance to arrive at a broader and more complete understanding of fashion—although, of course, in evaluating Garve's as well as other thinkers' views of fashion it must be taken into account what the real experience (or, as it were, the "empirical" practice) of fashion at the time was: for example, a practice that perhaps did not allow the same amount of differentiation and expression of individual taste as fashion has come to allow later.

4. Nineteenth-century developments: Post-idealism, Positivism, Pragmatism

Bypassing here some great philosophers who, like Kant, Hegel, Nietzsche, and still others, expressed an interest in fashion but only in the form of short aphorisms, brilliant mottos, or single and often brief sections of their otherwise long and complex works,[9] let us now take into consideration the perspectives disclosed by such authors as Hermann Lotze and William James. Lotze was one of the key figures in the history of nineteenth-century German philosophy as the promoter of a reinterpretation of idealism in terms of value-theory, and indeed the founder of the philosophy of value that was to have great influence in later developments of Neo-Kantianism and also phenomenology (see Schnädelbach 1984: 169–80). He dedicates a part of the second chapter of the fifth book of the second volume of his work in three volumes *Microcosmus: An Essay Concerning Man and His Relation to the World* (1856–64) to explaining the significance of dress in the context of a more general analysis of human sensitivity. Here, Lotze focuses his attention exclusively on "the source of the pleasure" that clothes "and other kinds of decoration afford to the human soul," and thus he intentionally (on the basis of his quite specific theoretical interest in inquiring into this subject) excludes from his perspective such aspects of our experience with clothes as their use "as a protection against the inclemency of weather" or "the sense of modesty that chooses them as a covering" (Lotze 1923, vol. 2: 206).[10] For him, "our pleasure in ornament and dress is derived from the sensations which both excite in ourselves," and depends in particular on "the consciousness of our personal existence [that] is prolonged into the extremities and surfaces of this foreign body." As a consequence, we experience "feelings now of an expansion of our proper self, now of the acquisition of a kind and amount of motion foreign to our natural organs, now of an unusual degree of vigour, power of resistance, or steadiness in our bearing" (Lotze 1923, vol. 2: 207–8). In short, Lotze is interested—in the context of the wide philosophical-anthropological and also metaphysical conception presented in his majestic systematic treatise *Microcosmus*—in the influence that clothes may have on our sensations, feelings, and moods, and this apparently draws his investigation close to some aspects of William James' famous *Principles of Psychology*.

As a matter of fact, in the tenth chapter (entitled "The Consciousness of Self") of his 1890 masterwork, *The Principles of Psychology*, James presents in a few lines what has been emphatically defined as a veritable "philosophy of dress" (Watson 2004). As is well known, James was the founding father, together with Charles Sanders Peirce, of the philosophical tradition of American pragmatism.[11] In this chapter, he moves from the idea of "the Self in its widest acceptation," then he distinguishes an empirical concept of the Self from a pure concept of the Self, and finally he defines the former as "all that [one] is tempted to call by the name of *me*," as "*the sum total of all that* [a man] *CAN call his*": hence "not only his body and his psychic powers, but his clothes and his house, his wife and children, his ancestors and friends, his reputation and works, his lands and horses, and yacht and bank-account. All these things give him the same emotions" (James 1950, vol. 1: 291). Once outlined this general view of the Self in the widest sense, James suggests to divide its history into three parts, respectively related to "its constituents," to "the feelings and emotions they arouse," and to "the actions to which they prompt." Then, he divides the constituents of the Self, in turn, into the following classes: "the material Self," "the social Self," "the spiritual Self," and finally "the pure Ego." And it is precisely at this point that clothes come into play, as he claims that, if it is true that the body surely represents "the innermost part of *the material Self* in each of us," it is also true that "the clothes come next. [. . .] The old saying that the human person is composed of three parts—soul, body, and clothes—is more than a joke," according to James. "We so appropriate our clothes and identify ourselves with them," he claims, "that there are few of us who, if asked to choose between having a beautiful body clad in raiment perpetually shabby and unclean, and having an ugly and blemished form always spotlessly attired, would not hesitate a moment before making a decisive reply" (James 1950, vol. 1: 292).

It is clear from these observations that Lotze and James are rather concerned with the experience of clothing broadly speaking than with fashion as such. Anyway, their views are also of great interest for us, inasmuch as they at least indirectly testify the central role assumed by these questions during the nineteenth century not only in such realms as poetry, literature, art criticism, essay writing, etc., but also in the realm of philosophy. From this point of view, the fact that such complex works as James' *Principles of Psychology* and Lotze's *Microcosmus*, dealing with such traditional and profound philosophical problems as mind, consciousness, language, truth, ethics, the nature of concepts, the perception of time, the theory of knowledge, the human/animal difference, or the body/soul relationship, also include what we may define as fragments of a philosophy of dress, is surely something worth thinking about.

Above all, it is important to notice that both Lotze and James essentially connect their cursory but nevertheless intriguing observations on dress to their general conceptions of the human nature and the human place in the world, arriving to define the "impulse" and need to dress up oneself as a somehow fundamental drive characterizing the human being as such. As a matter of fact, according to James human beings are characterized, among other things, by "a blind impulse to watch over [their] body" and "deck it with clothing" (James 1950, vol. 1: 292). Quite significantly, in dealing with this subject in *The Principles of Psychology* James precisely refers in a footnote to Lotze's "charming passage on the Philosophy of Dress" in his treatise *Microcosmus*, thus acknowledging him as a source of inspiration. Here, indeed, Lotze argues that, "of all living beings, man is the only one that from his natural defenselessness is forced to use implements in order to attain his ends" (Lotze 1923, vol. 2: 203). A basic insight into the fundamental defenseless nature of the human being, the latter, that *mutatis mutandis* underlies the entire tradition of German philosophical anthropology from Johann Gottfried Herder up to Nietzsche's famous idea of "man [as] the *as yet undetermined animal*" (Nietzsche 1966: 74) and up to such twentieth-century developments as Max Scheler's and especially Arnold Gehlen's philosophical anthropology. So, according to Lotze, among all living creatures only we, the human beings, "are impelled" to dress ourselves, and this happens indeed by virtue of "an original instinct" (Lotze 1923, vol. 2: 206).

Another philosopher who, during the nineteenth century, expressed a certain interest in the phenomena of clothing, in general, and fashion, in particular, is

Herbert Spencer. As is well known, with his ambitious multidisciplinary system of "synthetic philosophy" aimed at demonstrating that evolutionary laws and principles apply in such different domains as psychology, biology, ethics, and sociology, Spencer was one of the leading figures of nineteenth-century positivism. Worthy of interest in the context of the present historical-philosophical reconstruction are, for example, his 1854 article "Manners and Fashion," and the ninth and eleventh chapters of the fourth part of the second volume of his *Principles of Sociology* in three volumes (1874–75; 1879–82; 1885–96), respectively entitled "Badges and Costumes" (§§ 408–415) and "Fashion" (§§ 423–426).

According to Spencer, notwithstanding the commonsensical perspective on the origins of clothing that would lead us to think that human beings were "originally prompted to clothe themselves by either the desire for warmth or the thought of decency," the common root of the badge and the dress actually consists in that both are "at first worn from the wish for admiration" (Spencer 1966a, vol. 2: 180). Their common root thus lies in the deep-rooted need to express themselves also by adorning and decorating their bodies that is so characteristic of human beings and that represents one of the factors at the threshold between nature and culture that make humans such a peculiar and even "unpredictable species":[12] a strange kind of animal, so to speak, whose nature actually consists in overcoming nature in order to develop its own culture (or, as it were, its "second nature"[13]), thus including the manipulation and transformation of itself and the natural environment in order to create its own cultural-historical world. As Spencer explains, "the causes which have originated, developed, and specialized badges and dresses, have done the like with ornaments; which have, indeed, the same origins" (Spencer 1966a, vol. 2: 183). A question, the latter (namely, that concerning the ornamental origin of at least some cultural products characterized, among other things, by their specifically aesthetic significance) that has been variously addressed by several theorists and has been recently re-evaluated with regard to both the fine arts and fashion by Yves Michaud, for example.[14]

Spencer focuses on what he defines "further class-distinctions" (Spencer 1966a, vol. 2: 193–204), and then takes directly into consideration the phenomenon of fashion, defined as a "class of social observances" (Spencer 1966b: 28) or a "form of social regulation" that is "proper to the *régime* of voluntary co-operation" (opposed to the "*régime* of compulsory co-operation" that is characteristic of the ceremonial). According to him, fashion consists in a "behaviour resulting from imitation of the great" and an "accompaniment of the industrial type" (opposed, once again, to the ceremonial, interpreted as a "behaviour required by the subordination to the great" and an accompaniment of "the militant type"), and it typically displays "a compromise between governmental coercion and individual freedom" (Spencer 1966a, vol. 2: 205, 209–10). More precisely, with regard to this last point, Spencer explains that it is quintessential of fashion to be an "ever-changing compromise between restraint and freedom" which, however, during the modern age has constantly tended "towards increase of freedom" and has been paralleled by analogous developments in the domain of political regulation: "for while, on the average, governmental control of individual action" has decreased in modern societies, there has also been "a decrease in the rigidity of fashion," as is shown by "the greater latitude of private judgment exercised within certain vaguely marked limits" (Spencer 1966a, vol. 2: 210).

This is a highly significant aspect, especially if connected to what Spencer, evidently in full accord with other theorists, defines as the very essence of fashion, namely *imitation*. According to him, "in those modifications of behaviour, dress, mode of life, &c., which constitute fashion" it is indeed "likeness [that] is insisted upon," whereas in other "forms of social control" we see "enforced, not likeness, between the acts of higher and lower, but unlikeness": this is due to the fact that, as he explains, "fashion is intrinsically imitative" (Spencer 1966a, vol. 2: 205). Fashion, as he also claims in the article "Manners and Fashion," "originates by imitation of the behaviour *of* the great" and derives from "the habits and appearances exhibited *by* those in power" (Spencer 1966b: 28).

Quite interestingly, in *The Principles of Sociology* Spencer also seems to draw ethical and socio-political conclusions by combining these basic assumptions with an analysis of the development of fashion in the age of industrialism. So, he explains that "everywhere and always the tendency of the inferior to assert himself has been in antagonism with the restraints imposed on him," and that "a prevalent way of asserting himself has been to adopt costumes and appliances and customs like those of his superiors," namely to imitate them (Spencer 1966a, vol. 2: 208). However, during the modern age "the restraints [. . .] have been gradually relaxed" and fashion, imitative of the superiors "from the beginning," has progressively "tended towards equalization. Serving to obscure, and eventually to obliterate, the marks of class-distinction, it has favoured the growth of individuality," as he claims (Spencer 1966a, vol. 2: 208–10). From this specific point of view, Spencer's conception seemingly anticipates some processes that were to be rather typical of twentieth-century fashion: for example, the definitive coming to the foreground of the individual and, more in general, the widespread diffusion of a more democratic spirit as far as questions of taste are concerned. If observed from this perspective, fashion may appear to function as a social form capable of reducing and eventually suppressing (although only on a symbolic and aesthetic level) the distances and differences between individuals and even between social classes.

However, this interpretation of some *socio-political* effects of the ever-growing diffusion and significance of fashion does not prevent Spencer from expressing a negative evaluation of its effects on a strictly speaking *aesthetic* level. What we encounter here is in fact a variation on the much-repeated theme concerning the tendency of fashion to originate "numberless absurdities," "eccentricities," "extravagance[s]," and "follies," and to set them up "as standards for imitation" (Spencer 1966b: 29–30, 45–6). According to Spencer, this negative development is due to the fact that also fashion, like "other forms of rule," while initially promoting an "advantageous [. . .] imitation" of "the men of will, intelligence, and originality, who have got to the top," and who are, "on the average, more likely to show judgment in their habits and tastes than the mass," gradually undergoes a process of decay that ultimately leads it to "almost wholly cease to be an imitation of the best" and rather to become "an imitation of quite other than the best." Hence "the self-elected clique who set the fashion" can do it now "solely by unchecked assumption", and not "by intellect, by higher worth or better taste," and it is precisely by the "example of these sham great" that "society at large" now regulates "its habits" and, above all, "its dress." As a necessary and unavoidable consequence, the result for Spencer is "a reign of mere whim, of unreason, of change for the sake of change, of wanton oscillations from either extreme to the other," instead than a progressive development leading to "greater elegance and convenience" (which is clearly the *telos* or regulative idea, as it were, assumed by Spencer). So, he concludes that "life *à la mode*, instead of being life conducted in the most rational manner," has become today (namely, during his age) "life regulated by spendthrifts and idlers, milliners and tailors, dandies and silly women" (Spencer 1966b: 29–30).

Worthy of notice, in the same historical context of nineteenth-century culture, are also the ideas on fashion expressed by two German scholars: Friedrich Theodor Vischer and Friedrich Kleinwächter. Vischer was a pre-eminent representative of post-Hegelian aesthetics in Germany, his most famous and most important work actually being a long and systematic treatise entitled *Aesthetik oder Wissenschaft des Schönen* (1846–57). Beside this, he was also the author of two contributions on fashion: *Vernünftige Gedanken über die jetzige Mode* (1859) and *Wieder einmal über die Mode* (1879). His philosophical conception of fashion has been summarized, in general, with the emphatic expression "philosophy of history of fashion" (Neumann 2006: 192), and it might be perhaps connected to some of Spencer's abovementioned critical observations because of Vischer's criticism of the fashion of his time, seen as "a dangerous game" and even as a form of madness (Vischer 2006: 27–8, 31).[15] A criticism, the latter, that generates Vischer's (disappointed) hope in the possible rise of a new "reasonable form of dress" (Vischer 2006: 14) in an age of (in his eyes) growing irrationality and even perversity.

Vischer deliberately focuses on "fashion in clothing" and, in particular, on women's dress: that which may appear understandable, given that he (like other nineteenth-century thinkers) wrote on fashion during the age that has been interpreted by various scholars—following an insight originally provided by the psychologist John Carl Flügel in his famous *Psychology of Clothes*—as the age of the "great male renunciation" to adornment, style, and beauty in clothing. In his critical consideration of female clothing of his time, Vischer goes so far as to claim that women's fashion had now turned into no less than "a whores' fashion"! According to him, there are limits of decency that should be respected in clothing but "current fashions" clearly transgress these limits, inasmuch as they allow a woman to "park herself in front of the opposite sex" standing almost "naked in her clothes" (Vischer 2006: 15, 17–19). Such an extremely critical attitude probably represents one of the distinctive features of Vischer's contribution to nineteenth-century philosophy of fashion, although it must be also said that his way of approaching this subject is often ironic, rich in sarcastic observations, and so "one is never sure just how seriously he takes himself" (Purdy 2004: 153).

Anyway, without lingering on Vischer's criticism of women's fashion (in particular, the crinoline) and the reasons underlying his way of opposing fashion to style, to folk costume (*Tracht*), and even to good taste (Vischer 2006: 34–6, 50–4, 71–5), what matters for the specific purposes of this chapter is the fact that, according to him, fashion is characterized by a "levelling," "homogenizing," and "equalizing nature" (Vischer 2006: 56–7). This may be connected, once again, to what I have defined so far as the prevailing but one-sided interpretive paradigm based on *imitation* (see Pappas 2008: 10). This is testified, for example, by a passage in Vischer's essay where he takes a critical stance against French culture and costumes, and claims that whatever eccentricities, extravagances, or follies are "dictated from Paris today," there is no doubt that they will be "willingly, serviceably and dutifully imitated" by most everyone also in other countries (Vischer 2006: 26).

To be precise, the centrality of imitation in relation to the world of fashion is not attested here by means of a general theorization on this specific concept, but rather by means of a particular example (the imitation of French costumes) that, in turn, is also understood by Vischer as not only referring to an imitative process between individual subjects but also as referring to imitation processes involving different nations and cultures. Anyway, the point at stake here remains the same, namely the central role that is clearly played in all such theories (thus including also Vischer's) by the very idea of imitation. In Vischer's view, modern fashion (and in particular, as I said, women's fashion) seems to function as an emblem of imitative activities, i.e., activities based on imitative impulses or drives that thus deprive the individual of her real individuality and originality. This seems to be testified *ex negativo*, so to speak, by Vischer's reference to a previous age, namely to the people from the age of his grandfather, for whom "it was entirely natural that one man should wish to *distinguish* himself" through dress (Vischer 2006: 57 (my emphasis)). The basic parameter or rule for dressing in a fashionable way precisely consists in making oneself "inconspicuous by not deviating from everyone else in certain principle articles of clothing," although it must be also said that fashion for Vischer "does not request [full] homogeneity." "The canon of fashion," he explains, "is not a uniform" (Vischer 2006: 59–60).

However, in at least one passage of his essay Vischer seems to introduce a more nuanced view, as he claims that women's fashion often seeks "the conspicuous" and "grants the individual, within certain limits, a margin to *distinguish* herself." In fact, "it does not follow from the ban on conspicuousness that the individual woman is

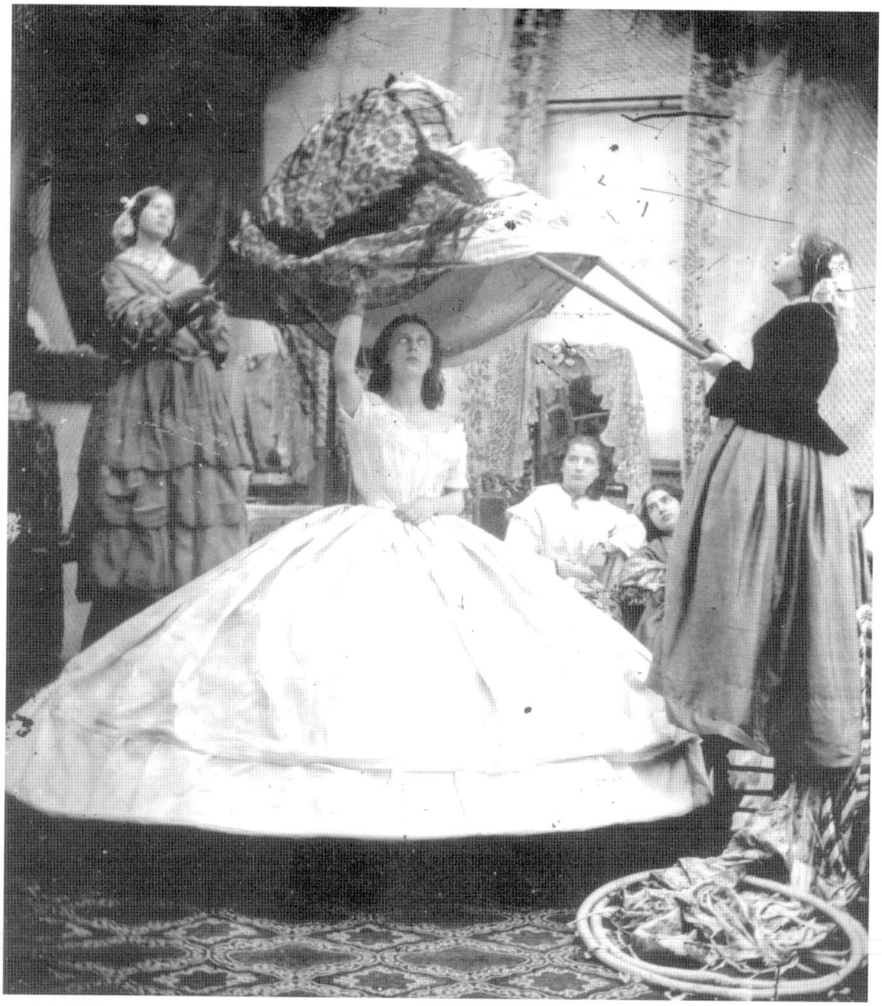

FIGURE 1.2 A woman being dressed with the aid of long poles to lift her crinoline dress over the hoops.

not left a significant leeway for her own inspirations and own personal vanity" (Vischer 2006: 58, 60 (my emphasis)). This seemingly points in the direction of a concept of fashion that also gives a certain importance to the dimension of distinction beside that of imitation. Vischer, however, does not take the further step, so to speak, that might have led him to a dialectical integration, as it were, of the two opposite drives, i.e., to a resolution of their mere contrast in a sort of higher and in-itself-mediated unity. Rather, in posing the deeply philosophical question "whether fashion allows individuals free expression or whether it is a slavish tendency that [even] proves that free will is a myth" (Purdy 2004: 153) he eventually invokes the authority of Kant's transcendental philosophy. As is well known, Kant only conceives of dialectics as inevitably generating unsolvable antinomies (juxtapositions of two statements, a thesis and an antithesis, with equal truth claims but mutually excluding one another[16]), and thus as bound to run aground, so to speak. As a result, Vischer develops a view of fashion as intrinsically contradictory, or better antinomic (Vischer 2006: 64–70), that does not arrive to a resolution of the contrast between the opposite tendencies that lie at the basis of fashion in a sort of higher and in-itself-mediated unity.

Arriving now to the conception of the second abovementioned author, namely the Austrian political economist and essayist Friedrich Kleinwächter, in his 1880 work *Zur Philosophie der Mode* he moves from the very general assumption that "fashion, as is well known, is a very peculiar and strange thing" (Kleinwächter 1880: 3). Then, borrowing a certain terminology from the science of morphology, and adapting it to the scopes of his inquiry into fashion, he recognizes heredity or the hereditary character (*Vererbung*) as one of "the moments that exercise a determining influence on the form of the dress." According to Kleinwächter, it is indeed impossible for us "to create something entirely new," so that we are somehow compelled to hold on to traditions and we "cannot find anywhere absolutely new forms of clothes" (Kleinwächter 1880: 4–5). In other words, due to limits that belong to our anthropological constitution, but also to limits that clearly derive from contingent economic and social conditions, as finite human beings we are not in the condition to produce or have access to what we may define as "the absolutely new." Rather, the playground in which our experience (including that of clothing) displays itself, so to speak, is that of the "in-between": in the present case, between tradition and innovation, and also between imitation and differentiation, as we have seen so far.

Kleinwächter—who, notwithstanding his relatively low celebrity and his being a minor author if compared to Spencer or James, according to some interpreters even anticipated some hypotheses that would be later presented with greater emphasis and systematicity by such famous theorists as Simmel and Veblen (see Meinhold 2013: 12)—distinguishes three different aims or fundamental dimensions characterizing our clothes: namely, a practical, a symbolic, and an aesthetic dimension (Kleinwächter 1880: 5–30). Just like some previous authors and also some later ones, he makes a fleeting reference to "fashion's abuses and sins against good taste and even against the human healthy understanding" (Kleinwächter 1880: 31, 41–4). But what matters the most for our specific purposes is the fact that near the end of his essay he too refers to "the category of imitation" and claims—in much the same terms that we have already found in Garve and still others—that "fashion is essentially a product of the imitative impulse (*Nachahmungstrieb*)" (Kleinwächter 1880: 37). This makes it possible to include him among the representatives of the one-sided interpretive paradigm centered on imitation that, in my view, has been predominant in the most part of nineteenth- and twentieth-century philosophical perspectives on fashion.

5. Twentieth-century perspectives: Humanism, *Lebensphilosophie*, Phenomenology

An author that, aiming at proposing "an idea of fashion capable of overcoming and getting better of several platitudes about it," instead than focusing on *imitation* that generates conformism rather chooses to focus on *differentiation* that generates "true originality" (Alain 2002: 56–7), is the French essayist, journalist, and humanist philosopher Émile-Auguste Chartier, commonly known as Alain. In the tenth lesson of his 1929–30 lectures on the fine arts (Alain 2002: 55–9), he takes into consideration clothing and fashion (on this topic, see also Alain 1963: 62–9).

After having defined "the empire of fashion" as something that is sometimes "capricious and even absurd," Alain claims that the first rule of fashionable clothing precisely consists in "the research of differentiation" that, in turn, is tightly and essentially (and indeed paradoxically) connected with its apparent opposite, namely "commonplace" (Alain 2002: 55–6). This is due to the fact that, according to Alain, in all fields of human experience "originality consists in the development of an imitable way of being like all others," inasmuch as "it is possible for one to elevate him- or herself only by using and making reference to standard means that are common to everybody," i.e., to criterions that are universally recognized by all. As a matter of fact, "exceptions always rest on prevailing rules," and "differences can emerge" (and thus be perceived as such) "only on the background of resemblances" (Alain 2002: 56). An intuition, the latter, that was also to be confirmed, among others, by Walter Benjamin, as he claimed that "each time, what sets the tone is without doubt the newest, but only where it emerges in the medium of the oldest, the longest past, the most ingrained. This spectacle, the unique self-construction of the newest in the medium of what has been, makes for the true dialectical theater of fashion" (Benjamin 1999: 64).

Anyway, moving from these presuppositions, Alain eventually arrives at defining fashion as "the commonplace in clothing" that bears in itself the possibility of originality, as "a refuge from which one may get out through dressy, much-sought variations" that make it possible for the individual "to be noticed just when and to the extent that he or she really wants to be noticed" (Alain 2002: 57). However, not even Alain does examine in depth the paradoxical (or, in the abovementioned Kantian terms, antinomic and thus dialectic) nature of fashion, although he, like some of the abovementioned authors, seemingly catches a fleeting glimpse of it. It was probably Georg Simmel the first thinker who, in his famous essay on fashion, developed in a really significant, systematic, and convincing way the fundamental dialectic between imitation and differentiation that seems to be required to do justice, at least on a basic level, to the *essence* of such a complex and plural phenomenon as fashion.

To be precise, one should not speak of Simmel's essay on fashion, in the singular, but rather of his essays on fashion, in the plural form. As a matter of fact, Simmel's interest in fashion remains constant during the development of his thought and he dedicates to this psychological-sociological phenomenon three German versions of his essay (1895, 1905, 1911), each somehow corresponding to a moment or phase of his philosophy. But beside the German versions of the essay we also have to mention the 1904 English version of the text, coinciding for the most part to the 1905 German version but characterized by a few passages that are only present in the English version, and thus at least to some extent understandable as still another version of the text. It is important to bear this in mind because it immediately throws light, so to speak, on the not at all ephemeral or short-lived character of Simmel's theoretical engagement with fashion. Referring here to the English translation of the 1905 version of the text that has been made available in the collection *Simmel On Culture*, as has been suggested we can assess the essay more clearly if we divide it into five parts (see Matteucci 2012: 33). However, for the more limited aims of my presentation it will suffice to understand its main points and emphasize the general themes we are pursuing.

Simmel's basic theoretical assumption is that fashion, understood as "a universal phenomenon in the history of our species," must be contextualized in the totality of "the phenomena of life," *all* resting on the interplay of "a multiplicity of elements," on the intertwinement of deep forces and "unresolved tensions" that confer to every phenomenon in "its visible expression" a dualistic character. However, this basic dualism underlying *all* aspects of the real and dimensions of life "cannot be described directly, but only in the individual antagonisms that are typical of our existence, and are felt to be its ultimate, structuring form." From his *lebensphilosophisch* point of view, *all* human experiences and practices must be dualistically understood as "unique way[s] of unifying the interest in duration, unity and equality, and similarity," on the one hand, "with that in change, particularity and uniqueness," on the other hand (Simmel 1997: 187–8). And it is precisely in this context that also fashion must be included. Fashion thus appears as a social form characterized by a dialectic between two fundamental drives: the tendency towards imitation, that "satisfies the need for social adaptation," and "at the same time, and to no less a degree, [...] the need for distinction, [...] differentiation, change and individual contrast" (Simmel 1997: 189).

This *twofold* nature is investigated then with regard to what we may define the social principle of fashion: namely, its being the effect of certain social processes and, in turn, its possible functioning as cause or origin of new social developments. From this point of view, fashion can be understood as both a *forma formata* and a *forma formans*, as both an effect and a cause of the typical accelerated rhythm of modern society (Perucchi 1996: 76). It is at this point of Simmel's essay that we also encounter his famous analysis of the trickle-down mechanism. An analysis that, however, must not be interpreted (as many commentators often tend to do, indeed ...) as *the* basic element upon which Simmel's entire inquiry into fashion is grounded. In fact, the trickle-down process rather represents for Simmel *a* consequence, on a quite specific and delimited level (namely, the level concerning the social diffusion of fashions), of the more abstract and theoretical view of "the essence of fashion" that, as such, is formed by the interplay between the "element of demarcation" and the "element of imitation" (Simmel 1997: 190). This is also confirmed by Simmel's fleeting but nevertheless significant hint at social structures that do not possess "any layered hierarchy of social strata, in which case fashion asserts itself in neighbouring strata" (Simmel 1997: 191), which means that, for him, the diffusion of fashion is not inevitably and ineluctably tied to a trickle-down process. In different social structures than the ones that Simmel lived in and could analyze in Europe in his age also the rules and processes of diffusion of fashion may and perhaps must be different.

Now, due to its distinctive *dialectical* nature, fashion is characterized, on a social level, by a sort of play "between the tendency towards universal acceptance and the destruction of its significance, to which this general adoption leads." And this confers to fashion "the peculiar attraction [...] of a simultaneous beginning and end, the charm of newness and simultaneously of transitoriness," the somehow miraculous capacity of being "simultaneously being and non-being" (Simmel 1997: 192). This leads to discovering significant implications on both a psychological and specifically aesthetic level. Simmel investigates indeed the way in which the "relations of equalizing unification and individual demarcation," previously analyzed on a social level, are also repeated "within the individual soul" (Simmel 1997: 200). And he also connects the results of such a psycho-sociological examination to the question concerning the ideal of beauty in fashion and the latter's relationship with "the forms of art, as they have developed historically": in particular, with the classical and the baroque (Simmel 1997: 204–5).

Beside all these aspects, there is also a substantial and indeed remarkable number of other important dimensions that Simmel takes into account in the relatively few pages of his essay. For example: the form/content relationship and the independence of fashion from any objective reason or material standard; the effect of money economy on accelerating the rhythm of fashion changes, which is connected, in turn, to the fundamentally accelerated rhythm of modern life in general; the psychological types of the "slaves to fashion," on the one hand, and those who deliberately clothe themselves in an unfashionable manner, on the other hand, as embodying opposite but equally one-sided attitudes towards fashion (say, "exaggeration" vs. "negation"); the role of fashion as a form of compensation for women, because of their lack of social position in the previous ages; the dialectical relationship between fashion and "inner freedom" vs. "social dependency." However, we do not need here full descriptions of each part of what Simmel is saying. What matters here is that Simmel proves to be able not to reduce fashion's complexity to just one of its components (imitation), but rather to conceptually grasp the elusive essence of fashion by emphasizing the latter's psychological and social relevance that precisely derives from its ambiguity. By doing so, he develops a full-blown interpretation that probably stands out from all the previous philosophical attempts in this field. We owe to Simmel an unprecedented understanding of the way fashion "both gives expression to the impulse towards equalization and individualization, as well as to the allure of imitation and conspicuousness" (Simmel 1997: 196). No wonder, then, if his essay soon became an essential and unavoidable reference point for all subsequent philosophical and sociological investigations of this phenomenon.

Notwithstanding the existence of several important philosophers who focused their attention on fashion after Simmel, the last thinker that I am going to focus upon in this contribution is the German phenomenologist Eugen Fink. This means that I am not going to take into examination here the perspectives disclosed, for example, by the leading theorists of the so-called Frankfurt School, like Walter Benjamin and his friend and colleague Theodor W. Adorno. In his monumental and unfinished *Passagen-Werk* Benjamin developed indeed a dialectical conception of fashion as something somehow suspended, or better placed on the threshold, "between carnal pleasure and the corpse," between "the organic world [and] the inorganic," between "frivolity and death," or even between "birth and death" (Benjamin 1999: 62, 69–70, 78). Whereas Adorno, although quite critical towards fashion because of its "obvious dependency [...] on the profit motive and its embeddedness in capitalist industry," nevertheless positively defined fashion in his likewise unfinished *Aesthetic Theory* as "art's permanent confession that it is not what it claims to be": namely, as something that, due to "its erotic element," can remind the arts "of what [they] never fully succeeded in sublimating" (Adorno 2002: 315–7). Beside them, other influential thinkers of the twentieth century who were interested in fashion are also, for example, Roland Barthes (1990), Jean Baudrillard (1981), Pierre Bourdieu (Bourdieu and Delsaut 1975; Bourdieu 1984), and Gilles Lipovetsky (1994). The choice not to linger on these as well other thinkers, and rather to only concentrate on Fink, is due to the fact that Benjamin's or Adorno's perspectives have been widely and accurately studied and interpreted by various scholars.[17] Vice versa, despite its length, systematic character, and its capacity to provide penetrating insights into various aspects of this phenomenon, Fink's contribution to the philosophy of fashion is still a relatively unknown and little studied contribution in the field of fashion theory, thus deserving a re-examination and rehabilitation. Whereas, as far as Barthes', Baudrillard's, Bourdieu's, and Lipovetsky's theories are concerned, it must be said that these authors have worked at the crossroad of philosophy, semiotics, social theory, and literary criticism. Furthermore, their theories are very well known, much studied, and much appreciated in the field of fashion studies. Therefore, despite their undeniable importance and influence, a presentation of their ideas is not strictly necessary, or at least less urgently required, in the context of this *cursory* historical reconstruction specifically focused on modern strictly speaking *philosophical* accounts of fashion.

Fink was a German philosopher belonging to the so-called phenomenological movement (for this definition, see Spiegelberg 1960 and Gadamer 1976). More precisely, he was one of the main representatives, beside Husserl and Heidegger, of the tradition of phenomenological philosophy at the University of Freiburg that is still alive and active today.[18] He is perhaps best known for being the author of a fundamental introduction to Nietzsche's philosophy and also for his ontological-cosmological interpretations of the concepts of play and world (for a biographical and philosophical sketch, see Sepp 2010). He is also the author, however, of a remarkable contribution to the philosophy of fashion published in 1969 under the title *Mode . . . ein verführerisches Spiel*.

The starting point and, quite interestingly, also the end and final result of Fink's investigation is represented by the claim that philosophy, despite its traditional suspiciousness towards everything that is merely superficial, should be open to "all phenomena that may give occasion to thinking," thus including such "a peculiar and ambiguous phenomenon" as fashion that, as he explains, is actually (and unsuspectedly, one may add) characterized by "an ontological" and "an anthropological relevance"[19] (Fink 1969: 15, 110, 113). It is important to lay emphasis on the philosophical-anthropological direction of Fink's investigation—which may be interpreted indeed as a *phenomenologically grounded anthropology of fashion*—because it actually represents one of the distinctive features of his approach. This emerges in the clearest way, for example, when he stresses the fact that the human being is "a peculiar creature," burdened with the need of self-structuring its life and characterized, among other things, by "a particular relationship to its own body." As a matter of fact, "our existence is embodied," "we are world-open in an embodied way (*leibhaft*)," and "a great variety of vital phenomena are bodily (*leiblich*) disclosed to us." In short, "the human body (*Menschenleib*) is not a thing," but it is rather "the human being's effective reality" that "gives expression to all of its essential existential structures" through words, actions, gestures and facial expressions, attitude and customs, "and finally also through the way in which one dresses up" (Fink 1969: 22–5, 34). In claiming this, and in insisting on the significance of the *bodily dimension* for the structure itself of our overall world-experience, Fink clearly relies on insights into the dual dimension of our bodily life—namely, into the dual way we can refer to our own body both as *Körper* (an objective body, i.e., a mere object, a thing among things examined on a third-person perspective) and as *Leib* (a lived body, the body of a living organism experienced on a first-person perspective)—that have characterized to a great extent the development of phenomenological philosophy from Husserl to Merleau-Ponty until today. As a matter of fact, according to phenomenological investigations, the body is not "one object among others," but rather:

> is considered a constitutive or transcendental principle, precisely because it is involved in the very possibility of experience. It is deeply implicated in our relation to the world, in our relation to others, and in our self-relation, and its analysis consequently proves crucial for our understanding of the mind–world relation, for our understanding of the relation between self and other, and for our understanding of the mind–body relation. [. . .] The lived body is neither spirit nor nature, neither soul nor body, neither inner nor outer, neither subject nor object. All of these contraposed categories are derivations of something more basic. [. . .] The body is not a screen between me and the world; rather, it shapes our primary way of being-in-the-world. [. . .] Moreover, all of [the] aspects of embodiment shape the way I perceive the world. [. . .] Since this is the lived body with which I perceive and act, it is in constant connection with the world. And this connection is not a mere surface-to-surface contact, as a corpse might lie on the surface of a table; rather, my body is integrated with the world. To be situated in the world means not simply to be located someplace in a physical environment, but to be in rapport with circumstances that are bodily meaningful.
>
> **GALLAGHER AND ZAHAVI** 2008: 135, 137

Far from being irrelevant for the specific purposes of a philosophical inquiry into fashion, this conception proves to be essential, inasmuch as it also opens up the possibility of a general *rethinking* of the body/dress relationship. In fact, "clothes serve as a cover, as a protection" for the human being, but also (if not in the first place) as "proximate, close-to-the-body (*leibnahe*) and skintight means of expression" (Fink 1969: 50). What emerges is thus a concept of dress, and "in particular fashionable dress," as a sort of "second lived body (*zweiter Leib*)" (Fink 1969: 69). A concept that is closely connected, in turn, to a general anthropological conception of the human being as a creature that obviously depends on natural processes and laws, but at the same time lives in a self-created, culturally conditioned, and historically determined world. Clothes appear then as a "second lived body" for such peculiar living beings as those we are, "inhabiting two dimensions," uniting in their life-experience "natural drives and freedom, desire and reason" (Fink 1969: 53, 62). Living beings essentially characterized, so to speak, by the possession of a "second nature": that is, by living in a cultural world that represents their natural environment but has been created and structured through a long and even distressing work of self-distanciation from nature in its immediacy.

Quite interestingly, in recent times somehow analogous observations have been made by Joanne Entwistle and Malcom Barnard. The former, in her influential study *The Fashioned Body* (2000), also speaks of dress as a sort of extension of our embodied Self, i.e., as a sort of "second skin."[20] While Barnard, for his part, explicitly refers to Entwistle herself and still other theorists, and argues that "while fashion may be about the body, [. . .] it is also [. . .] about the 'fashioned' body," by which he understands "*not a natural* [. . .] *body*" but rather:

> a "produced" and therefore "cultured" body. This is partly because one of the meanings of fashion (as a verb) is "to make" or "to produce", and partly because *there can be no simple, uncultured, natural body.* [. . .] Even when naked, the body is posed or held in certain ways, it makes gestures and it is thoroughly meaningful. To say that the fashioned body is always *a cultured body* is also to say that the fashioned body is *a meaningful body* [. . .]. This is because saying that fashion is meaningful is to say that *fashion is a cultural phenomenon.*
>
> **BARNARD** 2007: 4 (my emphasis)

With regard to this, it must be emphasized that a decisive element in Fink's conception is represented by the human capacity to assume a distanced position from *natural* impulses (especially those concerning natural attraction and seduction), to learn how to manage and control them, to establish a mediated relationship with them rather than immediately seek to satisfy them, and finally to sublimate such impulses by means of *cultural* activities. It is precisely at this point that *fashion* comes into play, inasmuch as the latter is precisely understood by Fink as "a seductive game," as a "sphere in between (*Zwischensphäre*)" or "field in between (*Zwischenfeld*)," namely as a space that is the result of the typically human process of "sublimation of impulses" but does not function as a means for the latter's mere repression or suppression, but rather leads to their intensification and even exaggeration, although always in the context of culturally domesticated activities (Fink 1969: 69–70. On fashion and seduction, see also Fink 1969: 100–1). In Fink's view, fashion thus shares with the human existence as such a fundamental *ambiguity*, or better it embodies the ambiguous character that is typical of the human being as *both* a natural and a cultural being, it takes this ambiguity on, and it actually brings it to extremes. "In the appearance of fashion," as Fink explains, we see "the flourishing of the ambiguous character of the human existence as such" (Fink 1969: 111–12).

Now, it is clear that making fashion's essentially ambiguous and multiform character fully explicit implies refusing to assume a simplifying or reductionist approach to this phenomenon. It is thus not by accident that Fink's conception shows a great complexity and what we may define, once again, as an eminently *dialectical* character (although clearly in a broad meaning of "dialectics," i.e., not referring this term only to dialectical philosophies strictly speaking, like Hegelian and post-Hegelian thought, etc.). This appears in the perhaps clearest way when Fink first points out that the "original drive to imitation"—contextualized as something belonging to the "public sphere (*Öffentlichkeit*)"—surely represents one of the fundamental "components of fashion," but then explains that the latter has a "twofold character (*zweifacher Charakter*)." In fact, it always oscillates between the two poles of "the public sphere," on the one hand, "and individuality," on the other hand (Fink 1969: 46–7). Once again, we thus see the dialectical relationship between opposite moments (imitation and distinction; conformism and originality; assimilation to others and individualism; public and private life) emerging as relevant and indeed decisive for the definition of fashion, where the latter is significantly understood as "a particular and particularly meaningful branch of culture industry today" but, contrary to the view of other theorists, not as a form of manipulation, empire, or even dictatorship, but rather as "a reservation of freedom" (Fink 1969: 46, 61, 95, 99).

On this basis, the phenomenon of fashion is defined by Fink as "multilayered and complex," "ambivalent and ambiguous," and "the fashionable dress" appears to him as characterized by an "intrinsic oppositive character":[21] that is, by a tendency to embody mutually opposite dimensions, inasmuch as it negates for example "natural nakedness," i.e., what we may consider as the merely natural condition of mankind, but at the same time "also negates the enveloping dress," i.e., what we may define as an excess of civilization (Fink 1969: 46, 53, 55). "The fashionable dress is dialectical," Fink eventually explains, and indeed "fashion as a whole, understood as an existential phenomenon (*Daseinsphänomen*), is dialectical: something that is neither determined by a one-sided positive character nor by a one-sided negative one, but rather presents itself as a choppy game made of antagonisms and contrasts" (Fink 1969: 113).

6. Fashion: An aesthetic topic

To summarize, the question "What is fashion?"—or better: "What is the law, mechanism or basic principle that fashion essentially rests upon?"—has been answered by most philosophers who deigned setting their foot in this field in terms of imitation, "in terms of unanimity and mass mutual mimicry" (Pappas 2008: 14). As I said, some of them also emphasized the importance of individuality and differentiation, but one had to wait until Simmel's work to find a theorization capable of equally emphasizing the significance of both moments, and above all of understanding them not as abstractly and dichotomically separated but rather as dialectically connected and intertwined with each other. Taking "human *imitativeness*" as "fashion's fundamental characteristic" implies describing it incompletely, inasmuch as social life is not reducible to this (although imitation surely plays a role in it) and rather appears as "a battleground between forces of assimilation and forces of differentiation": hence "social imitation" may be of course "a necessary condition" but "taken by itself it will not account for the phenomena of fashion" (Pappas 2008: 6, 14, 17). The same holds true, of course, for every attempt to take human *distinctiveness* alone as fashion's fundamental characteristic, as has been emphasized for example by Gilles Lipovetsky in his strong criticism of "the schema of social distinction" that, from a certain moment on (and probably more in sociological works than in strictly speaking philosophical works),[22] was assumed as "the sovereign key for understanding fashion." In Lipovetsky's view, however, this scheme gradually turned into "an obstacle to a historical understanding of the phenomenon," especially because it led to underrating the role played in the "empire of fashion" by "the cultural power of novelty," by "the thirst for novelty" (Lipovetsky 1994: 4–5, 153–4).

To be sure, as I have already explained in the first section of this chapter, I am not claiming here that nineteenth- and early twentieth-century philosophies of fashion can be reduced to the categories of imitation and differentiation alone. In fact, it is clear that the main philosophers of fashion of this age developed and applied several concepts in their attempt to arrive at an adequate understanding of this phenomenon. Among these *concepts*, one may mention, beside imitation and differentiation, also consumption and ostentation, class relationships and divisions, economic and symbolic values, psychosocial efficacy, rapidity in change, difference between ancient and modern ideals of beauty, or finally such conceptual pairs as essence/appearance, nature/culture, historical dependence/independence, deterministic/endogenous development, heteronomy/autonomy, and so on. Rather, what I have tried to point out is the fact that differentiation, and to a greater extent indeed imitation, have actually been given a greater significance than other concepts in the attempt to finally grasp the real *essence* of fashion.

Furthermore, with regard to these questions and these authors, it becomes clear that fashion, if interpreted from a *philosophical* point of view—and thus also considering the various sub-disciplines into which the field of philosophical studies in the broadest sense is articulated—is mainly an aesthetic subject, a matter of interest for *aesthetics*. This is already clear, for example, in Simmel's essay, as he takes into account the "complete indifference of fashion to the material standards of life" and to every kind of objective motivations or decisions, and then connects "the complete lack of objectivity" that is thus seen as quintessential of "the developments of fashion" (Simmel 1997: 190) to the latter's "aesthetic charm" or "appeal" (*ästhetischer Reiz*).[23] This particular charm is based on fashion's extraneousness to the realm of contents and meanings, on its fundamental frivolousness, on its being a mere play of forms that, however, is important for us precisely because of its superficial character: that is, because of its peculiar way of living on, and dealing with, the mere surface of things, and precisely for this reason acquiring a great relevance for us. But this results in a perhaps even clearer way from Fink's book, as he takes into account some objections against fashion that may be raised from an ethical point of view, and explains that "fashion does not deal with morality, [. . .] but is rather"—to express the concept in Nietzschean terms—"beyond good and evil, namely an aesthetic domain." According to Fink, "what is missing in moral interpretations of human clothing [...] is precisely the peculiar aesthetic function of fashion" (Fink 1969: 70–1) that should be thus interpreted as its fundamental dimension.

Finally, the pre-eminent *aesthetic character* of fashion also emerges from other contributions that, although not strictly speaking philosophical (that is, not produced by scholars who are active in the specific field of philosophical studies), are nevertheless of great interest also for philosophers. This is the case, for example, of Elizabeth Wilson's relevant study entitled *Adorned in Dreams*, where she repeatedly calls attention to the relevance of the aesthetic dimension of fashion, claiming that the latter actually represents "an aesthetic medium for the expression of ideas, desires and beliefs circulating in society," that "everywhere dress and adornment play symbolic, communicative and aesthetic roles," and that in various cases the theorists' attempts to reduce fashion to psychology or sociology have ultimately led to exclude, "or at best minimise, the vital aesthetic element of fashion" (Wilson 2003: 3, 9). Also, according to Wilson, fashion thus belongs to the realm of aesthetics, and in fact she proposes "an explanation in aesthetic terms": fashion is "a branch of aesthetics," she claims; it is "one among many forms of aesthetic creativity which make possible the exploration of alternatives"; in short, it is "a serious aesthetic medium" (Wilson 2003: 116, 245, 268).

From this point of view, the main reason why fashion undoubtedly represents an important element of our world, something that greatly conditions our lives and even contributes to the definition of the *Zeitgeist* of the present age (Vinken 2005), probably lies in its aesthetic potentialities. More precisely, it lies in the capacity of fashion to express by aesthetic means (that is, by means of variable combinations of forms, colors, structures, techniques, motifs, etc.) symbolic contents or ideas that come to play a relevant role in the definition of both our individual and collective identities. Beside this, the reason of its importance also lies to some extent in its capacity to call traditional aesthetic standards into question, thus promoting a general rethinking of the range, value, significance, and limits of the *aesthetic dimension* as such. For these and still many more reasons, fashion represents an object that philosophy, if it wants to remain loyal to its traditional goal to "comprehend what is"—namely, comprehend the real in its manifold forms and manifestations, without arbitrarily excluding one or more of them from its horizon—and thus to be "its own time comprehended" (Hegel 1991: 20), today more than ever cannot help dealing with.

Notes

* This work represents one of the outcomes of the research project *Fashion Theory in the Age of the Widespread Aestheticization of Everyday Life*. The project's development has

been supported by a postdoctoral fellowship of the Department for Life Quality Studies at the University of Bologna. The author would like to thank Giovanni Matteucci, an anonymous reader from Bloomsbury Press, and especially Nickolas Pappas, who have carefully read early versions of the text, providing valuable suggestions that were of great help for me and also some constructive critical comments that pressed me to clarify a few points of my text.

1 I have added "philosophy *and sociology* of fashion" just because some of the thinkers that I will take into consideration, like Spencer, Simmel, or Adorno, were both philosophers and sociologists.

2 An excellent presentation and discussion of this topic, also with regard to earlier studies on fashion, can be found in Esposito 2004: 7–16, 34–42, 65–73.

3 I distinguish here between the more general phenomenon of *clothing* and the more delimited or particular phenomenon of *fashion*, in the sense that, although clothing is not reducible to fashion (inasmuch as there are plenty of clothes that are not *a la mode* or trendy) and although fashion, in turn, is not reducible to clothing (inasmuch as it relies on psycho-sociological, anthropological, and aesthetic processes that also apply to other fields, perhaps even to all fields of human experience), it is nevertheless undeniable the existence of a special connection, so to speak, between the two. As has been convincingly pointed out by Lars Svendsen, "fashion is related to many areas of interest, such as clothing, the body, consumption, identity and art. [. . .] Fashion is not just a matter of clothes, but can just as well be considered as a mechanism or an ideology that applies to almost every conceivable area of the modern world." As he explains, "it is obvious that not all clothes can be included under 'fashion,' and as such the term 'fashion' has a *narrower* frame of reference than the term 'clothes.'" At the same time, however, "there is also a range of phenomena that are not clothes but which can also be described as 'fashion,' and as such the term has a *far wider* extension than 'clothes.'" The concept of fashion also applies to the world of "academics and intellectuals," inasmuch as they have to do with "which subjects are 'in' and which are 'out,' which approaches are 'sexy' and which are not": "philosophy does not change solely for rational reasons, but quite often for the sake of change itself," and this means to concede that "philosophy too, at least partially, is subject to fashion" (Svendsen 2006: 11, 13–16). In short, "although fashion exists in many areas of life, not only in the way we dress," it is precisely dress that most often "becomes the focus when fashion arises as a topic of discussion," so that "the discussion frequently centers on clothing" (Johnson et al. 2003: 1). Such different meanings of the notion of fashion, in turn, may be connected with the division existing "within the literature between studies of fashion (as a system, idea or aesthetic) and studies of dress (as in the meanings given to particular practices of clothing and adornment)" (Entwistle 2000: 3).

4 For a general overview, see the entries "Modisch/Mode" by Brunhilde Wehinger in the volume *Ästhetische Grundbegriffe* (Wehinger 2002, vol. 4: 168–83), and "Fashion" by Anne Hollander (sections "Dress in the World" and "La Haute Couture"), Richard Martin (section "Fashion as Art"), and Karen Hanson (section "Fashion and Philosophy"), in the volume *Encyclopedia of Aesthetics* (Kelly 1998, vol. 2: 147–60).

5 Recent works that have tried, at least to some extent, to overcome this well-established hostility or "fraught relationship" (as defined by Negrin 2012) between philosophy and fashion, and thus have proposed philosophical interpretations of various questions related to the world of fashion, include for example the collections edited by Scapp and Seitz (2010), and by Wolfendale and Kennett (2011).

6 A relevant exception is represented by an anthology edited by Daniel L. Purdy that, although not only concerned with philosophers, significantly focuses on "a philosophical lineage of fashion commentary that [had] previously not been recognized by American theorists," explaining that "for some 250 years, social theorists have acknowledged that fashion is a distinctive feature of modern life. [...] Its transitoriness, the conformity it inspires, the vast range of its influence, its reliance on opinion and media, its love of appearances all have made it a representation of modernity" (Purdy 2004: 3).

7 Garve's essay *Ueber die Moden* is only partially translated into English in the anthology *The Rise of Fashion* (Purdy 2004: 66–71). I will make reference to the page numbers of the original German text, although adopting the abovementioned English translation for those passages that have been anthologized in *The Rise of Fashion* (without explicit reference to the latter's page numbers). Otherwise the translations are my own.

8 I clearly assume here Lipovetsky's position on this point as representative of a great number of fashion theorists who, as I said, usually establish a clear connection between the essence or nature of fashion and what we may define the spirit of modernity. This does not exclude, however, the existence of some theorists who implicitly or explicitly agree with Garve's conviction about the universal character of fashion, the most important of whom is probably the German sociologist René König, who understands fashion as "*a total social phenomenon*" concerning "*the human being in its entirety*," and claims "the poor interpretation according to whom fashion is only 'a product of capitalism'" to be simply "absurd," inasmuch as "the roots of fashion" even lie in processes dating back to "the three phases of the Stone Age" (König 1999: 7–9).

9 See, for instance, Kant 2006 (142–3); Hegel 1975 (vol. 2: 742–50); Nietzsche 1996 (262–3, 363–5). Worthy of notice, both Kant and Nietzsche trace back the essence of fashion to our natural tendency to *imitation* (see Kant 2006: 142; and Nietzsche 1996: 262).

10 Lotze's passages on dress in his systematic treatise *Microcosmus* are only partially translated into English in the anthology *Fashion Foundations* (Johnson et al. 2003: 40–3). I will make reference to the page numbers of the original German text, although adopting the abovementioned English translation for those passages that have been anthologized in *Fashion Foundations* (without explicit reference to the latter's page numbers). Otherwise the translations are my own.

11 On the origins of American pragmatism *between* Peirce and James, see, for instance, the clear reconstruction provided by Murphy 1990: 7–57.

12 I borrow this last expression from Lieberman 2013.

13 I borrow some of these observations, abstracting from the epistemological context in which they had been originally developed and adapting them to the context of the present investigation of fashion, from John McDowell's influential perspective named "naturalism of second nature" (see McDowell 1996: especially 108–26).

14 "L'art signale les groupes humains, il marque leur identité. Culture et art, quelles que soient par surcroît leurs significations et leur fonctions plus profondes ou plus élevées, plus intellectuelles, plus inconscientes aussi, sont, pour tous les groupes, d'abord des formes de présentation de soi, des véhicules de leur identité. *Ce sont des parures.* [...] Dans un régime de l'art et de l'esthétique où prévaut le renouvellement continuel des événements, [...] seule la mode produit des différences. [...] De quoi la mode, si fugace soit-elle, est-elle donc l'expression pour porter ainsi seule la signification d'un monde

insignifiant? La réponse que je suggère est simplement que la mode est porteuse d'identité. [. . .] Elle est le point d'accrochage, le portemanteau des identités problématiques" (Michaud 2003: 194, 203–4).

15 Vischer's essay *Wieder einmal über die Mode* is only partially translated into English in the abovementioned anthology *The Rise of Fashion* (Purdy 2004: 154–62). I will make reference to the page numbers of the original German text, although adopting the abovementioned English translation for those passages that have been anthologized in *The Rise of Fashion* (without explicit reference to the latter's page numbers). Otherwise the translations are my own.

16 Kant's most famous antinomies are those concerning the "transcendental ideas" or "concepts of reason" in the *Critique of Pure Reason* (Kant 1998: 459–550), and taste and teleological judgment in the *Critique of the Power of Judgment* (Kant 2000: 213–21, 257–61).

17 For example, a detailed and convincing presentation of Benjamin's approach to the question concerning fashion is that provided by Lehmann 2000: 199–277.

18 See, in particular, the phenomenological hermeneutics developed in a very original fashion by Günter Figal (2010 and 2015).

19 In translating the German word *Bewandtnis* with "Relevance" I follow the suggestion of Joan Stambaugh, the English translator of one of the masterpieces of phenomenological philosophy that greatly influenced also Fink, namely *Being and Time*. In Heidegger's 1927 masterpiece, the concept of "Relevance (*Bewandtnis*)" plays an important role in the context of his analysis of "the worldliness of the world" and stands for "the being of innerworldly beings, for which they are always already initially freed. Beings are in each case relevant. Being is the *ontological* determination of the being of these beings, not an ontic statement about beings. What the relevance is about is the what-for of serviceability, the wherefore of usability. The what-for of serviceability can in turn be relevant. [. . .] The total relevance itself, however, ultimately leads back to a what-for which *no longer* has relevance, which itself is not a being of the kind of being of things at hand within a world, but is a being whose being is defined as being-in-the-world, to whose constitution of being worldliness itself belongs. This primary what-for is not just another for-that as a possible factor in relevance. The primary 'what-for' is a for-the-sake-of-which. But the for-the-sake-of-which always concerns the being of *Da-sein* which is essentially concerned *about* this being itself in its being" (Heidegger 1996: 77–8).

20 It is probably not by chance if Entwistle's original account relies, among others, also on phenomenological insights into the significance of the bodily dimension for the constitution of our world-experience in general. On this topic, see also Entwistle 2003.

21 The German word employed by Fink here and elsewhere in his book is *Gegenwendigkeit*, which is actually not easy to translate into English, inasmuch as it does not stand for a static quality or feature of an object (thus fixable, as it were, in a single and precise definition), but rather embodies the dynamic process of two elements mutually interacting or even turning against each other, thus establishing a dialectical relationship based on a polar opposition or contradiction (*sich gegen etwas wenden* means precisely "to oppose something, to turn against something"). I am grateful to my friend and colleague Julia Pfefferkorn at the University of Tübingen for the help provided in clarifying these semantic nuances in the term *Gegenwendigkeit*.

22 Lipovetsky especially stands up against what he calls "the prevailing sociological response," based on explanations in terms of "class competition and strategies of social distinction," that has been embodied, for example, by "Baudrillard's earliest work as well as that of Bourdieu." In his view, "the logic of distinction provides a crude map of the fashion economy [. . .]. The permanent installation of consummate fashion in our societies will never be understood until we restore cultural values to their rightful place, a place continually obscured by Marxism and sociology alike" (Lipovetsky 1994: 152–3).

23 This last passage, namely the one about fashion's peculiar kind of "aesthetic charm," is absent from the English translation based on the 1905 version of the essay, but is present in the 1911 text. Hence in this case the translation is mine (see Simmel 1986: 42).

Bibliography

Adorno, Th.W. (2002), *Aesthetic Theory* (1970), trans. R. Hullot-Kentor, London-New York: Continuum

Alain (Émile-Auguste Chartier) (1963), *Système des beaux-arts*, Paris: Gallimard

Alain (Émile-Auguste Chartier) (2002), *Vingt leçons sur les beaux-arts* (1931), digital edition ed. by B. Gibier in the context of the book series "Les classiques des sciences sociales." Available online: http://classiques.uqac.ca/classiques/Alain/vingt_lecons_beaux_arts/vingt_lecons_BA.html (accessed May 17, 2015)

Barnard, M. (2007), "Introduction", in M. Barnard (ed.), *Fashion Theory. A Reader*, 1–10, London-New York: Routledge

Barthes, R. (1990), *The Fashion System* (1967), trans. M. Ward and R. Howard, Berkeley: University of California Press

Baudrillard, J. (1981), *For a Critique of the Political Economy of the Sign* (1972), trans. C. Levin, St. Louis: Telos Press

Benjamin, W. (1999), *The Arcades Project* (1927–40), trans. H. Eiland and K. McLaughlin, Cambridge (MA)-London: Harvard University Press

Bourdieu, P. (1984), *Distinction: A Social Critique of the Judgment of Taste* (1979), trans. R. Nice, Cambridge (MA): Harvard University Press

Bourdieu, P. and Y. Delsaut (1975), "Le couturier et sa griffe: contribution à une théorie de la magie", *Actes de la recherche en sciences sociales*, 1 (1): 7–36

Carchia, G. (2005), "Moda", in G. Carchia and P. D'Angelo (eds), *Dizionario di estetica*, 185–6, Roma-Bari: Laterza

Entwistle, J. (2000), *The Fashioned Body: Fashion, Dress and Modern Social Theory*, Cambridge: Polity Press

Entwistle, J. (2003), "The Dressed Body", in M. Evans and E. Lee (eds), *Real Bodies: A Sociological Introduction*, 133–50, New York: Palgrave Macmillan

Esposito, E. (2004), *I Paradossi della Moda. Originalità e transitorietà nella società moderna*, Bologna: Baskerville

Figal, G. (2010), *Objectivity: The Hermeneutical and Philosophy* (2006), trans. Th.D. George, Albany: SUNY Press

Figal, G. (2015), *Aesthetics as Phenomenology: The Appearance of Things* (2010), trans. J. Veith, Bloomington: Indiana University Press

Fink, E. (1969), *Mode . . . ein verführerisches Spiel*, Basel-Stuttgart: Birkhäuser Verlag

Gadamer, H.-G. (1976), "The Phenomenological Movement" (1963), in *Philosophical Hermeneutics*, trans. D.E. Linge, 130–81, Berkeley-Los Angeles-London: University of California Press

Gallagher, S. and D. Zahavi (2008), *The Phenomenological Mind: An Introduction to Philosophy of Mind and Cognitive Science*, London-New York: Routledge

Garve, C. (1985), "Ueber die Moden" (1792), in *Versuche über verschiedene Gegenstände aus der Moral, der Literatur und dem gesellschaftlichen Leben. Teil 1 und 2*, in K. Wölfel (ed.), *Gesammelte Werke*, vol. 1: 117–294, Hildesheim-Zürich-New York: Georg Olms Verlag. Also available online: http://modetheorie.de/index.php?id=376 (accessed May 17, 2015)

Hanson, K. (1993), "Dressing Down Dressing Up: The Philosophical Fear of Fashion", in H. Hein and C. Korsmeyer (eds), *Aesthetics in Feminist Perspective*, 229–41, Bloomington-Indianapolis: Indiana University Press

Hanson, K. (1998), "Fashion and Philosophy", in M. Kelly (ed.), *Encyclopedia of Aesthetics*, vol. 2: 147–60, Oxford-New York: Oxford University Press

Hegel, G.W.F. (1975), *Aesthetics: Lectures on Fine Art* (1835–38), 2 vols, trans. T.M. Knox, Oxford: Clarendon Press

Hegel, G.W.F. (1991), *Elements of the Philosophy of Right* (1821), trans. H.B. Nisbet, ed. A.W. Wood, Cambridge-New York: Cambridge University Press

Heidegger, M. (1996), *Being and Time* (1927), trans. J. Stambaugh, Albany: SUNY Press

Hollander, A. (1998), "Dress in the World" and "La Haute Couture", in M. Kelly (ed.), *Encyclopedia of Aesthetics*, vol. 2: 147–60, Oxford-New York: Oxford University Press

James, W. (1950), *The Principles of Psychology* (1890), 2 vols, New York: Dover Publications

Johnson, K.P., S.J. Torntore and J.B. Eicher, eds (2003), *Fashion Foundations: Early Writings on Fashion and Dress*, Oxford-New York: Berg

Kant, I. (1998), *Critique of Pure Reason* (1781; 1787), trans. P. Guyer and A.W. Wood, Cambridge-New York: Cambridge University Press

Kant, I. (2000), *Critique of the Power of Judgment* (1790), trans. P. Guyer and E. Matthews, Cambridge-New York: Cambridge University Press

Kant, I. (2006), *Anthropology From a Pragmatic Point of View* (1798), trans. R.B. Louden, Cambridge-New York: Cambridge University Press

Kawamura, Y. (2005), *Fashion-ology: An Introduction to Fashion Studies*, Oxford-New York: Berg

Kleinwächter, F. (1880), "Zur Philosophie der Mode", *Deutsche Streit- und Zeitfragen. Flugschriften zur Kenntnis der Gegenwart*, ed. by F. von Holtzendorff, 9 (129): 3–44. Also available online: http://modetheorie.de/index.php?id=553 (accessed May 17, 2015)

König, R. (1999), *Menschheit auf dem Laufsteg. Die Mode im Zivilisationsprozeß* (1985), in *Schriften. Ausgabe letzter Hand*, vol. 6, ed. by H. von Alemann, H.-J. Hummell, O. Konig and H.-P. Thurn, Opladen: Leske + Budrich

Lehmann, U. (2000), *Tigersprung: Fashion in Modernity*, Cambridge (MA)-London: The MIT Press

Lieberman, P. (2013), *The Unpredictable Species: What Makes Humans Unique*, Princeton (NJ): Princeton University Press

Lillethun, A. (2007), "Introduction: Fashion Theory", in L. Welters and A. Lillethum (eds), *The Fashion Reader*, 77–82, Oxford-New York: Berg

Lipovetsky, G. (1994), *The Empire of Fashion: Dressing Modern Democracy* (1987), trans. C. Porter, Princeton (NJ): Princeton University Press

Lotze, H. (1923), *Mikrokosmos. Ideen zur Naturgeschichte und Geschichte der Menschheit. Versuch einer Anthropologie* (1856–64), 2 vols, Leipzig: Felix Meiner Verlag

Martin, R. (1998), "Fashion as Art", in M. Kelly (ed.), *Encyclopedia of Aesthetics*, vol. 2: 147–160, Oxford-New York: Oxford University Press

Matteucci, G. (2012), *L'artificio estetico. Moda e bello naturale in Simmel e Adorno*, Milano-Udine: Mimesis

McDowell, J. (1996), *Mind and World* (1994), Cambridge (MA)-London: Harvard University Press

Meinhold, R. (2013), *Fashion Myths: A Cultural Critique*, trans. J. Irons, Bielefeld: Transcript Verlag

Michaud, Y. (2003), *L'art a l'état gazeux. Essai sur le triomphe de l'esthétique*, Paris: Éditions Stock

Monneyron, F. (2006), *La sociologie de la mode*, Paris: Presses Universitaires de France

Morini, E. (2012), "Creatore, artista o designer? Il problema della legittimazione", in M. Pedroni and P. Volonté (eds), *Moda e arte*, 35–50, Milano: Franco Angeli

Murphy, J.P. (1990): *Pragmatism: From Peirce to Davidson*, Boulder-San Francisco-Oxford: Westview Press

Negrin, L. (2012), "Fashion and Aesthetics—A Fraught Relationship", in A. Gecky and V. Karaminas (eds), *Fashion and Art*, 43–54, London: Bloomsbury

Neumann, M. (2006), "'das Abstractum: Mode': Über Friedrich Theodor Vischers *Mode und Cynismus*", Appendix to F.Th. Vischer, *Mode und Cynismus. Beiträge zur Kenntniß unserer Culturformen und Sittenbegriffe*, ed. by M. Neumann, 181–208, Berlin: Kulturverlag Kadmos

Nietzsche, F. (1966), *Beyond Good and Evil: Prelude to a Philosophy of the Future* (1886), trans. W. Kaufmann, New York: Random House

Nietzsche, F. (1996), *Human, All Too Human: A Book for Free Spirits* (1878–80), trans. R.J. Hollingdale, Cambridge-New York: Cambridge University Press

Pappas, N. (2008), "Fashion Seen as Something Imitative and Foreign", *The British Journal of Aesthetics*, 48 (1): 1–19

Perucchi, L. (1996), "Simmel e la moda", Appendix to G. Simmel, *La moda*, ed. by L. Perucchi, 71–8, Milano: SE

Purdy, D.L., ed. (2004), *The Rise of Fashion: A Reader*, Minneapolis: University of Minnesota Press

Riello, G. (2012), *La moda. Una storia dal Medioevo a oggi*, Roma-Bari: Laterza

Scapp, R. and B. Seitz, eds (2010), *Fashion Statements: On Style, Appearance, and Reality*, New York: Palgrave Macmillan

Schnädelbach, H. (1984), *Philosophy in Germany 1831–1933*, trans. E. Matthews, Cambridge-New York: Cambridge University Press

Sepp, H.R. (2010), "Eugen Fink (1905–1975)", in H.R. Sepp and L. Embree (eds), *Handbook of Phenomenological Aesthetics*, 119–21, Dordrecht-Heidelberg-London-New York: Springer

Simmel, G. (1986), "Die Mode" (1911), in *Philosophische Kultur: Über das Abenteuer, die Geschlechter und die Krise der Moderne. Gesammelte Essais* (1923), Berlin: Klaus Wagenbach

Simmel, G. (1997), "The Philosophy of Fashion" (1905), trans. M. Ritter and D. Frisby, in D. Frisby and M. Featherstone (eds), *Simmel On Culture: Selected Writings*, 187–205, London-Thousand Oaks-New Delhi: Sage Publications

Spencer, H. (1966a), *The Principles of Sociology* (1874–96), 3 vols, Osnabrück: Otto Zeller (reprint of the 1902 edition)

Spencer, H. (1966b), "Manners and Fashion" (1854), in *Essays: Scientific, Political & Speculative*, in *The Works of Herbert Spencer*, vol. 15: 1–51, Osnabrück: Otto Zeller (reprint of the 1891 edition)

Spiegelberg, H. (1960), *The Phenomenological Movement: A Historical Introduction*, 2 vols, The Hague: M. Nijhoff

Svendsen, L. (2006), *Fashion: A Philosophy* (2004), trans. J. Iron, London: Reaktion Books

Vinken, B. (2005), *Fashion Zeitgeist: Trends and Cycles in the Fashion System*, trans. M. Hewson, Oxford-New York: Berg

Vischer, F.Th. (2006), "Wieder einmal über die Mode" (1879), in M. Neumann (ed.), *Mode und Cynismus. Beiträge zur Kenntniß unserer Culturformen und Sittenbegriffe*, 11–82, Berlin: Kulturverlag Kadmos. Also available online: http://modetheorie.de/index.php?id=939 (accessed May 17, 2015)

Watson, C.A. (2004), "The Sartorial Self: William James's Philosophy of Dress", *History of Psychology*, 7 (3): 211–24

Wehinger, B. (2002), "Modisch/Mode", in K. Barck (ed.), *Ästhetische Grundbegriffe. Historisches Wörterbuch in sieben Bänden*, vol. 4: 168–83, Stuttgart-Weimar: Metzler

Wilson, E. (2003): *Adorned in Dreams: Fashion and Modernity* (1985), London-New York: Tauris & Co.

Wolfendale, J. and J. Kennett, eds (2011), *Fashion—Philosophy for Everyone: Thinking with Style*, Malden (MA)-Oxford: Wiley-Blackwell

2 FASHION: A CONCEPTUAL CONSTELLATION

Giovanni Matteucci

Fiat modes pereat ars

MAX ERNST[1]

From a philosophical point of view, fashion represents a bundle of irregularly interconnected questions. Some of the problems raised by fashion concern social relationships, while others concern psychological processes within the individual; some questions concerning fashion have to do with the ethical dimension of life, while others are basically related to the aesthetic domain of taste, and still others emerge from the order of symbolic-cultural questions or even from that of practical and economic relationships. This irregular complexity of fashion contributes to making at least in part understandable an uncontroversial matter of fact: namely, the fact that fashion, despite its being one of the most pervasive and powerful phenomena of today's so-called global civilization, has not yet been investigated in a way capable of grasping its full potentialities and all its implications. So, although one might reasonably claim that fashion is one of the key features and distinctive phenomena of the most recent part of our history, namely since the last decades, fashion still remains a subject that is mostly neglected by intellectuals. And this is quite paradoxical, inasmuch as intellectuals, in general, and philosophers, in particular, are (or should be) bound to critically analyze and reflect upon their respective historical situations, with special attention to those phenomena that appear as pre-eminent in the various historical periods.

It is my aim in this contribution to show how fashion weighs on, i.e., has great impact on, four fields of inquiry, revealing with regard to each of them one of the specific features that make it an *aesthetic* phenomenon. On this basis, I will thus try to sketch a conceptual map which will prove to be useful in order to understand a phenomenon like fashion, namely a phenomenon that, due to its inner tensions and intrinsic antinomies, rather looks like a constellation than a figure characterized by clear and univocally determinable contents.

1. The cultural problem of fashion: The aesthetic as everyday practice

That fashion is an aesthetic phenomenon is made clear by the simple fact that, both in fashion activities (i.e., practices, productions, etc.) and fashion theories, such typical aesthetic concepts as beauty, pleasure, style, etc., are commonly and widely employed. These elements refer to and rely on categories that ever since the eighteenth century have formed the specific content and heritage assigned to the philosophical discipline concerning taste and art, namely aesthetics. However, it is not enough to simply remind of the fact that it has often made great use of these categories in the field of fashion. Rather, emphasizing the relevance of these concepts in the field of fashion means posing difficult and hard-to-answer questions. As a matter of fact, the attempt to merely put fashion side to side to art, i.e., the attempt to merely juxtapose them, is not something self-evident that can be simply taken for granted. As a consequence, one might be tempted to doubt that it is possible and indeed legitimate to consider fashion as a proper subject of inquiry for aesthetics, namely for the field of philosophy that has traditionally dealt with questions concerning the fine arts (with regard to this, see also Negrin 2012).

There have been various attempts during the last two centuries to find a solution for the question concerning the "artistry," i.e., the artistic status, of fashion. The result of these various attempts was a series of complex and controversial developments that leave the observer with the sensation of finding herself in front of a quite paradoxical situation. In fact, if one exclusively employs the label "art" to indicate what is understood today as art by common sense (where on closer inspection it becomes clear that this widespread common sense is still bound to nineteenth-century artistic conceptions and traditions), then one will be hardly inclined to also include fashion among the arts. To the utmost the honorary title of "artistry" will be appointed to the production of particular dresses and costumes or luxuries, but these practices will be anyway regarded as nothing more than minor and ancillary activities if compared to the visual arts (Hollander 1993) or architecture (see, for instance, Alain 1931). This latter case characterized indeed an epoch in which, due to the spiritual climate influenced by the *Art Déco* and probably on the wave of the appreciation of Paul Poiret expressed by art critics of the late French *Liberty* (as shown by Morini 2012: 40–3), a definitive acknowledgment of the artistic value of the great *couturier* of the time was nearly achieved.

It was a great event when the world of art, so to speak, opened up the door to fashion: an event that produced remarkable results, such as those connected to

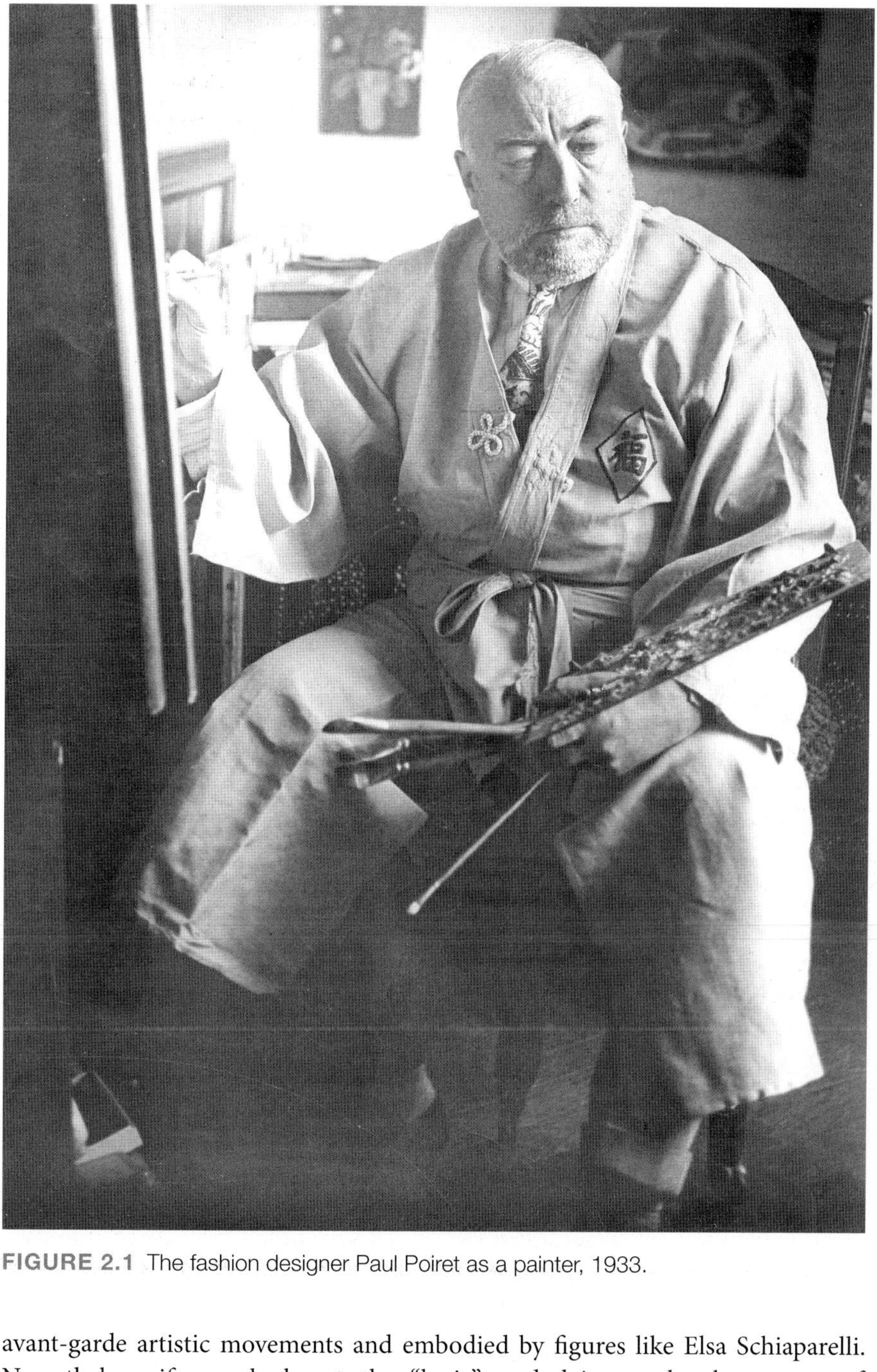

FIGURE 2.1 The fashion designer Paul Poiret as a painter, 1933.

avant-garde artistic movements and embodied by figures like Elsa Schiaparelli. Nevertheless, if one looks at the "logic" underlying such phenomena of acknowledgment and appreciation of the *couturier* by the world of art, it is clear that the attempt was basically that of assimilating single episodes and aspects of fashion to already existing and established fine arts, rather than that of conferring to fashion as such the status of a true form of art.

If one looks instead at the achievements of some twentieth-century researches on the various expressive languages, and properly assesses those artistic developments that led to delegitimize (or at least to radically undermine) such traditional aesthetic concepts as "genius," "artwork," "intuition," "non-practical function of art," etc., what results then is a very different picture. It might even be argued that in the last part of the twentieth century there has been a mutual convergence of fashion and art, and a sort of juxtaposition and interlacing between them in the context of a general field of aesthetic practices in which all differences of rank and relevance appear now as definitively dissolved. It is often the case that artistic practices today are also, or perhaps above all, industrial and spectacular processes implying multiple and jointly connected subjectivities as far as both art creation and enjoyment are concerned. Following these practices the concept of the aesthetic object as an oeuvre has been irremediably replaced today by the concept of an aesthetic *event* that is activated by an experiential device; the objective component of experience acts as interactive interface and thus no longer functions as a pure content of consciousness to be merely contemplated by assuming an aesthetic attitude clearly modeled along the lines of the modern, Cartesian-like, idealized conception of cognitive acts. Fashion has become today one of the most paradigmatic expressions of these kinds of processes that affect and deeply characterize the realm of the aesthetic in our time. Together with design, popular music, and film, fashion has become in the contemporary age the main form of a kind of aesthetic practice that is definitively built upon the "tension plus ou moins intense du commercial et du créatif" which is "constitutive de l'organisation bipolaire du capitalisme artiste" (Lipovetsky and Serroy 2013: 44).

This discourse can also prove to be useful in order to introduce another essential difference between the traditional reference points of aesthetics and the reality we effectively experience today. According to what we may define the aesthetic common sense, grounded on a traditional conception of art, the latter represented a noble and refined domain designated to shape people's taste in certain institutional circumstances in which everyday life was somehow interrupted or suspended (as it still happens today in museums, art galleries, concert halls, theaters, and academies). But the dynamics presiding over the shaping and education of taste today are vice versa nearly completely coincident with those experienced in our "high-aesthetical" everyday lives, namely in the "aestheticized reality" that represents the ideal setting for the cultivation and diffusion of processes that are primarily embodied by fashion. It is not coincidental that the difference between art creations, entertainment performances, and fashion events has grown increasingly imperceptible as far as both the participants to the events, the logic underlying them, the way they take place, and finally the institutional settings of these happenings, are concerned.

One may try to understand these differences by examining the question from a historical-cultural point of view. In the first half of the eighteenth century aesthetics was grounded as a specific theoretical discipline in order to allow philosophy to deal with, and take charge of, the unprecedented and unexpected problems raised at the time by a new conception of the world and the human being. The birth of aesthetics in that historical juncture actually required an act of reduction, inasmuch as the honorary title of "fine art" was not acknowledged and awarded to all human creative and productive techniques, but only to those endowed with such imitative and/or expressive features that would make them appear as weighty and meaningful to the sensibility of the time, that was shaped on the standards of the particular historical-cultural situation of the age. This, however, also implied an act of delimitation and reduction of the realm of the aesthetic in its entirety: if compared to the wider anthropological dimension underlying the dimension of taste, it is clear indeed that modern aesthetics' fundamental approach was to isolate and assume as philosophically relevant only single and restricted aesthetic contents.

Almost correspondingly the current crisis of the arts—namely, the fact that the boundaries that the advocates of a rigid delimitation and reduction of the domain of art have appealed to, no longer appear as reasonable—has produced a sort of emancipation of the aesthetic phenomenon from any pre-established cultural framework or scheme. The experience of the aesthetic that is characteristic of our time is irrespective of the question concerning the boundaries of art. And it is precisely fashion that represents the cross dimension in which this kind of experience of the aesthetic—which is subsequent to the invention of the perimeter of the fine arts—occurs today. In the age when the aesthetic seems to have reached its highest degree of dissemination it is consequently fashion, rather than any of the arts belonging to the limited and elite group of the "fine arts," that soars to the height of key-phenomenon through which the predominant logics of taste consolidate themselves today. As a result, in the age of the widespread aestheticization of everyday life it is not fashion that necessitates being acknowledged and legitimated as art, but it is rather art that appears in need of learning from fashion such strategies and logics that may allow it to regain efficacy, pervasiveness, and communication strength.

In short, and expressing the concept with terms that are frequently used in current philosophical debates, the question is not whether fashion can or even should be "artified"—artification being a neologism that refers to "situations and processes in which something that is not regarded as art in the traditional sense of the word is changed into something art-like or into something that takes influences from artistic ways of thinking and practicing," as explained by Naukkarinen and Saito (2012). Rather, the real question is if (and, if so, to what degree) it is appropriate that fashion contaminates, so to speak, artistic practices. This is proved *e contrario* by the failure of all attempts to appeal to the logic of artification in order to explain the relationship between fashion and art in the contemporary cultural scene. As a matter of fact, every time someone tried to follow this kind of argumentative strategy what resulted was the impossibility to follow it all the way down until arriving to a good conclusion, which is due to the fact that the attempt itself of simply applying the concept of artification implicitly or explicitly implies assuming a limited and traditional idea of art. It is easy and even trivial to notice that fashion is not an Art producing Works that can be considered as creations of the Genius and must be kept in Museums so that they can be offered to spectators capable of a genuinely and totally Disinterested Contemplation. Fashion instead is an industrial process that produces devices offering pleasure (also of a strictly hedonistic kind), in which even the symbolic dimension is turned into economic value, i.e., merchandize, and cynically used for a merely emotive way of communication. So, while the presumption concerning the possibility of the artification of fashion proves to be structurally, intrinsically limited because it fatally presupposes a restricted and highbrow concept of art to which, by means of a "generous" act of ennoblement, fashion would be elevated, the contamination of the world of art by the world of fashion appears instead as a real feature of our time. Namely, as something that has characterized the Western civilization at least since the time when Andy Warhol and pop culture gave birth to the system of the so-called "aesthetic economy" (Böhme 2001). Hence—especially if one looks at the development of aesthetic practices in the last one hundred years—we could have the suspicion that the general paradigm of art is the latter, which is currently widespread, rather than the limited and extremely refined paradigm that monopolized our attention from the all in all quite short period ranging from the mid-eighteenth century to the first half of the twentieth century.

If this is true, then it becomes clear that fashion represents a veritable and indeed complicated challenge for philosophy. And it must be also acknowledged that fashion can play an important and positive role in the field of aesthetics in order to debunk a general conception of philosophical aesthetics that was originally built upon the aversion to face the ghost of what Western thought historically never accepted. Fashion represents indeed the place of the ephemeral, the illusory, the cyclical, the metamorphic, and the multifarious: that is, it is precisely the place of what Western philosophy has always demonized but has also become predominant in the global culture of our time. Hence the theoretical interest raised by fashion in recent times can be described as a sort of "return of the repressed." From this point of view, it is not by accident that the history of the progressive expansion and success of fashion actually coincides with the history of the construction, and then exhaustion and decay, of the modern subject. This coincidence is clear both if one focuses on the positive, affirmative side of the history of the modern subject, and if one investigates instead the "hidden shadow" that has always gone with the construction process of the modern subject—as Lipovetsky (1987) and König (1971; 1985) have done, although from different and indeed opposite perspectives. The few great contemporary authors who have dealt in a convincing way with fashion have always paid close and specific attention precisely to these kinds of processes (see the valuable survey provided by Lehmann 2000).

The liberal teaching, so to speak, that one may derive from these observations is the following: the challenge of fashion consists in an invitation to understand the realm of the aesthetic as a complex domain of mutually intertwined everyday practices, rather than as a domain made up of clearly defined and indeed idealized cultural contents. Namely, as a domain that—in order to be properly understood—requires a careful and patient analytical work free from prejudices deriving from prebuilt hierarchies, such as those that have ultimately led to the oppositions between highbrow and lowbrow culture, between refined and popular arts, or even between art and non-art.

2. The categorial problem of fashion: The aesthetic as dynamic field

Anyway, even in case it was generally accepted to understand fashion as the manifestation of a particular aesthetic dimension that cannot be reductively assimilated to the domain of those activities that, on the basis of a certain historical-cultural perspective, have been and are commonly defined as the "fine arts," there would still remain an open question. Specifically, that of defining which is the best way to bring into focus, and thus correctly identify and analyze, the functioning of the respective category. So, problems connected to the intrinsic logic of the concept of fashion overlap with the abovementioned problems connected to the need to provide a cultural contextualization of the phenomenon of fashion.

The proximity of fashion to the arts and its inseparable relationship to the aesthetic realm also give us a clue in order to set up this question. In fact, it may prove to be useful to approach this question by acquiring some elements and ideas from some important positions that have characterized aesthetic debates in our time. My attempt, then, will be that of applying different conceptual and interpretive frameworks, emerged in the context of aesthetic debates in the last fifty years, to the contents and features that are characteristic of fashion.

2.1. Fashion and extensionalist approaches

The first conception that I will take into consideration is that of Nelson Goodman (1976), who aims at providing a unitary account of the various symbolic articulations and, by doing so, also of the various artistic phenomena. This conception is basically characterized by two elements. On the one hand, it is characterized by a kind of *anti-essentialist nominalism* (a) that does not allow speaking of entities or universal essences unconnected to specific symbolic systems. From this perspective, what a certain thing is, namely the way something is what it is, is due to the way it works into a particular reference system. On the other hand, and actually combined to the first aspect, this conception is also characterized by a no less radical *anti-psychologistic extensionalism* (b), according to which the relationships between symbols are only conceivable in referential terms, thus excluding any appeal to mental entities as sources of meaning. The result of this combination of (a) and (b) is the abandonment of any kind of realism about entities and the obliteration of any kind of ontological difference between sign and referent, whose difference is rather conceived only in terms of their respective way of functioning. Inasmuch as something "functions" as a sign only in relation to a certain symbolic system that confers it its particular meaning, the idea of something like intrinsic properties of signs loses all its value and importance.

It is precisely by means of an analysis of the way in which certain objects ("signs") function within certain symbolic systems, and thus acquire the status of works of art, that Goodman arrives at establishing one of his best-known distinctions, namely that between autographic and allographic arts. In the first case, a work is recognized as an artwork thanks to its relation with a certain context of production, so that the decisive role is played here by the signature, by the author's mark. The latter acts as a proof of the history of the work's production and thus probates the validity and originality of a particular item in comparison to all its possible copies. The autographic system is exemplified in the best way possible by such arts as painting and sculpture. In the second case, instead, it makes no sense to pose the question about the originality of the single item, since the allographic system is based on the fact that every instantiation acts as an actualization of the artwork. This is exemplified in the best way possible by the performance of a musical piece that—if performed correctly—does not represent a mere "copy" but rather the fulfillment of the piece.

Now, the attempt to apply this distinction to fashion is not schematic and automatic. As has been noted (Luchetti and Tota 2012: 89–90), the general concept of fashion surely includes such creations as high fashion clothes or other accessories and items whose unique value depends on the style of their authors, and which have therefore the typical features of an autographic work of art. Such products meet the requirements of the logic of falsifiability, i.e., the possibility of being falsified. From a historical point of view, until the 1950s fashion production was directed and aimed (at least as far as its basic ideology was concerned) at realizing these kinds of items, inasmuch as fashion seemed to coincide totally and in an exemplary way with *haute couture*. Not by chance, it was precisely in this age that the abovementioned operation called "artification" was brought to its highest degree. Afterwards, however, the advent of *prêt-à-porter* and so-called *street styles* made it possible and indeed necessary to include under the general concept of fashion also productions whose main feature is precisely the serial character of their performance or fulfillment. The most dangerous threat for these kinds of creations is not represented by falsification but rather by plagiarism: in fact, as it typically happens with performance arts, single and multiple interpretations of a serial product are all legitimated to strive for being acknowledged as "authentic."

If compared to the double paradigm that Goodman conceived exclusively with regard to, and consequently only applied to, the realm of the fine arts, the ongoing and ceaseless fluctuation between autographicity and allographicity that is so typical of fashion leads to define a different kind of relation. Namely, a sort dynamic relation between different poles, in place of the schematic and merely contrastive relation between opposite systems that extensionalist aesthetics ultimately reduces all artistic languages to.

2.2. Fashion and interpretive intensionalism

Another interesting—and actually antipodal to Goodman's extensionalism—conception is that advanced by Arthur C. Danto (1981). At the core of Danto's aesthetics we find the basic conviction that (in given historical circumstances) any object may become a work of art by means of an interpretive and "transfiguring" act which provides it with a special ontological status. Thanks to this transfiguration into art, the object acquires a second nature besides the first, trivial nature represented by its mere real existence—just like a person (according to the Christian religion) after being baptized becomes a member of the city of God beside its being obviously a member of the earthly city.

In order to provide foundations to this aesthetic conception and prove its correctness, Danto draws upon a series of arguments that put into the foreground and emphasize the intensional character of aesthetic experience, namely the cultural contents of belief, historical perspective, personal definition of style, and capacities of reception. According to Danto, such contents and dimensions do not influence nor change in any way our perceptual relationship to the object that has become a candidate for acquiring the status of a work of art; rather, they attach an extra-perceptual dimension to the latter, namely to the object, that is the properly artistic dimension.

Fashion items also contribute to highlight the harmful rigid, schematic, and one-sided character of this second conception. It is true indeed that fashion accomplishes a "transfiguration of the commonplace" almost every day, namely every time it transforms any kind of accessory in our lives or any kind of dress in our wardrobe into a distinctive and socially incisive symbol. However, fashion achieves this aim by means of promotion and intensification of the perceptual, formal, concrete part of the object itself that thus acquires a completely different perceptible aspect. Even the eyes with which one looks at the item are subject to change. In fact, there is a function at work in human perception that acts as an intensification factor of aesthetic qualities and, for this reason, turns fashion devices into something extremely incisive and assures them widespread diffusion, *pace* the modular and cognitivist framework that Danto remains stuck to. As has been convincingly pointed out by Thomas Leddy in his defense of an everyday-aesthetics conception critically oriented towards Danto, the extraordinary significance that fashion practices confer even to ordinary things of our everyday life is still connected to the perceptual dimension. "When the ordinary becomes extraordinary, when it is transfigured," Leddy explains indeed, "it begins to enter into a space that is *perceived as* or *as like* a sacred space" (Leddy 2012: 76). There is no need to further discuss this point with regard to fashion, inasmuch as plenty of examples can be easily found in which the world of fashion turns into a sort of sacred-like space (or space for a parody of the sacred) that sheds new light on ordinary items and bestows on them a new aspect, even arriving sometimes to extreme degrees of fetishism. Fashion thus attests the existence of a reality in which what is essentially required is not the capacity of interpreting differently a certain "given," but rather the ability of perceptually moving within an aesthetically thick space that requests extraordinary, non-trivial reactions following the acknowledgment of the object's aesthetic richness.

2.3. Fashion and institutional theory

This last observation helps to highlight the fact that the aesthetic content that is characteristic of fashion has to do with the effective, concrete practice of taste. Direct experience represents a basic and indeed essential, unavoidable element of the aesthetic, to whose preservation fashion greatly contributes even in contrast to such dogmatic conceptions of art as that fostered by Danto (and, in some sense, also by that of hermeneutical aesthetics in the context of continental philosophy). This proves to be particularly important if one takes into consideration a third conception that has emerged within the philosophy of art, namely the so-called institutional theory.

According to this aesthetic conception, the definition of art depends on a world of institutions whose existence and possibility, in turn, depend on the actions of various subjects, or better agents, who are qualified to carry out their roles. Museums, art galleries, academies, concert halls, theaters, specialized magazines, and Master's degrees may be numbered among the institutional forms that, through their respective officers, decide whether the acknowledgment of the artistic status of a certain object or event is felicitous or infelicitous. Philosophers like George Dickie (1974; 1984) and sociologists like Howard Becker (1982) have put at the center of inquiry the particular domain called "the *artworld*." However, notwithstanding the surely interesting and useful hypothesis about the modes of operation of the institutional dimension of art offered by these authors, the final result of their investigations is often a cul-de-sac. In fact, their inquiries appear unable to provide convincing analyses of the way in which this dimension gets formed and subsequently develops, although it must be said that the processes leading to the transformation and sometimes even to the overcoming of the existing conditions are definitely not irrelevant. Moving, as Dickie does, from the hypothesis—that sometimes turns out to be indeed a hypostasis—of the artworld that the artwork "institutionally" belongs to (which is quite different from the idea of a world that "intensionally" belongs to an artwork, as Danto argues), leads to concealing the processes that actually shape this "world," and hence to preventing oneself from understanding its modes of alteration, decay, disintegration, and potentially also reactivation. It is clear that this concept of "world," inasmuch as it already raises various doubts and objections when applied to the fine arts, will prove to be almost untenable and inapplicable to a world characterized by extreme fluidity, inconstancy, and dynamism like that of fashion.

In order to get round this kind of rigidity and avoid falling into a merely justificational attitude it is preferable then, when dealing with the aesthetic dimension, the usage of the term "field" (borrowed from Bourdieu) as "a field of forces within which the agents occupy positions that statistically determine the positions they take with respect to the field, these position-takings being aimed at conserving or transforming the structure of relations of forces that is constitutive of the field" (Bourdieu 1996: 30). As Bourdieu explains, in such a "structured social space" that "contains people who dominate and people who are dominated" (Bourdieu 1998: 40–1), "the agents react to these relations of forces, to these structures; they construct them, perceive them, form an idea of them, represent them to themselves, and so on. And, while being, therefore, constrained by the forces inscribed in these fields and being determined by these forces as regards their permanent dispositions, they are able to act upon these fields, in ways that are partially preconstrained, but with a margin of freedom" (Bourdieu 1996: 30).

As a matter of fact, the concept of field—for example, the way it is employed by modern physics—has the advantage of immediately expressing an intrinsic dynamicity. A field is a reality that reveals itself through the externalization of its potentiality, as *dynamis* and interaction between the various vectors that are active and operating in it. We arrive at gaining knowledge about a field only inasmuch as we analyze the interactions between the phenomena that take place and occur within it. While there is always the risk of mistaking the *world* for just a part of it, and thus of erroneously advancing new essentialist definitions that ultimately turn single phenomena into something inflexible and assume them as paradigmatic or quintessential for the entire dimension that is at issue, there are no such risks when one adopts the concept of *field* that is in principle impossible to specify and define by abstracting from all its vectors. Furthermore, while the concept of world basically depends on a logic of exclusivity, the concept of field instead is inherently inclusive, since its interactive nature does not exclude *de iure* any vector. And still, if the concept of world may lead to the illusion that it is simply possible to occupy any desired position in it once one has accessed it, the space of action of a certain field only allows one to occupy those positions that are made available by the field lines that innervate the field with diminishing intensity, so that there will always be an unstable osmosis between "inside" and "outside" at the edge of the field, up to the point of determining a veritably undecidable condition as far as one's belongingness to the field is concerned. A *world* represents a continuous space whose only constraint factors are situated at the edge, due to the existence of boundaries regulating the possibility to access it; vice versa, a *field* is a discreet and densely conditioned, i.e., packed with various constraints, space devoid of any substantial incoming limitation.

Against all kinds of justificational attitude, adopting the field-perspective (see, for instance, Bourdieu 1996) immediately leads to shift the focus of attention from existing *institutions* as such to the process of *institutionalization* (i.e., of *instituting* and *institutionalizing*) of the operational dimension within which temporarily effective relationships are determined. At this threshold work and attitude, namely the two sides of the aesthetic that are obviously connected to each other, do not appear as original sources but rather as mutually integrated parts. This is extremely important and useful in order to account for the way in which the definition of standards of taste, intended as generative principles of common sense, is finally configured in the field of fashion, as well as (and perhaps even before than) in the field of art. Fashion repeatedly crosses the interactive threshold that generates the subject/object, work/attitude, and taste content/taste act circular relationships, and it cannot avoid crossing that threshold because fashion will never find its justification in a single object or find the reasons of its pervasive power in a specific subjective attitude. Fashion connects aesthetics institutions to the social constitution and, in doing so, it can just be and work as a practice of taste that evolves by means of trends that are either destined to become inflexible and turn into something else (for example, into enduring standards that, inasmuch as they persist and never decline, ultimately step out of the field of fashion) or destined to fade and disappear, and thus leave space and nourishment to new trends.

The proposed revision of the institutional perspective takes inspiration from two very influential authors. The first one is, once again, Nelson Goodman. This time, however, Goodman is not referred to because of his famous autographic/allographic distinction, but rather for his advice to replace the essentialist "What-question" (for instance, "What is art?" but also "What is fashion?": i.e., two questions that are destined to remain unanswered inasmuch as they lead to a domain disconnected from the practices that characterize their respective "symbolic" systems) with the "When-question" concerning the effective way in which such labels as "art" and "fashion" function—and, in the latter's case, to opportunely shift the focus of attention from the usual question about "style" to that concerning the dynamics of tendencies and trends that are intrinsic to the field of fashion (see the widespread research of Loschek 2009, and also Franci 2014). What "generates fashionableness" are not only the things produced, the single objects, but also the symbolic-representational system that is involved in this process in much the same way every single statement holistically implicates language in its entirety (on this subject, see also the contributions gathered in the first part of Wolfendale and Kennett 2011: 13–49). The second influential figure is obviously Pierre Bourdieu, not only and not so much because of his investigations of fashion and taste as such (see Bourdieu and Delsaut 1975; and Bourdieu 1979), but rather for his abovementioned theoretical development of the concept of field that he has offered in critical comparison to the institutional concept of world (see Pedroni and Volonté 2012: 13–16).

2.4. Fashion and form of life

Fashion thus corroborates the current need to overcome the static and justificational conception underlying the use of the concept of world, and rather moves towards an aesthetic conception inspired by the metaphor of the field. Adopting this last notion also helps to deal with the crucial dynamic tension existing between the instituting practices of taste (namely, the practices that concretely shape or ground taste preferences: gestures, inscriptions, expressions of appreciation, etc.) and the institutional practices into which those same exercises of taste ultimately result.

Such a scheme seems to be well supported by a fourth and last position that can be identified within current aesthetic debates. This position has found its most important configuration in Richard Wollheim's inquiry on art. Instead of attempting to formulate a univocal definition of art and the aesthetic, Wollheim (1980) argues that philosophers should rather begin their investigation from the analysis of the ways in which we effectively relate (by means of perception, imagination, critique, etc.) to what presents itself as an aesthetic experience. Some aspects and functions ("representation," "expression," "sign," the intransitivity of the aesthetic predication, etc.) that assume a certain value depending on the various artistic modalities are hence examined. They therefore converge into a cluster of traits that, not necessarily in a systematic manner, outline what is today understood as art and as aesthetic.

In order to stress this peculiarity of the aesthetic field, Wollheim turns to a concept originally thematized by Wittgenstein. As he observes, "art is, in Wittgenstein's sense, a form of life. The phrase [form of life] appears [in Wittgenstein] as descriptive or invocatory of the total context within which alone language can exist: the complex of habits, experiences, skills, with which language interlocks in that it could not be operated without them and, equally, they cannot be identified without reference to it" (Wollheim 1980: 104). If we describe the aesthetic as a form of life, that would imply the consideration of experiential practices that are both perceptual and cultural, in which "to express" is not synonymous with appending a sign, an index or, so to speak, a mask on "the face of things." Contrariwise, it means making the physiognomy of things emerge, to the extent that such familiarity, which reveals the reality with which we daily relate to in our life environments, is justified. Following this interpretation line, the aesthetic dimension (and fashion within it) becomes more prominent as a form of life rather than as a language game (see Matteucci 2013). A form of life is what appears as a "given" inasmuch as it always remains on the background; it is what compels philosophical reflection to finally resign but only after that philosophy, in its attempt to grasp it, has experienced the fruitful impact or collision with it. "What has to be accepted, the given, is—so one could *say—forms of life*" (Wittgenstein 1953: 226): namely, it is not something ineffable or non-analyzable, but rather "the fact that we act in such-and-such ways, e.g. *punish* certain actions, *establish* the state of affair thus and so, *give* orders, render accounts, describe colors, take an interest in others' feelings" (Wittgenstein 1980: I, § 630). Now, it is clear that one must also include exercises of preferences and taste among such "facts," that are carried out by means of acts which are almost interiorized by subjects who are used to them in a specific context, so that their usage results as more or less spontaneous. This is a process of "embodiment" (*á la* Bourdieu) that takes place in a shared *medium* which allows—when a number of its aspects becomes significant—a perception of the aesthetic content that is more naturally adequate to its referent, as it precisely happens in the case of taste tendencies.

From this point of view, the contiguity of the aesthetic to the form of life—intended as the space in which grammatical, "institutionalizing" but not "institutionalized" practices arise: practices that possess a normative, binding, and distinctive character without being prescriptive or discriminating—becomes fully clear. It is possible to assume the pervasive character of this domain as a fundamental and programmatic theme for a new approach to everyday aesthetics aimed at providing a non-ideological basis for the investigation of the processes that have turned the contemporary world into an increasingly aestheticized reality. It is precisely in this context that fashion—intended here as a peculiar conceptual and categorial structure—can and indeed must be situated with full rights.

3. The anthropological problem of fashion: The aesthetic as construction of the identity

The critical comparison of different positions in current aesthetic debates has showed how the attempt to understand fashion requires adopting a conception capable of holding aesthetics close to the analysis of the effective practices of the forms of life. This is important exactly because aesthetics has to do with taste, intended as the domain that plays an instituting or institutionalizing—rather and before than a merely institutional—role with regard to the creation and development of the common sense that even social structures rest upon. And this can explain why it is precisely fashion—in a historical time, like ours, in which art is affected by a growing and indeed unprecedented crisis as far as the delimitation of its boundaries is concerned—that plays a primary role today and has gone so far as to become the most important sphere for the establishment of the standards of taste. It is as if the field of the aesthetic, once the purely artistic structures that had been strongly emphasized in the last two centuries have been weakened in their significance and prestige, was finally able now to retrieve its deep dynamicity by abandoning all abstract ideals of purity and, conversely, achieving a new kind of socio-anthropological incisiveness.

With regard to this, it is apparent that Georg Simmel, already at the end of the nineteenth and the beginning of the twentieth century, had guessed it right in choosing to focus his attention on fashion in order to investigate the logic of the social relationships characterizing the metropolitan environment of his age. Simmel's inquiry in his 1911 essay on fashion was entirely developed on the basis of a group of polar oppositions, thus confirming the importance and value of the dynamic structure of the *field* that in the previous section I have set against the static character of the *world*. We can find here a renewed confirmation of our idea of fashion as something intrinsically and extremely fluid, mobile, and variable, which is thus impossible in principle to reduce to just one fixed and stable component that would presumably justify it. In order for movement and dynamicity to occur and be real, what is required is the possibility of at least a double positioning. Fashion defines this unceasing, ongoing oscillation between different and indeed opposed poles, and through its subversion of consolidated aesthetic categories it perfectly embodies the expressive nature of a yet undetermined (and probably never fully determinable) creature as the human being. Furthermore, inasmuch as the human being is a social animal, it comes as no surprise to discover that the aesthetic dimension, once its aspect of practice and exercise of taste has been rehabilitated, also appears as a space of experimentation and manifestation of nucleuses of social cohesion or social opposition (see Edwards 2011). From this point of view, the aesthetic also represents one of the test-beds of the social and the political.

As already noted by Immanuel Kant, common sense—in which the political has its foundations—always has also an aesthetic root. By the time when the need for a philosophical aesthetics based on the well-delimited domain of the fine arts was expressed, namely by the mid-eighteenth century, the subject that was asserting herself on the scene of history was the Western bourgeois individual as the bearer of new citizenship rights (see Ferry 1990). Analogously today, once it has been set free from its subjection to the aesthetic ideology of the fine arts, fashion (intended as one of the spaces for the development of aesthetic common sense) makes it possible to have first-hand experience, so to speak, of new social contents and even to deal in full autonomy with complex ethical issues. For this reason, it is correct to consider fashion as the current "matrix" for the definition of both individual and collective identities.

When playing this role, however, it always does it with a sort of inattentive and often ironical attitude, thanks to its characteristic levity that also means disengagement and detachment from contents. It is precisely here that the philosophical enigma of fashion lies, namely in the question asking how is it possible that something apparently unimportant or even insignificant, as far as existentially binding decisions are concerned, turns into the battlefield in which struggles and conflicts for the affirmation and even imposition of identity are primarily fought and resolved. We all owe to Simmel the clearest investigation to date of the various and gradually more essential levels that the peculiar power of fashion rests upon: specifically, the level of social symbols, the level of interpretive categories, the level of psychological tensions, and the level of taste preferences that represents the basic root of our decisions and then also of conflicts (see Matteucci 2015). The result of such an interference between different levels and strata is the construction of identity: a concept, the latter, that we must assume and use today with a projectual and functional, rather than substantive, meaning. In fact, it has now become clear that the root of the definition of one's identity does not lie in constative acquaintances but rather in (self-)representation acts. Fashion is precisely a system of these kinds of acts. In recent times, due to its tendency to articulate itself in the forms of the Self's *mise-en-scene* by leveraging the complex pair made up of the opposite tendencies to originality and conformism, fashion has functioned as one of the most powerful means for the definition of identity.

Analogous presuppositions had already been set up by Eugen Fink, a German phenomenologist that most scholars and recent interpreters have unfortunately not paid enough attention to (see Fink 1969: 20–6). More recently, these kinds of presuppositions have re-emerged in the important work of Elizabeth Wilson (*Adorned in Dreams: Fashion and Modernity* (1985)), which moves from the basic assumption according to which clothing implies a symbolic system of decisive importance, in general, for the human being. Clothes connect our biological body to our second nature of social agents, and thus also the public dimension to the private dimension of our lives, therefore functioning as a sort of bivalent threshold, as much uncertain as it is essential. Convincingly relying on some of the results achieved by Mary Douglas' researches (see Douglas 1966), Wilson observes that clothing ambiguously marks this equivocal ridge, thus belonging to the group of the symbolic and ritual systems that have been created throughout human history by various cultures in order to strengthen and consolidate the borders that make it possible to keep purity intact. Since it belongs to the group of the typical factors of anthropization, clothing "not only links [the] body to the social world," thus operating as a means of intersubjective communication, but "also more clearly separates the two": it embodies "the frontier between the self and the not-self," and thus functions as a decisive element for the constitution of identity (Wilson 1985: 3).

The human being can be viewed as that particular animal characterized not only by the use of the hand or the possession of language, but also by the tendency or habit to cover its body and leave marks on it, i.e., decorate it. More precisely: by the inclination to modify the surface (which is ineffable in itself) that naturally separates what belongs to the individual from the multitude of stimulations, potential dangers, and positive expectations, that looms over her. The skin can be understood as the page upon which pictorial gestures and engravings are drawn that are aimed at emphasizing the fact that *there is* actually a difference within the complex of interrelations connecting and tying the *Homo sapiens* to the environment. It is this kind of artificial manipulation of the surface of our skin that, by laying claim to shared and public attention, makes it possible to intervene in such a way as to let emerge *sub specie aesthetica* the real *nature* of both our lived body and the surrounding environment that belongs to this body and that, in turn, this body belongs to. Creating, producing, and finally wearing clothes is a non-forced and non-compelled prosecution of all of this. From this point of view, clothes represent an absolutely natural institution for the human being: more precisely, an institution that appears as completely natural once that the illusion of a mythical Edenic condition has dissolved.

This is the reason why—returning now to Wilson's observations—"in all societies the body is 'dressed', and everywhere dress and adornment play symbolic, communicative and aesthetic roles": that is, "dress is always 'unspeakably meaningful'" (Wilson 1985: 3). The expression "*unspeakably* meaningful" is revealing, and there would be a great deal to say about it. The aesthetic device embodied (in the literal meaning of this term) by tattoos, scarifications, ornamentations, and clothes proves to be here the original source of a particular kind of significance or meaningfulness that is not possible to paraphrase or express differently inasmuch as it is specifically aesthetic and not yet properly conceptual. It is felt in the very act of being performed rather than properly known or consciously grasped; namely, it is a kind of significance that generates and yields the denotative function of language, and that is certainly intertwined with the latter (just like depiction) but not at all derived from it.

Such minimal observations about the anthropological significance of clothing prove to be useful at least for the attempt to sketch out the basic presuppositions for an inquiry into the more specific question concerning fashion, whereas the latter definitely represents a qualitatively different phenomenon. What I am referring to here is not a merely historical matter: that is, the question at issue here is not to define when fashion began, or to decide whether it is legitimate and appropriate to properly speak of fashion only with regard to the Western societies of the last two centuries or if, vice versa, it is also possible to recognize the existence of fashion in pre-modern societies. Even regardless of the fact that fashion does not only concern clothing, it is anyway clear that, just like the history of painting does not coincide with the history of the ways in which colors have been used, so also the history of fashion does not coincide with the history of clothing and the development of dress. Far from being a merely historical matter, the question concerning fashion is a conceptual (and also anthropological, of course: see Meinhold 2005) question, inasmuch as it has to do with the differentiation factor that defines the narrow but undeniable divide between the development of systems and codes of clothing, on the one side, and the actual dynamics and processes characterizing fashion, on the other side.

This factor clearly lies in the way in which *change* intrinsically determines the development of fashion, where the latter consists of a process of unceasing transformation exclusively aimed at its own perpetuation that, at a certain point in history, began to control the systems (and the codes) of clothing. We are faced here with one of the most typical features of fashion, always hanging in the balance between originality and conformism precisely because of its being subjected to the "golden rule" of change for change's sake. As a matter of fact (and as has been often noted), this gives rise to the contradictory nature of fashion that surely strengthens the typical sensation of having to do with a groundless and frivolous thing, thus justifying those who relegate fashion among the questions that appear as unimportant if viewed from a theoretical and cultural point of view. There being no functional criteria, any plausible reason for change fails, and the result is a sharpening of the sensation of the seeming irrationality of fashion. Hence, though, at the same time the intrinsic social significance of the abovementioned open dialectics between originality and conformism finally and fully emerges. The rule of change for change's sake derives indeed from a basic principle of social unity that finds its proper manifestation in the tension between conformism (conventional dress) and individualism (eccentric dress). And it is not hard to realize how important this aspect can be in the bourgeois society, in particular during its mature stage. It is therefore not by accident that fashion has gradually become a means to express a critical stance towards the society, besides being also a means to integrate oneself into society. Such phenomena as the 1960s hippie style or the late 1970s punk clothing must be understood both as declarations of dissent regarding supposedly respectable conformism and as an innovative search for unprecedented fashion styles, in particular if one takes into consideration their extraordinary ability to reach a widespread and transverse diffusion.

In order to achieve a disenchanted point of view on fashion, it is necessary to take into account the complex character of this phenomenon and thus abandon the somehow lazy tendency to simply classify fashion as a trick of the marketplace (a sort of ephemeral catalyst of cultural homogenization) or as a phenomenon that only concerns niches of luxury consumers. It is precisely because it intrinsically partakes in the laws according to which social groups are defined that fashion feels the effect of the success of mass production so strongly, thus experiencing throughout the twentieth century a sort of polarization between elitist enjoyment and widespread consumption that is absolutely analogous to that experienced meanwhile by the fine arts. Fashion must be connected to both stylistic developments in the domain of high and avant-garde culture and art, and to popular culture and taste. It is precisely for this reason that it must be considered with full rights as an aesthetic means to express ideas, desires, and beliefs. Thanks to its aesthetic characteristics, fashion is able to express them and "to resolve formally, at the imaginary level, social contradictions that cannot be resolved" (Wilson 1985: 9).

As a consequence, the way fashion plays with appearances acquires a remarkable significance and affects the processes of defining one's identity by means of *mise-en-scene* and socio-communicative interactions. The outbreak of fashion as one of the most pervasive phenomena in Western societies dates back to the mid-nineteenth century: that is, exactly from the time when "appearance became more and more mixed up with identity. It was—as Wilson argues—the beginnings of the idea of the Self as a Work of Art, the 'personality' as something that extended to dress, scent, and surroundings, all of which made an essential contribution to the formation of 'self'—at least for women." It was indeed by the mid-twentieth century that:

> a special emphasis on what was called "the art of being a woman" reached its zenith. The women's magazines urged every woman to discover her "type" and yet to dress to "be herself": the paradox of artificially created spontaneity. To reconcile the desire to look "different" with the simultaneous yet conflicting compulsion to conform was the tightrope along which millions of women teetered.
>
> **WILSON** 1985: 123

Paradoxically strengthened by its relativistic character, fashion thus attests the artificial nature of the social order and the arbitrary nature of conventional behavior and moral habits, in the first place with regard to the decisive element that stands at the very basis of every kind of substantiality, namely the identity of the Self. Therefore a subtle self-ironic capacity constitutionally belongs to fashion, when the latter, by elevating the ephemeral to something worthy of worship, reveals itself as a "double-edged" phenomenon (Wilson 1985: 10). And it is precisely for this reason that, as has been convincingly pointed out by Winfried Menninghaus (2003: 66 ff.), one must also ascribe to fashion a leading function in the logic of evolution itself.

This last aspect should come as no surprise. As a matter of fact, even if it is perhaps possible to overlook the early attempt of George H. Darwin, one of Charles Darwin's sons, to pull fashion and evolutionism together (see Darwin 1872), it is impossible however not to mention the fact that Simmel had already made extensive reference to issues concerning evolution theory in his own treatment of the question concerning fashion. Simmel defines the polarity that is predominant in the field of fashion through a set of opposite conceptual pairs that is ultimately grounded on two antagonistic principles: heredity and variation. In the domain of human society, the heredity principle finds its fulfillment in the drive to imitation, conformism, assimilation to the people that one wants to be integrated with and recognized by. From this point of view, fashion works as a means of transmission and dissemination of homogeneity through mechanisms of social mimicry. Variation, instead, i.e., the possibility of introducing innovations that may allow the individual to reach a better and more efficient adaptation to the environment in comparison to other members of the species, finds its fulfillment in the domain of human society in the drive to individual differentiation, in the search for self-affirmation, and hence in a basically exasperated individualism. This clearly highlights how the two aspects towards which fashion is polarized, namely the tendency to conform oneself with the group and the opposite tendency to individual differentiation, are somehow grounded on key principles of Charles Darwin's theory of evolution. If one understands the human being as someone who no longer reaches her natural fulfillment merely through biological life but rather by means of cultural development, then fashion will appear as something that works both as a selection factor and an evolution element.

4. The experiential problem of fashion: The aesthetic as appearance of the ephemeral

Due to its ability to produce a sense (or at least a semblance) of identity irrespective of substantial grounds, fashion represents an excellent test-bed to evaluate and assess the ambitions of an anthropology of contemporaneity: an age that, as we have seen, is characterized by a widespread aestheticity. Thanks to its capacity to punctuate and spell out, so to speak, the stream of experience that today seemingly cannot find any stable pivot or any previously defined and fixed principle (as, instead, it once happened in the aesthetic world centered on the fine arts), fashion becomes indeed the instrument allowing one to simply slide on the surface of things without at the same time losing him- or herself in a vague and indeterminate flow. From this point of view, the inner relationship connecting fashion to the ephemeral proves to be an extraordinary strong point to release oneself from a situation in which all criteria grounded on cognitively determinate or determinable contents have been dismissed. And this is exactly the specific feature of the present human condition, in which the ongoing and widespread (but never really subversive) transformations of taste and its devices have replaced the search for innovation intended as avant-garde, tradition-breaking, revolutionary action. As a consequence, also our perspective on fashion, i.e., the way we look at this peculiar phenomenon in terms of a current aesthetic practice, has changed.

These aspects of fashion have been clearly highlighted by Yves Michaud at the end of his inquiry, in the book *L'art a l'état gazeux*, into the way in which the aesthetic domain has emancipated today from the exclusive principles that had been established in relation to the ideology of the fine arts.

> When what is new was conceived as founding and instituting, fashion was condemned as empty, superficial and illusory: it was the scum of the time, the inessential that conceals what is really new, the appearance that distracts one from what is really important. However, when there is nothing else than renewal, fashion becomes the only way to mark the time. Through fashion the utopian promise to abolish one day the passing of time turns into a promise of repetition, a refrain: fashion never stops abolishing time because it always restarts with the new trend. Fashion itself becomes a permanent utopia living from day to day that has no time or place, that always renews itself and never stops reappearing. Fashion is thus invested of a strange quality: it becomes the only force that is capable of producing differences in a world in which there are no differences anymore. That way fashion represents the spirit of the time in any sense, i.e., both in the Hegelian and the ordinary sense of this expression.
>
> **MICHAUD** 2003: 175[2]

Fashion thus represents the last anthropological reserve of meaningfulness in a meaningless age as the present one, but this paradoxically happens only by virtue of its lack of any substantial meaning. As Michaud explains indeed:

> there is actually something that makes sense in the present age without for this reason representing an exception to its general lack of sense: it is fashion—that is the sense of a world devoid of sense, the meaningful singularity of a world in which there is nothing else than meaningless singularities.
>
> **MICHAUD** 2003: 178[3]

It is perhaps possible to find here one of the original sources of the power that has turned fashion into an irresistible and overpowering phenomenon of our time. It finds its nourishment in the juxtaposition of two antinomic temporal dimensions, namely linear development and circular direction, which we find reflected then in the polar relationship between innovation and stability that essentially characterizes this particular aesthetic practice, and compensates for (and indeed exploits) its inescapable and undeniable lack of determinate contents. It is precisely this antinomic origin that confers a central significance to the principle of the "trend," where the latter has basically to do with something equipped with the ability to affirm its presence in a very intense but also very limited way. The aesthetic field thus encompasses an intertwined play of trends that ultimately replaces the mere sequence of different styles envisaged by a historiography of the aesthetic and the artistic inspired by the criterion of the discontinuity between determinate and determinable contents. A trend is something that gives an articulation and structure to a flow without at the same time compromising the continuity and unpredictability of the latter's development; something that emerges as a result of a temporary constellation and finds its fulfillment in mere appearance as a celebration of the ephemeral. The form that results from such an aesthetic practice must be neither interpreted as a predefined idea or an ideal content, nor be understood as a determinate and fixed feature of the real. Neither *eidos* nor *morphé*, it rather appears as an extemporaneous configuration that results in a *Gestaltung* that is by its very nature metamorphic, serial, and incomplete.

This is the reason why evolutionism, ever since Darwin, has always taken seriously into account the aesthetic feature of experience and has thematically drawn upon the concept of fashion, as clearly testified by Winfried Menninghaus' (2003) studies in this field. There are rules of definition of taste at the basis of the process of sexual selection that can be connected to the pleasure deriving from a beauty determined by tendencies that reach such a degree of success as to become predominant and pervasive, and consequently originate imitations that make a selection of features that ultimately acquire a hereditary character. There is no functional, cognitive, or biological justification for such taste preferences and choices. They are the manifestation of a kind of specifically aesthetic significance or meaningfulness that sometimes even arrives at "prizing" the uselessness of the attraction we feel for merely ephemeral beauties. It is as if a certain kind of beauty was at the very basis of our skill to generate meaning where meaning does not yet exist or—as it happens in the contemporary age—where meaning is no longer. However, this is a very different kind of beauty if compared to that traditionally referred to, at least for the reason that it has no reasons (no determinate contents) to strive to an unlimited life and, for it has the character of a trend, it rather accepts the fact of being destined to disappear immediately after having reached its greatest degree of success.

In order to understand this kind of practice of beauty, Menninghaus (2003) suggests reconsidering and rethinking the experience of the beautiful that pivots on the mythological figure of Adonis.

Having been challenged by Persephone and Aphrodite because of the extraordinary and silent beauty of his body and form, Adonis falls victim to the jealousy of Ares (or, as in other accounts, Apollo). The jealous god sends to him a wild boar, against which young Adonis, who is incapable of becoming a man and a hunter, cannot defend himself. Once dead, he is transformed into an anemone.

Adonis' is a human beauty that appeals to the gods and evokes a desire so violent that it results in the murder of its bearer, when it becomes clear that full and exclusive possession of that beauty will be impossible. So, the crime that the gods commit is the price of their worldly fall: they have, in fact, dealt with man. Pouncing upon he who had sparked their desire with his mere presence (talentless Adonis can do nothing but look beautiful), the gods almost totally remove their proximity to man. As with the beauty of another, which was also more ardently desired than consumed (Narcissus), the beauty of Adonis is turned into a flower, a vegetable. No longer even an animal, Adonis survives due to a cyclic nature that nullifies every progression, every direction, and every production of sense. With his animal characteristics of linearity and mobility clouded, Adonis' sub-animal characteristics of cyclicity and immobility prevail within him. These are precisely the aesthetic and daily practices of beauty: consider fashion, which incites a desire that is never really satisfied and which exhausts its erotic energy in the recurrent chase of trends.

I would like to use Adonic beauty in order to complete an ideal grid that considers four typologies. The other three have been well described by the same number of renowned concepts, as defined by Nietzsche: the *Apollonian*, which requires contemplation; the *Dionysian*, in which chaos reigns; the *Socratic*, which prompts reflexivity. The fourth type of beauty, the *Adonic,* merely incites a desire to "ruin" in unexhausted practical commerce. It therefore differs from beauties that are to "live deeply" (Dionysian), or to "purely contemplate" (Apollonian), which represent the two extremes of the divine, the underworld and the celestial. Man is thus placed in between these extremes and strives for the horizon, which itself develops between the pseudo-Apollonian reflexivity (Socratic) and the pseudo-Dionysian desire (Adonic). Hence, the four modes of beauty do not form a hierarchical pyramid, but draw out two orthogonal axes.

The vertical axis conveys the polarity of the divine and stretches from the depths to the sublime. The depths are the Dionysian: intoxication, chaos, loss of identity; total dissolution of individuality in the terrestrial force of nature. The sublime is the Apollonian: formal, frozen, contemplative, theoretical from a purely spectatorial standpoint; contactless observation; total detachment and total extraneousness of the corporeity of what is purely contemplated, even with the pure mind's eye. At one end of the horizontal axis, conversely, is the Socratic: reflexivity, intellectual inquisition that further leads to the cunning of the technique in the construction of the form and artistic object, as well as the respective understanding in its consumption. At the other end, therefore, we find the Adonic, which seeks bodily contact with what is longed for and produced, in an experience that thrills and torments, thus recalling the eroticism of the aesthetic. Therefore, if the Socratic embodies the reflexive-intellectual dimension of the pleasure of beauty, the Adonic moment of beauty refers to the desire and investment of the *libido* on appearance. Fashion is indeed emblematic of this.

Here is then a sort of recapitulation of the aesthetic challenge represented by fashion. Contradicting the traditional concept of beauty, what appears as beautiful in the field of fashion is absolutely interesting up to the point of resulting erotically powerful. It winks at the possibility of not letting itself be purely gazed at, but at the same time it is exclusively liable to being exhibited. It lets itself be contaminated by

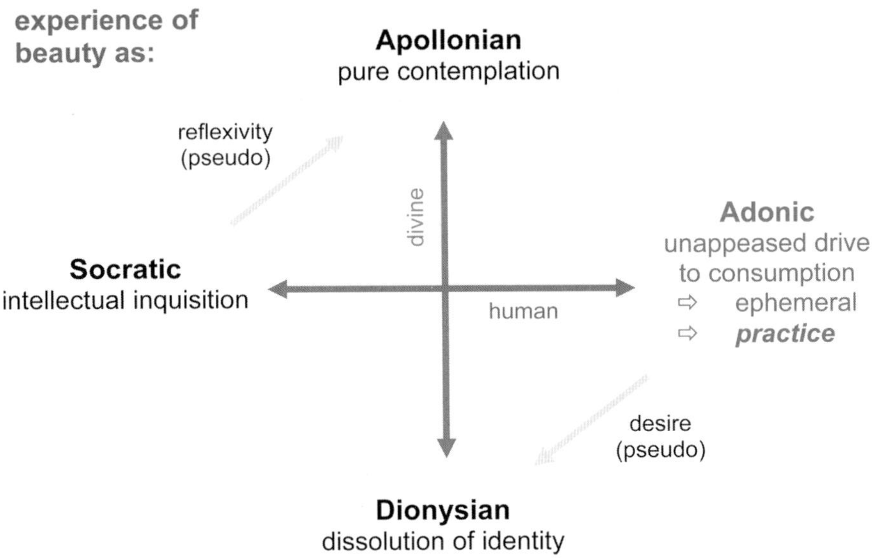

FIGURE 2.2 Different kinds of experience of beauty.

taste compromises that, at least from a general and also ideological point of view, purely artistic beauty would rather be inclined to delete. It outlines an experience of the ephemeral that almost leaves no trace and shies away from museums because, rather than defining standards, it represents a temporary, cyclical, "trendy" articulation of taste. Disinterested in acquiring a determinate form, fashion finds its fulfillment in something that takes shape in the performance of the event that exhausts it. It is therefore as *practice* of beauty that fashion coincides with the ephemeral emergence of sense.

Notes

1 "*Fiat modes pereat ars*" ("Let There Be Fashion, Down with Art") is the title of a series of lithographs designed in 1919 by the pioneer of Dada and Surrealism Max Ernst. The title is clearly aimed at announcing the end of traditional art and derives from a paraphrase and ironic inversion of the famous Latin saying "*Fiat justitia et pereat mundus*" ("Let justice be done, though the world perish").

2 "Lorsque le nouveau était conçu comme fondateur et instaurateur, la mode était dénoncée comme vide, superficielle et illusoire: elle était l'écume des jours, l'inessentiel qui dissimule le vrai nouveau, l'apparence qui distrait de ce qui seul importe. Lorsqu'il n'y a plus que du renouvellement, la mode devient l'unique scansion du temps. La promesse de l'utopie d'annuler un jour le temps devient à travers la mode une promesse à répétition, une rengaine: la mode ne cesse d'annuler le temps pour qu'il reparte avec la mode suivante. Elle devient elle-même une utopie permanente

et à la petite semaine qui n'a ni temps ni place, qui se renouvelle et ne cesse de réapparaître. La mode ce retrouve ainsi investie d'une étrange qualité: elle seule est capable de produire des différences dans un monde où il n'y a plus de différences. Par là elle figure l'esprit du temps, à tous les sens, hégélien comme ordinaire, de l'expression."

3 "[...] il y a effectivement quelque chose qui fait sens dans le présent sans faire exception à l'absence générale de sens: c'est la mode—qui est le sens d'un monde dépourvu de sens, la singularité signifiante d'un monde où il n'y à plus que des singularités insignifiantes."

Bibliography

Alain (Émile-Auguste Chartier) (1931), *Vingt Leçons sur les Beaux-Arts*, Paris: Gallimard

Becker, H.S. (1982), *Art Worlds*, Berkeley-Los Angeles: University of California Press

Böhme, G. (2001), "Zur Kritik der ästhetischen Ökonomie", *Zeitschrift für kritische Theorie*, 12: 69–82

Bourdieu, P. (1979), *La distinction. Critique sociale du jugement*, Paris: Minuit

Bourdieu, P. (1996), "Champ politique, champ des sciences sociales, champ journalistique", *Cahier de Recherche*, 15, Lyon: GRS; Engl. transl.: "The Political Field, the Social Science Field, and the Journalistic Field", in R. Benson and E. Neveu (eds), *Bourdieu and the Journalistic Field*, 29–47, Cambridge: Polity Press

Bourdieu, P. (1998), *On Television*, New York: The New Press.

Bourdieu, P. and Y. Delsaut (1975), "Le couturier et sa griffe: contribution à une théorie de la magie", *Actes de la recherche en sciences sociales*, 1 (1): 7–36

Danto, A.C. (1981), *The Transfiguration of the Commonplace: A Philosophy of Art*, Cambridge (MA)-London: Harvard University Press

Darwin, G.H. (1872), "Development in Dress", *Macmillan Magazine*, 26: 410–6

Dickie, G. (1974), *Art and the Aesthetic: An Institutional Analysis*, Ithaca: Cornell University Press

Dickie, G. (1984), *The Art Circle: A Theory of Art*, New York: Haven

Douglas, M. (1966), *Purity and Danger. An Analysis of Concepts of Pollution and Taboo*, Harmondsworth: Penguin

Edwards, T. (2011), *Fashion in Focus: Concepts, Practices and Politics*, London-New York: Routledge

Ferry, L. (1990), *Homo aestheticus. L'invention du goût à l'âge démocratique*, Paris: Grasset et Fasquelle

Fink, E. (1969), *Mode ... ein verführerisches Spiel*, Basel-Stuttgart: Birkhäuser Verlag

Franci, S. (2014), "Quando è moda. Dallo stile al trend", *Aracne. Rivista d'arte on-line*, 4 (1). Available online: http://www.aracne-rivista.it/index%20editoriale%20moda.html (accessed May 17, 2015)

Goodman, N. (1976), *Languages of Art: An Approach to a Theory of Symbols* (1968), Indianapolis-Cambridge: Hackett Publishing Company

Hollander, A. (1993), *Seeing Through Clothes* (1975), Berkeley-Los Angeles: University of California Press

König, R. (1971), *Macht und Reiz der Mode*, Düsseldorf-Wien: Econ-Verlag

König, R. (1985), *Menschheit auf dem Laufsteg. Die Mode im Zivilisationsprozeß*, München-Wien: Carl Hanser Verlag

Leddy, Th. (2012), *The Extraordinary in the Ordinary: The Aesthetics of Everyday Life*, Peterborough (Ontario): Broadview Press
Lehmann, U. (2000), *Tigersprung: Fashion in Modernity*, Cambridge (MA)-London: The MIT Press
Lipovetsky, G. (1987), *L'empire de l'éphèmère. La mode et son destin dans les sociétés modernes*, Paris: Gallimard
Lipovetsky, G. and J. Serroy (2013), *L'estétisation du mond. Vivre à l'âge du capitalism artiste*, Paris: Gallimard
Loschek, I. (2009), *When Clothes Become Fashion: Design and Innovation Systems*, Oxford-New York: Berg
Luchetti, L. and A. Tota (2012), "Abiti che fanno opinione", in M. Pedroni and P. Volonté (eds), *Moda e arte*, 87–101, Milano: Franco Angeli
Matteucci, G. (2013), "Towards a Wittgensteinian Aesthetics. Wollheim and the Analysis of Aesthetic Practices", *Aisthesis. Pratiche, linguaggi e saperi dell'estetico*, 6 (1): 67–84. Available online: http://www.fupress.net/index.php/aisthesis/article/view/12838/12160 (accessed May 17, 2015)
Matteucci, G. (2015), "Simmel on Fashion. A Commented Reading of the 1911 Essay", in F. Muzzarelli (ed.), *Culture, Fashion and Society's Notebooks 2015*, 1–46, Milano: Pearson-Bruno Mondadori
Meinhold, R. (2005), *Der Mode-Mythos: Lifestyle als Lebenskunst*, Würzburg: Königshausen & Neumann
Menninghaus, W. (2003), *Das Versprechen des Schönheit*, Frankfurt a.M.: Suhrkamp
Michaud, Y. (2003), *L'art a l'état gazeux. Essai sur le triomphe de l'esthétique*, Paris: Éditions Stock
Morini, E. (2012), "Creatore, artista o designer? Il problema della legittimazione", in M. Pedroni and P. Volonté (eds), *Moda e arte*, 35–50, Milano: Franco Angeli
Naukkarinen, O. and Y. Saito, eds (2012), *Artification* (Special Volume), *Contemporary Aesthetics*, 4. Available online: http://www.contempaesthetics.org/newvolume/pages/journal.php?volume=49 (accessed May 17, 2015)
Negrin, L. (2012), "Fashion and Aesthetics—A Fraught Relationship", in A. Gecky and V. Karaminas (eds), *Fashion and Art*, 43–54, London: Bloomsbury
Pedroni, M. and P. Volonté (2012), "Introduzione. Oggetti, pratiche e istituzioni di due campi sociali correlati", in M. Pedroni and P. Volonté (eds), *Moda e arte*, 9–32, Milano: Franco Angeli
Simmel, G. (1911) "Die Mode", in *Philosophische Kultur*, Potsdam: Gustav Kiepenhauer Verlag; partial trans. M. Ritter and D. Frisby, "The Philosophy of Fashion", in D. Frisby and M. Featherstone (eds), *Simmel On Culture: Selected Writings*, 187–205, London-Thousand Oaks-New Delhi: Sage Publications
Wilson, E. (1985): *Adorned in Dreams: Fashion and Modernity*, London-New York: Tauris & Co.
Wittgenstein, L. (1953), *Philosophical Investigations*, trans. G.E.M. Anscombe, Oxford: Basil Blackwell
Wittgenstein, L. (1980), *Remarks on the Philosophy of Psychology*, vol. 1, Oxford: Blackwell
Wolfendale, J. and J. Kennett, eds (2011), *Fashion—Philosophy for Everyone: Thinking with Style*, Malden (MA)-Oxford: Wiley-Blackwell
Wollheim, R. (1980), *Art and Its Objects* (1968), Cambridge: Cambridge University Press

3 ANTI-FASHION: IF NOT FASHION, THEN WHAT?

Nickolas Pappas

1. A philosophical question for fashion

Sooner or later everything comes to interest philosophy. There is a view of the field according to which philosophy once encompassed every inquiry and went on to lose parts of itself one by one as each field saw how to be scientific. On that view philosophy keeps eroding to nothing. But the opposite progress is more closely true, that philosophy's curiosity continues to seize on more of what is said and done and has not yet been brought into philosophy's consciousness. If it's brain science and film today it was relativity a century ago, and before that Europe's discovery of the world's cultures.

In antiquity we have Socrates, credited with bringing philosophy down from the heavens to human affairs. Human affairs included what humans wear. It sounded like folly to Callicles that Socrates asked about clothing and shoes, as if philosophers should keep their minds on grander realities, but Socrates kept at it, was even said to spend days in a cobbler's shop.[1] Now the subject has followed his ancient lead and we are talking about shoes again.

It took until recently for philosophers to engage with fashion. Comments appear in Thoreau (*Walden*: chap. 1 ("Economy"), discussed below) and Santayana (1905: III, chap. 7 ("Reason in Religion")), asides from Rousseau and Kant (*Discourse on the Arts and Sciences*: Part I; and *Anthropology from a Pragmatic Point of View*: § 71).[2] But in the present generation philosophers have written full-length books, and edited anthologies, that dwell on fashion in a sustained and attentive way. The books by Gilles Lipovetsky (1994) and Lars Svendsen (2006) are widely known and deserve to be, but Karen Hanson's articles (1990; 1998) are also examples of how much philosophers can add to our understanding of fashion.[3]

2. What is not fashion?—Or, what fashion is not

Speaking philosophically of fashion can mean a splendid variety of things. Philosophers often do ask "What is it?" as Socrates did, except that they are more likely to be chastised for that tendency today than indulged. They have developed other techniques for approaching the beings of things, though, some of those successful in the philosophical classroom (and not only there).

For instance, when you find a student appealing to what is natural, it is not a bad exercise to step away from the "nature" in that heartfelt appeal and look for its absence. What are they opposing "natural" to? Eyeglasses are not naturally occurring objects, in the sense of being artifacts, and such examples make the *natural* seem opposite to the *artificial*. But it also might not be natural for you to wake up every half hour; here what is not natural is the *unaccustomed*. A third example—a turtle born with two heads—might bring your student to see the opposite of the natural as the *abnormal* or monstrous.

Such an exercise trips up what had looked like ironclad appeals to natural behavior. Where "nature" is denied in such different ways, the accusations of "unnatural" sound more equivocal than they had before. And students are readier to hear other challenges to *prima facie* oppositions.

So, now that philosophers can bring to fashion the tactics and techniques we call philosophical, it might be worth asking as one preliminary taxonomical question whether more than a single opposite to fashion exists. What is clothing or dress in the absence of fashion? What is fashion *not*?

I suspect that the "unfashionable" will not be the place to look. When clothes are judged to be unfashionable, that almost always means either that they were fashionable once and ceased to be, or that they are vulgar or otherwise failed attempts to imitate something fashionable. Wide neckties and women's padded shoulders looked just right and then did not. Counterfeit Prada bags do not look sufficiently like the real thing. What those unfashionable items have in common is their closeness to fashion not their difference from it. They are, unfashionably, what had been in fashion; or they are unfashionably like (maybe we'd want to say: merely *like*) what is in fashion now.

It would be dull-witted to deny the importance of understanding these distinctions between success and failure, but they are important only within a domain that recognizes small distinctions as essential, for they are after all small distinctions. The unfashionable travels alongside the fashion, and much about dress lies a distance away from either.

A larger contrast with fashion looks back to the time before fashion began. It is commonly observed that the word for "fashion" in several European languages is the same as the word for "modernity": *moda*, *la mode*. And with good reason. In its broad sense fashion began around 1300 with the stitching and fitting of clothes to replace gowns or robes,[4] while on the more precise meaning of the word the fashion industry came into existence in the nineteenth century (Lipovetsky 1994: 55–87). So fashion generally speaking shares a birth with other modern institutions, while a fashion world that is conscious of itself as an enterprise is contemporaneous with a modern world conscious of itself as a problem. And given this modernity of fashion there may be a point to seeking what is not fashion in the same place one finds what is not modern. That alternative might appear more easily in pre-modern times than it does in the modernized present.

Ancient and medieval people did dress. Often enough they had reasons to dress finely. Their ways of dress changed, sometimes on a large scale and sometimes in a detail. Rome's emperors were clean-shaven until Hadrian, then mostly bearded until Constantine, and then clean-shaven again. Do such shifts in presentation imply that fashion existed before 1300?

It is not an idle question. Someday historians of dress may arrive at a consensus very different from today's about the modernity of fashion. But unless they assert (what is surely false) that all clothing entails fashion, what matters for our discussion is that fashion exists now and once did not exist. Whether it began in 1850, in 1300, or during the fifteenth ancient Olympic Games in 720 BC, there was an era and a stretch of time before the beginning of fashion. That much is enough. Let fashion be the system for evaluating dress that exists today and make its opposite the way of dress belonging to whatever the earlier era was, where "way of dress" can encompass customs, judgments about those customs, and stories of how they began (fig leaves and animal skins). It will only not encompass fashion.

There is a point to imagining such a past. Even fashion's fans sometimes weary of the demands it creates. And when you weary of fashion you might spare a nostalgic look for that earlier time that was innocent of fashion decisions. It is a harmless look back, like thinking of the time before air travel, or before there was such a thing as calculus. And for the purpose of understanding what fashion is there is a point to contrasting it with that earlier time.

But from the practitioner's point of view a thought-experiment that produces *this* distinction between fashion and non-fashion has limited usefulness, as imagining a state of nature has limited value for political theorizing in the midst of artificial and sometimes monstrous societies. An earlier lost-time innocent of fashion will not contain the answers you seek if you are a person getting dressed in the morning and wondering how to go about getting dressed, and wondering whether any alternative exists to dressing fashionably or unfashionably (the former if you try and succeed, the latter if you try and fail). A time innocent of fashion had no experience of turning away from fashion, any more than a being innocent of sin has experience at turning away from sinning, and what you want to know when you're wearying of fashion is how one might turn away and to what. All by itself, looking to the past is like asking how animals dress. The very obliviousness to fashion that gives antiquity its charm in this respect makes it an incomplete guide for those who seek an alternative.

There is a meaningful opposition to be drawn here, in other words. But it is not the only opposition one might want.

In language from Genesis, the problem is this. Adam and Eve were naked and unashamed. We might think we would like to go back to being naked, or something close to naked, as well as to being unashamed. There are moods in which it would be nice to present your body naturally, without affectation or deceit; without sin. But we are not ready to give up the knowledge of good and evil that makes us so similar to gods.

3. Anti-fashion is the rejection of fashion

What one might want from an opposite to fashion, when antiquity's obliviousness is not enough, is a way of performing the delicate task that *ignoring* fashion consists in. How much can you know about something and still ignore it? You have to know something; otherwise you are ignorant, which is not the same thing as ignoring. But too much awareness of the thing to be ignored and you risk merely *trying* to ignore it, or *seeming* to.

According to Anne Hollander's history, one rejection of fashion began almost as soon as fashion itself did, among aristocrats who wanted to ignore the new bourgeoisie's sartorial displays of wealth. To show that they rose above such vulgarities the aristocrats dressed in the same baggy clothes from year to year, making it clear that they paid no mind to the changes fashion brought. Hollander calls this aristocratic turn away from fashion the first *anti-fashion.* Let fashion change. Anti-fashion would remain as it had been (see Hollander 1975: 363).

Anti-fashion behavior enhanced its air of seriousness by signifying not only difference from the bourgeoisie but distance from all indulgence, still in the early centuries of modernity. Philip the Good, Duke of Burgundy through the middle of the fifteenth century, dressed in black all the years that he was duke (Harvey 1995: 52–6). His sartorial abstemiousness read as moral seriousness. Wearing black showed that Philip continued to mourn his father, and it also let him stand outside the cycles of fashion that symbolize the never-sated desires of the body.

Hollander does not mention Philip, but she does recognize the special status of the color he wore. Black clothing, she says, is "one steady current in the course of fashion that always gains power [. . .] from its ancient flavor of antifashion" (Hollander 1975: 365).

If Hollander had spoken of Baldesar Castiglione's character the Magnifico Giuliano, she would have to count him as an advocate of anti-fashion too. In Castiglione's *Book of the Courtier* (Book II: §§ 26–7), written in 1528 (after the death of Philip the Good), the Magnifico Giuliano dispenses advice to courtiers on all matters of character and deportment. Naturally he arrives at the question of what to wear; and Giuliano proposes moderation. He surveys the range of styles

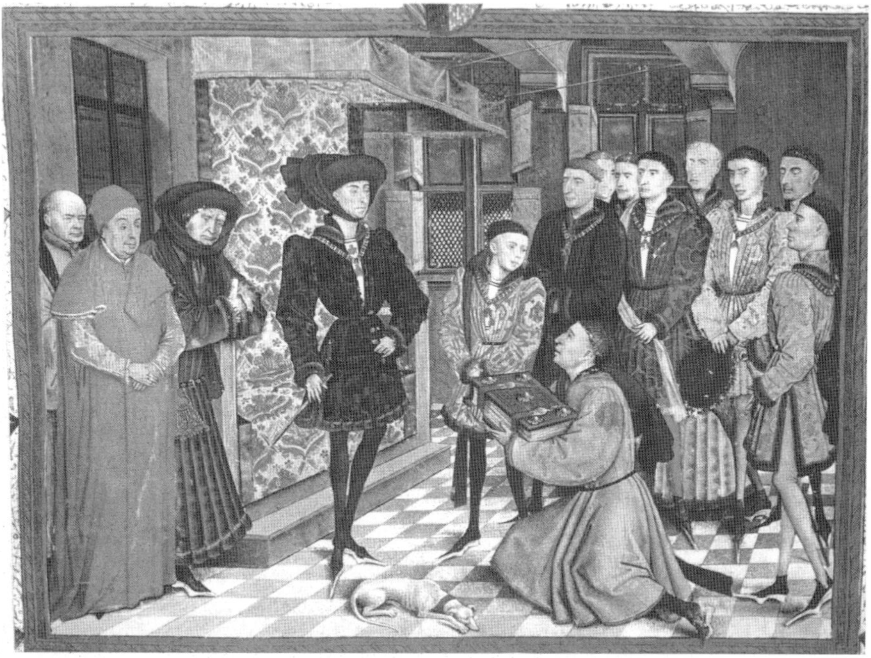

FIGURE 3.1 Ms. 9243 Chroniques de Hainault, Dedication page: Filippo III il Buono di Borgogna riceve un manoscritto. Bibliotheque Royale Albert I, Bruxelles.

and hues that the different nations wear. It is best not to belong to any one camp, he says. Black is the best color, for it refrains from all fads.

Where a curmudgeonly aristocracy wore the same thing forever to avoid variations over time, Giuliano proposes a black wardrobe as an alternative to variations that exist at any one time across the continent. Anti-fashion seems to see itself as a default condition of dress: a fashion, as it were, that does not change.

4. Must fashion change?

This minimal introduction to anti-fashion is enough to trigger an objection. Someone might smell a contradiction in the very description of anti-fashion, and accuse me of having sidestepped the problem with the phrase "as it were" when I called anti-fashion a fashion that does not change.

Thus in one article from the recent anthology *Fashion—Philosophy for Everyone*, Jesse Prinz and Anya Farennikova dismiss the very possibility of unchanging fashion. By definition, they say, there can be no such thing. That would seem to rule out anti-fashion as an alternative, except in the charmless sense that 7 + 5 = 13 is an alternative to arithmetic (Prinz and Farennikova 2011: 13–30).

Prinz and Farennikova's is one of the best-argued contributions to a book that contains many good philosophical looks at fashion. Along with others in that book their article is a reminder of how philosophy can present an activity back to itself—how well philosophy can look and listen. But this one remark is a misstep, the idea that unchanging fashion amounts to contradiction. Such an assertion presupposes that change is of the essence in fashion. It rests on an insistent belief that whatever other features we also discover in fashion phenomena, we are required to find variability over time. "Fashions change" is an *a priori* truth on this approach—which ought to suggest to other interested parties that it is an assumption in need of interrogation.

The same belief about change comes up insistently among other philosophers today, sometimes as a description of fashion and sometimes at second order as a description of how philosophers have seen fashion—which is then to say, a reason philosophers have had to oppose fashion. Both of the book-length treatments of fashion that I am aware of by philosophers, by Lipovetsky and by Svendsen, understand philosophers' reactions to fashion in the same terms. Fashion is bound to change and philosophers bound up against its changeability.[5]

Whether or not you agree that changeability determines fashion, and even if you agree that changeability by itself is enough to do so, there is a caricature of philosophy at work here: philosophy with a distaste for change. Grant that on a standard reading of Plato he finds nature's changes a problem in need of solution. Give him Parmenides and Melissus for company. There is still a long silence from the centuries that follow this group instead of the chorus of philosophical voices denouncing change that Svendsen and Lipovetsky seem to be assuming.

In fact, as I have argued elsewhere, on the occasions that past philosophers *did* speak to the un-sublime subject of fashion, what stands out in their condemnations is not that fashion changes, not even that it pertains to one's body[6] (for again, Plato has many successors who do not mind the body), but that it arises out of the spirit of imitation (see Pappas 2008). Fashion means no more than this for Rousseau, Thoreau, and Santayana, that everyone who observes its rules is copying someone else (copying someone who is also observing those rules as well as reinforcing them). Herd mentality gives you fashion, understood as everyone's attempt to resemble everyone else.

In some theorists' hands the account in terms of mass imitation might become the more specific thesis that the poor imitate the rich.[7] But that specification does not have to be part of the story. I am not requiring it and I even doubt that it has been the prevailing imitative impulse for a century or more. It suffices that one dresses as "they" dress, to name the mob of others that Thoreau blames fashion on. The result will be pathological attentiveness to one's fellow humans—worse than that, attentiveness to their pathological attentiveness. You don't get up in the morning and put on clothes you like the look of. You do not even put clothes on that you think other people will like, because that will fail to make you fashionable if those other people are conscious of the demands of fashion. They might take pleasure in what you are wearing but not respect or recognize it as fashionable. In order to be fashionable you put on clothes that you think other people will think that *other* other people will like. One now begins picturing human society as a large cave in which arguments are held over shadows.

If, together with Thoreau and the other philosophers, you should perceive fashion's imitative impulse as more fundamentally generative of fashion than its changeability alone is, then the prospect of a persisting fashion loses some of its sense of contradictoriness. If it does not arise out of the imitative pathology, that which remains the same (not eternally, but at least through repeated cycles) will not qualify exactly as a fashion, but it could still stand among fashions, somewhat as their peer; a recognizable alternative; a legitimate opposite.

5. What is not merely social

The worry that fashion rests on mass mutual imitation raises other questions about what the opposite to fashion must be like. Leave aside some of the questions that matter most, such as whether it is true that fashion works through imitation alone (I wonder how it could do that and continue to change, if everyone always aims at resembling everyone else. This problem might account for the recurring move to blame foreigners for all innovations—remember Zephaniah [1.8], calling God's punishment down on "all who are dressed in foreign clothing"—as if the herd at home lacks the independence of mind to vary what they wear). For my purposes it will be enough that people have seen it that way. Fashion can be justified only socially, on this view.

To say that fashion can be justified only socially is to say that while one still has reasons for wearing something rather than nothing—weather, morality, enemy swords—one has only social reasons, and reasons that are *known on all sides* to be social, for wearing this coat rather than that one, or for wearing this color, or this or that haircut. Dressing in recognition of fashion begins with the acknowledgment that fashion is a mutually imitative social experience. In this respect we have no need of fashion-sophists to come and reveal to us naïfs what the old sophists felt compelled to reveal, that what we do is *nomos* (custom, law, convention) rather than *phusis* (nature). A way of dressing that worked as an alternative to that would seek reasons for the choice of clothing that exceeded the merely social.

Let me emphasize that by "social" I mean what everyone recognizes to be nothing above and beyond the social. Morality may well be a social phenomenon, but at least some people believe that moral laws have a basis outside of what is social. So I am not including morality among the considerations that are known on all sides as social.[8]

One magisterial alternative to what acknowledges itself as social is the religious or the magical, inasmuch as the participants in a religion or a magical method believe it to derive its power (whatever outsiders may think) from something transcending an orchestrated human trust. Some recognized anti-fashions begin in ritual wear and ritual practice. One example already mentioned, black dress, has multiple origins in ritual, from its ancient use as a cloth of mourning to the medieval sorcerer's black clothes. Aeschylus and Euripides make much use of the adjective *melagchimos*, a poetic form of *melas* (black), to describe clothes for mourning, a ram's fleece offered at a grave, or the grave itself.[9] In medieval Europe both monks and magicians dressed in black robes.

As it happens, the magicians in Roman Egypt sometimes stripped naked to perform their spells (Graf 1997: 104, 115). This might make the same point, for I believe that male nudity functioned as an anti-fashion among the archaic Greeks and in later ancient centuries;[10] and male nudity among the Greeks seems more likely to have begun in initiation rituals than anywhere else.[11]

But there is no need to remain in the ancient world to find anti-fashion conjoining with religion and magic. There are magicians among us today, at least in the US, and they wear another kind of anti-fashion, the formal black suit that is known in America as the tuxedo. Another religious officer, the Protestant minister, wears the man's suit, yet another recognized anti-fashion (thus Hollander 1994: 79). Clothing with a religious or ritual significance does sometimes show the influence of fashion. Christian clergymen who once wore robes now walk the streets in trousers. But fashion affects these garments much more slowly, weakly, and partially than it changes anyone else's clothes.[12]

There are sources for anti-fashion besides cult and worship. In secular societies, anti-fashions arise that have no evident ties to magic or religion. The least controversial example are jeans—or, if you believe that jeans have now succumbed to the pressures of fashion, then jeans as they were until the mid-1970s; but I think they are still anti-fashion to a substantial degree. I would add tattoos and the shaved head, even if those examples take us away from fashion considered narrowly as dress, i.e., uses of fabric on the body.

Of the secular examples, tattoos carry some associations with magic. Egyptian women used certain tattoos to enhance their fertility or improve their sex lives. There has been much discussion of a passage from the Babylonian Talmud that seems to call Jesus a magician, saying he returned from Egypt with charms scratched into his skin, i.e., tattooed on him, evidently a practice among Egyptian sorcerers.[13] The male shaved head may or may not derive its appeal from those traditions in which clergy had no hair on their heads. The Egyptian priests of Osiris seem to have shaved their heads, as many Buddhists do today. When Joseph leaves prison to see the Pharaoh he first shaves, probably all the hair off his body, as palace protocol dictated.[14] These are only traces of old religion, though, now far from ongoing practice. And any connection between denim and religion would have to be indirect, and metaphorical in the extreme.

These examples that lack a sacred aspect share other features of anti-fashion. They are all famously long-lasting. Black dress has carried its significance for so long that when any other color threatens to become the new standard or default color it is named "the new black." The man's suit changes, but only in some details. In fact it is striking that the suit pattern itself seems to dictate which particulars may change: lapels wider or narrower, the number of buttons climbing up as high as a peak of three before plunging to two. And then one may have cuffs or not. That the suit tradition dictates the acceptable domains for its own variation indicates that the normal rules of fashion are not at work in this special area; and the suit has proved remarkably resistant to shifts in fashion since its full modern appearance more than a century ago (and when I speak of the suit I mean a suit worn with a shirt and the right kinds of shoes, and almost always a necktie. It is a further remarkable feature of suits that the items accompanying them have altered as slowly as the jacket and trousers themselves. Thus despite appearances a suit is not a single thing but almost always a thing imbedded in a whole context).

The long-lasting fashion becomes literally long-lasting, or enduring at the level of particular objects—the token not only the type enduring—in the case of jeans. As fashion, jeans continue to look much as they did in the 1950s, and individual pairs of jeans endure longer than most trousers that face the same rough treatment. Then there are tattoos. If any fashion item has some traits by definition, tattoos have the quality of lasting. For tattooing to belong in the domain of fashion, it must reflect the wish for a fashion that does not change. I do not claim that they succeed at that goal, and that tattoos achieve a state of transcendence from fashion. Still I am impressed with how long tattoos in their contemporary form have been among us, without as you might say fading away. Tattoos have made a start toward anti-fashion status, and they are surely intended to be anti-fashion.

Not all these examples are masculine, but there is no denying the male tendency in them. Jeans and tattoos were exclusively male once even though they are not today. Athletic nudity in Greece was exclusively male, and the tuxedo still is. The smooth-shaven head might be hard to read *except* as masculine, or masculinizing. So it might be a sense of the masculine as standard that brings anti-fashion into this association with a gender. The unmarked sex is the one we would expect to dress without the identifying markers of fashion. But I do not insist on this reading of the fact; I only note the maleness of much anti-fashion as a fact, maybe a fact in need of interpretation.

The features of anti-fashion work to maintain a nervous balance between anti-fashion and fashion, and possibly an impossible balance. The anti-fashion item goes where fashion items go. In this respect it is a fashion possibility. At the same time it marks a place for itself that is not on the spectrum of fashion's possibilities. Everything you wear must be some color (unless you wear colorless transparent clothing; and no one does). But regarding black one can make the case for either calling it a color or not. It is interesting that you might say the same about another anti-fashion hue, the color of undyed cotton or linen; what is called "natural."

A shaved head likewise takes its place on the spectrum of haircuts, or just off the spectrum. Or really, it is neither clearly on the spectrum nor clearly off. Shaving the head is something you can do with your hair, as haircuts also are. Yet it is only a haircut in some special sense of the word. Aristotle might call it a hairstyle in name only, in the same limited sense that he says a dead man's hand is a hand (*Politics*: I, 2, 1253a 19–34). Decisions about hair have been ruled out when the head is smooth, as the color black implies that there will be no color-decision made, and as (in another respect) wearing a tuxedo means not deciding what to wear.

That any one feature of this group should only apply to some members of the group, another feature to others, is to be expected. It is of the nature of a genre that some of its features fit emphatically in one case, tenuously or metaphorically in another. The *abiding* quality of the items I have listed, their (frequent) *masculinity*, and (sometimes) their echoes of *religion*, overlap to describe a plausible kind of dress. But something is still missing if we want more than description and more along the lines of explanation.

If I speak more freely in the rest of these remarks (where "freedom" means: without proof), it is because some explanation strikes me as called for, even if that has to be a speculative account. By virtue of *what* does anti-fashion dress escape the transparently social reality of fashion? How can salmon be this year's color for neckties and cede the ground to olive, while black remains a kind of tie so special that the phrase "black tie" stands for an entire outfit and mode of social presentation? What gives anti-fashions the exceptional status they possess? Will that source for their singular place among fashions also account for their durability, masculinity, and sacredness?

6. Natural dress

Think of the double condition of anti-fashion as its extension along two dimensions, possessing both length and height. Horizontally considered, anti-fashion exists among other ways of dressing, including fashion, uniforms, and traditional costume. These all recognize one another, not to the point of anti-fashion's *passing for* a fashion, but enough so that it is one thing you can do, among others, to present your body in public.

And then, in addition to this coexistence with fashions, anti-fashion has what you may call a vertical dimension. The frequent religious associations that anti-fashions carry offer one kind of basis for dress that runs perpendicular to what fashion has made the usual basis—or rather, perpendicular to what fashion has tried to make the only basis imaginable.

So how can you tell that a vertical dimension exists, let's say if you are among those who dwell horizontally and you come across this anti-fashion neither succeeding nor failing at the task fashion sets itself? The religious element or history is not always there; and even where it is present in a garment's history it tends not to announce itself. The religious tradition is not a public feature of dress.

This is not so much the question how anti-fashion justifies itself in fact as the question of how it can be glimpsed among fashions. How does the rejection of fashion show itself to eyes that know only fashion?

For me the path to an answer arose out of the earliest articulation I have found of the problem that I am calling the problem of perpendicular assessments. That articulation comes in Book 5 of Plato's *Republic,* when Socrates is envisioning life in the good city. Having proposed equality among men and women in the guardian class, Socrates describes the extent of that equality. For example all the guardians will exercise together. In Greek, *gumnastikê* (exercise) necessarily or etymologically means activity in which one is *gumnos* (naked), so it follows that those women who serve in the army and help to rule the city will strip alongside their male colleagues.

Socrates and his interlocutors observe the danger of this innovation. People will laugh (only later do they worry about the guardians' sexual arousal). But then if people laugh the new practice will never get started. The laughter that Socrates imagines is hard and censorious, the public giggling at the sight of women who leap and run with men, especially at the sight of the old lady guardians (Plato, *Republic*: 452a–b).

Ah, but remember what happened when *male* athletic nudity began among the Greeks, Socrates says, in Crete and Sparta first and then elsewhere. It was not a long time ago. Actually this isn't true, and it matters that it isn't true. Nudity had to have come to Athenian gymnasia between two and three centuries before the conversation in the *Republic.*[15] Plato is pretending to remember what the change is like, very probably because he can make the change take the form that seems right to him. So Socrates reminds Glaucon and Adeimantus what happened when nudity arrived in Athens, with the implication that male-and-female nudity can catch on under the new constitution according to the same logic that male nudity followed during the present regime.

What happened first, Socrates says, was that people laughed. No one laughs any more. But on this newly remembered account the change did not take place as mere habituation, the nudity turning unfunny as it became accustomed sight. Vision played the crucial role in the change, and indeed two warring roles of human vision. First athletic nudity was made fun of because it looked funny, when people judged it with their eyes; and then they "saw," as Socrates says, that nudity was better. *To en tois ophthalmois dê geloion* (what was funny in the eyes), what the eyes deemed to be ridiculous, fell away in the face of *tou en tois logois mênuthentos aristou* (what in arguments was disclosed as best). Being funny-*looking* wasn't

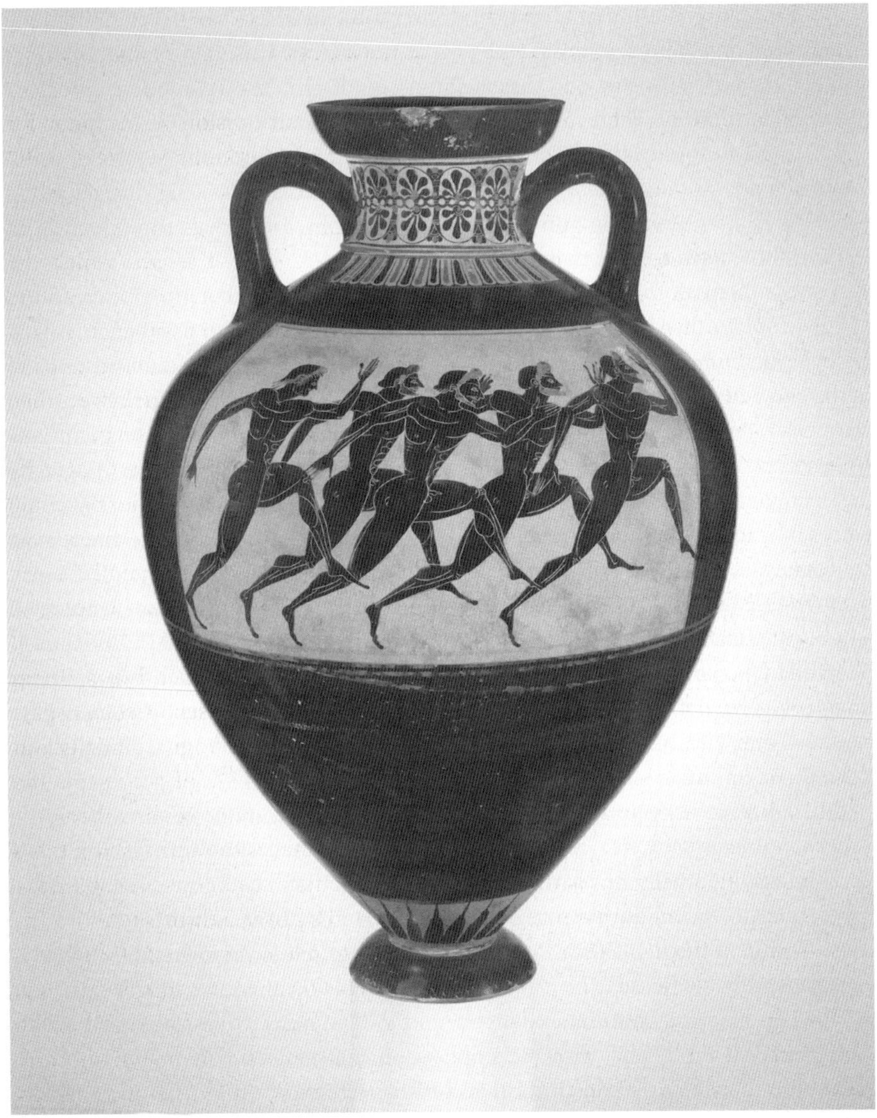

FIGURE 3.2 Panathenaic prize amphora (*c.* 530 BC), attributed to the Euphiletos Painter.

funny anymore. "Only what is bad is truly laughable." For it *ephanê* (appeared), Socrates says, that it was better to disrobe, but *this* appearing comes through arguments and comes to the mind not to the eyes. It is bootless trying to raise a laugh with reference to any other *opsin* (sight, spectacle) besides the sight of the *aphronos* (the silly, foolish), a category that apparently includes the folly of remaining dressed during exercise (Plato, *Republic*: 452d–e). Once people understood that there was nothing artificial or abnormal about the practice, their minds' eyes grew accustomed to the sight.

It has become a cliché to say that philosophers make vision a metaphor for knowledge. As usual the truth is more intriguing than the half-truth of cliché. If the *Republic* treats knowledge as metaphorical sight, it also makes sight metonymic ignorance. That is to say that vision is a metaphor for knowledge by virtue of the resemblance between them. But sight is also one among the senses, which the *Republic* treats as obstacles to knowledge and often enough enticements away from philosophy's knowledge, and by virtue of its adjacency to the other senses it metonymically represents sense as such, therefore serving as metonym for ignorance.

The *Republic* tends to keep the two meanings of vision distinct, letting metaphor prevail in one passage to explain knowledge visually while turning to metonym elsewhere to contrast knowledge with the visible realm. Some arguments make vision a ringer for knowledge while in others it is a ringleader for the mindless senses. What makes the page about nudity in Book 5 so striking is that vision carries both associations simultaneously. People "see" nudity as better, in the sense of reasoning that it's better, where they once "saw" it as ridiculous in the sense of *not* reasoning about it.

Now suppose Greek athletic nudity belongs with the other anti-fashions. I even think this passage from Plato makes it the first, if knowing oneself as such is part of being an anti-fashion, although nothing turns on this chronological priority. But if nudity is an anti-fashion, the doubled vision I am speaking of represents the second-guessing that always accompanies anti-fashion, and its two dimensions of existence. Seen, which is to say sensed, treated as a spectacle, the anti-fashion takes its place among other ways of dress; but seen, which is to say known, along what I am calling its vertical dimension, the anti-fashion exhibits its advantages.

Imagining ancient athletic nudity as a heuristic for modern anti-fashions guided me toward the undressed body, an opposite to fashion in probably the most obvious sense. Of course tattoos and shaved heads evoke the undressed human body too. They put the body on display as fashion does not—not because fashionable clothes are compelled to hide the body, but because fashions do not take the body for their justification. Even when fashionable clothing does not hide the body it does display itself.

At first sight the man's suit might seem to violate my generalization about anti-fashion and the body. In fact it provides the most satisfying support to that generalization. I am persuaded by Anne Hollander's study (1994), which argues that the contours of what we know as a man's suit, in particular its jacket, represent the contours of the idealized male body. She tells how long it took for England's tailors—unless *pace* Hollander it was the French[16]—to master the cutting and shaping of cloth that made the lapels lie flat on a jacket's front. Then, in a cartoon version of the V-shaped build, the lapels started out waist-level with nothing, meeting at a button (over the navel or belly button) in a wasp waist, widening and parting as they rose into a broad lapel-chest below what now looked like two stuffed and squared-away shoulders: "the perfect classical body, aptly translated into the modern garments that were the most traditionally 'natural' in themselves." The man in the suit becomes an "unfallen Adam" because he is a man in his own body now. "The perfect man, as conceived by English tailors, was part English country gentleman, part innocent natural Adam, and part naked Apollo."[17] Thus the suit persists as standard dress because it connotes undress.

Jeans are bodily in more self-evident ways. They shrink against the legs to show what the naked leg would look like. They wear out on the legs to create a visible record of how this body's lower part customarily or naturally moves. Lucinda Ballard, the costume designer for both stage and film versions of *A Streetcar Named Desire*, washed Brando's jeans until they clung to his skin and even cut out their inner pockets. Brando approved. "I think that Stanley would have liked to push his hands in his pockets and feel himself" (Manso 1995: 228).[18] His reaction sounds close to, and shares an idea of anti-fashion with, what Thoreau says about *his* idea of necessary dress:

> [O]ur shirts are our liber, or true bark, which cannot be removed without girdling and so destroying the man. I believe that all races at some seasons wear something equivalent to the shirt. It is desirable that a man be clad so simply that he can lay his hands on himself in the dark.
>
> **THOREAU**, *Walden*: chap. 1, § 37

The shirt lets you put your hands on your own body and know your body, where fashion forces its followers to guess how everybody else plans to dress. For Thoreau the shirt is a human standard, having grown on bodies as if naturally, the way that a bark or liber grows on a tree.

Liber was also the name of the patron deity of Rome's plebeians and emblem of their freedom. And rightly so. If anti-fashion is possible, then human dress can speak of human commonality without proclaiming slavish conformism. If anti-fashion clothing keeps the body that it dresses in another way undressed, then something of the undressed body, unshamed by fashion, is back in the domain of dress. The eyes see nothing special, whether fashionable or laughable. The mind's eye sees the body, or the idea of the body. And the idea is what philosophers know as a universal term.

Notes

1 Socrates brought philosophy down from the heavens (cf. Cicero, *Tusculan Disputations*: 5.10). Diogenes Laërtius speaks similarly, locating Socrates' interest in matters *en* *megaroisi* (indoors) (*Lives of the Eminent Philosophers*: 2.21). On Socrates on clothing and shoes, see Plato, *Gorgias* 490d–e; in the shop of Simon the shoemaker, see Diogenes Laërtius, *Lives of the Eminent Philosophers*: 2.122.

2 I discuss these authors' remarks on fashion in *The Philosopher's New Clothes* (see Pappas 2016).

3 Two rich anthologies are Scapp and Seitz (2010), and Wolfendale and Kennett (2011).

4 Thus Hollander 1975: 17, 90. For a typical account, see Nunn 2000: 13; and also Lipovetsky 1994: 15, 19–20, 35, 46.

5 See Svendsen 2006: 22, 25–6, especially 28 on fashion and *the new* (a point at which Svendsen follows Adorno); and Lipovetsky 1994: 15, 20, 27, 41, 64, 135, 157.

6 *Pace* Hanson, for whom squeamishness about the body as the object of attention lies at the heart of philosophers' resistance to fashion.

7 Kant speaks this way explicitly in *Anthropology from a Pragmatic Point of View* (§ 71); and compare Adam Smith (*The Theory of Moral Sentiments*: I. III. 34). Lipovetsky attacks the version of this view found in Gabriel de Tarde (1962): see Lipovetsky 1994: 126, 227. But Lipovetsky argues as though calling fashion imitative had always implied the imitation of rich by poor.

8 I am grateful to an anonymous reader from Bloomsbury Press for a remark that inspired this response.

9 *Melagchimos*: mourning clothes (see Aeschylus, *Choephoroi*: 11; Euripides, *Phoenician Women*: 372); fleece (Euripides, *Electra*: 513); grave (Euripides, *Rhesus*: 962). Cf. "black-clad Death" (Euripides, *Alcestis*: 843–4).

10 I develop this claim in "The Naked Truth of Anti-Fashion Philosophy" (Pappas 2010). Also see the relevant sections of my book *The Philosopher's New Clothes* (Pappas 2016).

11 The place to begin any inquiry into Greek nudity is Bonfante 1989; for the origins of adolescent male nudity in religious ritual (most likely the initiation rites of early antiquity), see 551. On "the festival of stripping" and other appearances of nudity in ancient initiations, see Burkert 1985: 261.

12 I am grateful again to the anonymous reader who pressed me to clarify this point.

13 On tattooed Egyptian artifacts, see Pinch 1994: 126, 131. On women's tattoos of Bes, see Pinch 2002: 118. On Jesus and inscribed magic charms, cf. Babylonian Talmud, tractate on Shabbat. 104b.

14 Egyptian priests: cf. Apuleius, *The Golden Ass*: 11.10; but see Swetnam-Burland 2011: 346–7. Joseph: cf. Genesis: 41.14. Cf. Numbers: 6.18 on the head's being shaved in fulfillment of a Nazirite's vow; and Jeremiah: 16.6 on head-shaving in mourning as exclusively gentile practice.

15 Not long since Greeks laughed at male nudity (Plato, *Republic*: 452c). Of Plato's contemporaries, only Thucydides (1.6.5) makes the same claim about the recent date of this innovation. But in fact the *Republic*'s conversation is set around 420 BC, and later writers like Pausanias date the beginning of athletic nudity to the fifteenth Olympiad, 720 BC. In any event the practice seems to go back to 700 (see McDonnell 1991). Some historians argue that athletic nudity was not established practice until as late as 650 (thus Scanlon 2002). But even that date is as far away from Socrates' discussion as George Washington's presidency from the present.

16 Hollander presents the evolution of the suit as purely English, but the English themselves spoke of a foreign contribution. In 1835, *The Gentleman's Magazine of Fashions* in London depicted a frock coat with a sewn-on lapel, credited to the famous Parisian tailor Straub. Straub claimed to have invented this technique of cutting the lapel and re-sewing it to the jacket front to improve the way it lay against the chest. See Breward et al. 2004: 41.

17 Hollander 1994: 87–8 ("perfect classical body"), 88 ("unfallen Adam"), 92 ("perfect man"). Hollander writes that the suit "replaced the same scheme of nude muscles that had been the classical expression" of honesty and rationality (Hollander 1994: 91).

18 See Sullivan 2006: 87–8.

Bibliography

Bonfante, L. (1989), "Nudity as a Costume in Classical Art", *American Journal of Archaeology*, 93 (4): 543–70

Breward, C., E. Ehrman and C. Evans (2004), *The London Look: Fashion from Street to Catwalk*, New Haven: Yale University Press

Burkert, W. (1985), *Greek Religion*, trans. J. Raffan, Cambridge (MA): Harvard University Press

Graf, F. (1997), *Magic in the Ancient World*, trans. F. Philip, Cambridge (MA): Harvard University Press

Hanson, K. (1990), "Dressing Down Dressing Up", *Hypatia*, 5 (2): 107–22

Hanson, K. (1998), "Fashion and Philosophy", in M. Kelly (ed.), *Encyclopedia of Aesthetics*, vol. 2: 147–60, Oxford-New York: Oxford University Press

Harvey, J. (1995), *Men in Black*, Chicago: University of Chicago Press

Hollander, A. (1975), *Seeing Through Clothes*, Berkeley: University of California Press

Hollander, A. (1994), *Sex and Suits*, New York-Tokyo: Kodansha International

Lipovetsky, G. (1994), *The Empire of Fashion: Dressing Modern Democracy* (1987), trans. C. Porter, Princeton (NJ): Princeton University Press

Manso, P. (1995), *Brando: The Biography*, New York: Hyperion Press

McDonnell, M. (1991), "The Introduction of Athletic Nudity: Thucydides, Plato, and the Vases", *The Journal of Hellenic Studies*, 111: 182–93

Nunn, J. (2000), *Fashion in Costume 1200–2000* (1990), Chicago: New Amsterdam Books

Pappas, N. (2008), "Fashion Seen as Something Imitative and Foreign", *The British Journal of Aesthetics*, 48 (1): 1–19

Pappas, N. (2010), "The Naked Truth of Anti-Fashion Philosophy", in R. Scapp and B. Seitz (eds), *Fashion Statements: On Style, Appearance, and Reality*, 143–58, New York: Palgrave Macmillan

Pappas, N. (2016), *The Philosopher's New Clothes: The Theaetetus, the Academy, and Philosophy's Turn against Fashion*, Oxford-New York: Routledge

Pinch, G. (1994), *Magic in Ancient Egypt*, London: British Museum Press

Pinch, G. (2002), *Egyptian Mythology*, Oxford: Oxford University Press

Prinz, J. and A. Farennikova (2011), "What Makes Something Fashionable?", in J. Wolfendale and J. Kennett (eds), *Fashion—Philosophy for Everyone: Thinking with Style*, 13–30, Malden (MA)-Oxford: Wiley-Blackwell

Santayana, G. (1905), *The Life of Reason*, New York: Scribner's

Scanlon, Th.F. (2002), *Eros and Greek Athletics*, Oxford: Oxford University Press

Scapp, R. and B. Seitz, eds (2010), *Fashion Statements: On Style, Appearance, and Reality*, New York: Palgrave Macmillan
Sullivan, J. (2006), *Jeans: A Cultural History of an American Icon*, New York: Gotham Books
Svendsen, L. (2006), *Fashion: A Philosophy* (2004), trans. J. Iron, London: Reaktion Books
Swetnam-Burland, M. (2011), "'Egyptian' Priests in Roman Italy", in E. Gruen (ed.), *Cultural Identity in the Ancient Mediterranean*, 336–53, Los Angeles: Getty Research Institute
Tarde, G. (1962), *The Laws of Imitation* (1890), trans. E. Clews Parsons, Gloucester (MA): Peter Smith
Wolfendale, J. and J. Kennett, eds (2011), *Fashion—Philosophy for Everyone: Thinking with Style*, Malden (MA)-Oxford: Wiley-Blackwell

4 FITS OF FASHION: THE SOMAESTHETICS OF STYLE

Richard Shusterman

1.

Most of my ideas in philosophy derive more from personal experience than from the reading of theoretical texts. Those texts, however, are crucial in helping to shape those ideas in clearer form by lending them an appropriate, academically established vocabulary to communicate them—and, of course, to give them academic credibility. Normally, my philosophical essays begin with a detailed critical discussion of influential theories dealing with the topic at hand. On this occasion, however, with the generous permission of this book's editors, I begin by explaining the source not only of my interest in fashion but also of my experience with its professional practice. That personal experience forms the perspective of this essay.

For most of the decade from 1992–2002 I lived in the fashion capital of New York City, sharing my Chelsea apartment with the Japanese-American designer Erica Ando. With her Master of Fine Arts background in sculpture, she began her artistic career with fabric installations for the gallery but then evolved to hand-dyed hemp shawls at craft shows and finally into her own small fashion company, which confined itself to accessories such as scarves, shawls, wraps, and cloth handbags that were sold at trendy boutiques and some high-end department stores. Among the steps in her evolution from a sculptor to a fashion designer with her own company, Erica interned with Marc Jacobs and then worked for Armani and Perry Ellis, accumulating both the professional know-how and the capital to launch her own business.

Her chapter with Perry Ellis was the longest, and for me the most significant and instructive. It revealed to me the existence and function of the fit model in fashion, a crucial but largely hidden role in the fashion industry. Clothes are supposed to fit, and fit models are chosen and labor (along with designers and pattern makers) to make them fit our bodies properly. Ironically, the fit model function is also one of the key reasons why clothes (more often than not) do not really fit as well as they should. This apparent conflict or contradiction is one of fashion's many paradoxes. There are indeed so many that fashion might be described as a complex, paradoxical enterprise of trying to reconcile contrasting elements into a compelling fit. The fit model can usefully symbolize the diverse paradoxes and fits of fashion that my essay will discuss.

What, then, is a fit model? We can begin to define its paradoxical identity by what it is not. Though employed by the fashion industry and essential to its success, the fit model is not a fashion model. Fit models do not walk the fashion runway or pose for fashion photographs. They do not need to be physically attractive; nor are they enviably, fashionably thin or tall. Indeed if they were captivatingly long and slender, then they could not fit their job. Their job is to work with the fashion company's designers, pattern makers, technical designers, and sample makers to test and adjust the fit of the sample garments that the fashion company must create before they actually manufacture them industrially. These samples play a crucial role in the company's complex and costly processes of design, manufacture, and marketing that must be completed in order for the final fashion articles to become available for purchase in the stores.

Fit models can be men or women, adults or children. I will speak of the adult male fit model, since it is through that particular gendered role that I learned what fit models are and do. No, Erica did not recruit me as a fit model at Perry Ellis. But she might have, since it turned out that I was exactly the size of the adult male fit model they were using to make their samples. I learned this when a variety of shirts, sweaters, jackets, and pants that Erica brought back for me from special "sample sales" turned out to fit me perfectly, as if they were made to measure for my body. To understand the logic for these sales requires more detail about the use of samples and the role of fit models in the fabrication of those samples and in the subsequent manufacture of the clothing for which they are samples.

Manufactures do not initially produce garments in the whole range of sizes in which they will eventually sell the garment. That would be insanely wasteful in both time and money. Manufacturers instead wait until they have a clear knowledge of the quantities of the given garment (in all the various sizes being offered) that they will need to produce to fill the orders of the retail stores and outlets who will eventually sell the garments. Those quantities are decided by the "buyers" for the retailers, who also decide which garment styles will be ordered at all (These buyers, employed by the retailers and sometimes including the retail company's managers, are of course different from the ordinary customers who buy the garments from the retailers rather than for the retailers). The buyers determine the orders on the basis of their judgment of the sample garment the manufacturer shows them. The buyers may initially see a sample at a fashion show, but they typically will want to have a sample sent to their company's store or office so they can examine it more closely and show it to their superiors and other high executives who will need to sign off on the order and determine how large it will be.

The manufacturer thus needs to send a sample garment to each company interested in buying the garment for subsequent retail selling. After making their decision (which may be a negative one to place no order at all), the retail company's buyer returns the sample garment back to the fashion company. At the end of a particular season, the fashion company accumulates a significant number of these returned samples. It cannot sell them on the open, retail market because the fashion company is not equipped or licensed for such sales. Moreover, the revenue would be minimal. Frequently these samples are simply ripped and discarded. But sometimes, when the fashion company's designers don't have the heart to destroy these beautiful clothes (and the samples are often quite beautiful), they quietly organize a private "sample sale" that is open only to trusted employees of the fashion company and where the garments are offered at "give-away" prices: such as 5 dollars for a shirt; 5 or 10 dollars for a sweater or sports jacket or pair of trousers, but occasionally for nothing at all.

When Erica went to her first sample sale she picked up a few items for me, and they turned out to fit me perfectly. Thereafter, I waited eagerly for each new sample sale, with Erica returning with an abundance of perfectly fitting clothes in the latest Perry Ellis styles. My tiny Manhattan closet was so bursting with fine clothes that I had to use my office to hang some of my trendy shirts, embellished with the signature Perry Ellis pleat (where the sleeve meets the shoulder) that the designer (who died in 1986) even trademarked (calling it the "dimple" or the "Perry Pleat").[1] I never met the fit model, but being his size made him my distinct yet mysterious benefactor, while making me the most fashionably dressed man in my philosophical circles (Of course, I didn't have much competition. When Erica accompanied me to her first philosophy conference, her first remark was that she never saw so many poorly dressed men with facial hair).

What size was the fit model, besides being my size? He was the standard size for fit models, which is the average size of the projected customers, or more precisely the average or median size for the range of sizes that the fashion manufacturing company will be offering in that particular line of garments or specific garment type. So, for a woman fit model, if the size range is 0–12, the fit model would be a 6. For a man, if the sizes run from XS–XL, the fit model would be a medium. Because different fashion companies manufacture different kinds of garments for different kinds of customers, fit models also vary in their actual body size.[2] For example, sizes vary with the projected sales region and customer, as well as with the price of the clothes. More expensive, big-city oriented product lines usually use a smaller-sized fit model because their target consumers of wealth urbanites are usually thinner. I was very lucky that Erica's company had a body like mine as its own desired average. I had always implicitly sensed that I was average size, but the fact just made me feel average. Now suddenly, being average was a wonderful distinction.

This reveals another dimension of the fit model paradox. Chosen for simply being an average body, the fit model is then transformed into the somatic ideal that determines the precise cut of clothes for the entire size range of the garments he models for. Designers, pattern makers, and sample makers closely examine how the garment fits him; where it may be too loose, too tight, or not very flattering; how it drapes, hangs, or creases. Besides showing them how the garment looks on a real, living, breathing, moving (walking, sitting, bending) man rather than a static manikin, the fit model enables the design team to learn how the garment feels on the body, how easy it is to put it on or take off, how it affects his bodily movements, influencing the ease, efficacy, and grace of such habitual movements as walking, sitting, reaching. Although this aspect receives little attention in fashion magazine images with their exclusive focus on visuality, the somaesthetic success of great clothes depends not only on how they look but on how they feel when they are worn.[3] The design team will ask for the fit model's input on how the garment feels, but will also watch him as he changes into and out of the garment to determine whether the practicality of its fit for dressing and undressing or for bending, twisting, and other movements needs to be improved and how it could be improved without harming the garment's visual design qualities. The design team will then adjust and finalize the sample garment pattern and make the soon-to-be marketed samples as a result of this input from the fit model's look and experience in wearing the sample.

The sample garment whose precise design is based on how it fits the fit model's body is extremely important. It not only functions as a marketing tool but also provides a prototype and pattern for all sizes of the size run in production. In other words, fashion companies do not produce carefully fitted and tested samples for every size. They provide one such sample design prototype for their average size based on the fit model's particular body. Thereafter, the production patterns made for the other sizes are simply extrapolated through complex mathematical calculations based on average variations in bodily dimensions as one moves away from the fit model's defining standard size. In short, the patterns that determine the fit for all the other sizes of the garment (and all their thousands of actual instances) are never fitted on real people but are only fitted to mathematical ideals or virtual forms. No wonder it is hard to find clothes that fit if you are very big or very small or just not averagely shaped. For those schooled in Platonic forms, the fact that mathematical ideas are ancillary and inferior to the fit through the particular, material body of the fit model adds further irony to the already mentioned paradox that fashion transfigures the fit model's merely average material body into the transcendent ideal that determines the form of all garments produced in the given fashion garment line.

2.

Having established the fundamentally paradoxical nature of the fashion fit model, we can turn to some of the other paradoxes of fashion that this occupation can symbolize. Fashion can be seen as a complex process of fitting a striking variety of conflicting forces together in a productive and dynamic balance. Because of these complex contrasts, the notion of fashion embraces considerable ambiguity. It would be tediously inelegant in this essay to present an exhaustive analysis of these contrasts, though this might be the fashion of academic philosophical writing. This sentence already exemplifies one ambiguity of the concept of fashion: it is both descriptive and evaluative. We can praise a person's way of dressing for being fashionable but we can also use the term more neutrally to say that her fashion of dressing shows bad taste. We can even say that her "fashion" of dressing is fashionable but lacking in elegance or style. Being fashionable here means simply being in accordance with the current fashion without any quality of distinctive chic.

This leads to a second ambiguity or contrast. Fashion is both generic and particular. Different groups have different fashion styles which often serve to support and display group identity. Different ethnicities have different fashions of dress that identify them. In much earlier times, artisans belonging to various guilds but also servants and officials of various aristocratic households or governing institutions could be distinguished by their particular uniforms or liveries that they were required to wear to demonstrate their group affiliation. In modern times (and apart from professions requiring uniforms), we have considerable choice in what we wear but we often use that choice to identify ourselves with certain social groups or classes. Some of those fashion social groups are related to other cultural tastes such as music. Hip-hop fashion (with its baseball caps, gold chains, and expensive sneakers) and country-music fashion (with its cowboy hats, jeans, and cowboy boots) are examples of generic fashion. These fashion-taste groups are prevalent with lower social classes in American culture. Other fashion-taste groups—the preppy look—are connected with more affluent classes.[4] More generally, being fashionable means belonging to the class of fashionable people, being in the "in group," however the relevant culture or subculture defines that group in fashion. But if fashion serves to link people together, its equally powerful function is to divide people by excluding other groups as being "out" or not fashionable. That is one of the reasons why fashion is always changing. When excluded people threaten to push their way into the "in group" by imitating its fashionable attire, the fashion setters change what is fashionably chic in order to preserve their stylistic distinction and dominance by the continued exclusion of others.

However, despite this intrinsic group-related character, fashion is also an individual affair. It is where the individual has a realm of choice in how she displays herself, expressing (along with her group identity and values) her personal taste, not only in clothing but also through fashion accessories such as jewelry, fragrance, and cosmetics. Fashion involves a balancing act between the contrasting forces of group affiliation and individual assertion, of conformity and independence, dependence and freedom. Having already discussed this paradoxical dialectic of standing out while fitting in (or fitting in while standing out) when I provided detailed analyses of the logics of style and of architecture, I will not pause to rehearse those analyses here (see Shusterman 2012: 225–6, 322–5)

Instead consider how the undeniable fact that individuals use fashion to express their individuality with clothes seems paradoxical because the clothes that most people wear today to express their individuality are not custom tailored for them by taking the individual's bodily measurements and making one particular pattern to fit the particular individual's body but are instead produced in bulk on the basis of patterns deriving from the pattern defined by the fit model. But even a century ago when fashionable clothes were not mass produced *prêt-à-porter*, a deeper paradox of fashion's individuality existed. People's desire to assert their special individuality by calling attention to themselves through distinctive fashionable clothes may contrastingly reflect, if one examines the matter critically, a lack of substantive, confident individuality. Instead, as architect Adolf Loos argued a century ago, it tends to "display a dandyism that betrays their servility and lack of real individualism." Those "whose individuality is [truly] strong [. . .] cannot bring themselves to express it with the aid of garish colors, plumes or elaborate modes of dress. Woe to the painter expressing his individuality with a satin frock, for the artist in him has resigned in despair" (Loos 2011: 16, 30). Fashion's individual expression comes paradoxically through the form of fashionable conformism rather than through the manifestation of a completely individualistic attire, which would not be fashionable but instead eccentric. Loos preferred sartorial conformity to the correct fashion norm (which he argued was determined by what is most eminently modern and practical and affiliated with society), since fashion conformity allowed the urge for individual expression to be channeled more powerfully into more significant aesthetic domains.[5] We could express this idea in another fashion paradox: if being fashionable adds a touch of prestige as a sign of one's social and personal distinction, then it also conversely signals that one requires this added prestige to validate or boost one's status.

In speaking of fashion's simultaneous logic of inclusion and exclusion, we noted its crucial engine of change. There is no disputing that change is essential to fashion, but fashion's logic of change also embraces some paradoxes. As Georg Simmel argued in his day, although current fashion must eventually change because the lower unfashionable groups begin to imitate it, the highest social groups are not those who initiate new fashions. Because the superior classes do not require fashion to mark their distinction, the need for changing fashion comes from the middle classes who use their status as fashionable to climb higher in social recognition. They hope that when the higher class imitates their new fashion, they will become more closely affiliated with that class and thus gain in status. After a century of democratic social evolution and commercial development, Simmel's fashion formula of "imitation from below and the flight towards novelty above" might need some adjustment and greater complexity (Simmel 1997: 190). If certain subcultures with low social status (such as hip-hop) can also set fashion trends (perhaps even as much as the middle classes), then we also need to consider youth culture as a very powerful force in driving changing fashion, along with the profit-seeking force of the fashion industry that requires change for continued profits and deploys youth culture (with its ever-new generations of consumers) as fuel for its capitalist machinery.

We find further paradoxes and balancing contrasts in the change of fashion. We speak so frequently of fashion's fleeting or ephemeral nature that we forget its contrasting permanence. I am not speaking merely of the permanence of change, but of the fact that fashion must last long enough to establish itself as a fashion. *Women's Wear Daily* (WWD) was the daily fashion rag Erica read over our morning coffee, but there is no fashion that lasts only for a day. That would be too short for the long period of work required to design, produce, market, and sell the fashion garments. The very minimum fashion duration seems to be a season; but for fashion, as I learned from Erica's line of products, there are, paradoxically, more than four seasons. Along with the four standard seasons there is "holiday" and "resort"; while autumn sometimes divides into two fashion seasons—early and late fall. Some fashions can last more than a year or evolve very slowly for a certain period with but minor variations. For such reasons, we speak frequently of fashion styles in term of decades: a 1960s, 1970s, or 1980s look. These old fashion styles succeed in being both past and present, because their key design elements are recycled in more contemporary fashion.[6] We enjoy fashion's paradoxical novelty of the old not only because a very old style brings back fond memories but also because its long absence from view makes it more refreshing than the by now too familiar fashions of recent years.

The social philosopher Georg Simmel, who rejects (like Loos) the idea that fashion is concerned with aesthetic values, insists it is ruled by "other motivations, namely with formal, social ones" that involve social values of group and personal identity and prestige (Simmel 1997: 190). Nonetheless, he explains the social drives and change of fashion in terms of deeper physiological and even metaphysical grounds. Fashion's mix of change and permanence rests on the fact that our "physiological foundation [. . .] requires motion as well as rest," as we are part of a universe that is involved in permanent but often stable and gradual change.

Likewise, fashion's balancing of group identity and personal differentiation is linked to the deeper balance between our drive for unity or generality (which give our mind rest) and our interest in the particular which "causes us to *move* from case to case" (Simmel 1997: 187). Fashion, though essentially a social and cultural product, thus paradoxically appears to derive from the deeper physiological and psychological essence of human nature. One way to explain this apparent paradox is with another one that Helmut Plessner famously pronounced, that "man is 'by nature' artificial," that humans can only be what they are through the social-cultural world they inhabit and incorporate (Plessner 1981: 199).

If clothing originally evolved for practical reasons of protection from the cold and other elements, then fashion balances the practical with the decorative. Biblical narrative offers a different origin for fashion—the sin-inspired shame of nakedness that led Adam and Eve to conceal their private parts by sewing fig leaves into aprons. But fashion paradoxically reveals the body it conceals precisely by concealing it. This is done by highlighting the concealment of the body part in a way that imaginatively reveals it, often by only partially concealing it (as in plunging necklines, semi-transparent fabrics, body-clinging fits, etc.). In explaining this paradox of suggestively revealing concealment in women's fashion, Loos reinterprets the Genesis story: it was not "modesty that made woman adopt the fig leaf" since modesty, which requires developed "cultural structures, was alien to the primitive human race." Eve covered herself to maintain Adam's affection. "Unclothed she can certainly arouse a man's passion, but not maintain his love. [. . .] Woman clothes herself and thereby made herself a mystery to man in order to fill his heart with a longing to solve the mystery" (Loos 2011: 63). Men's fashion is not very different in imaginatively heightening the appeal of male body parts by their suggestive concealment that often involves a play of concealing and revealing (think of the old codpiece or the padded shoulders of a suit jacket or sheer shirts through which the skin and nipples are somewhat visible).

Though clothing is not strictly speaking part of one's body in the way that a tattoo belongs to it, our bodies shape our clothes in ways that they do not shape more external fashion accessories. A pair of jeans will stretch, crease, and fashionably fray in terms of our particular bodies and our habits of using them in walking, sitting, bending, kneeling, and other actions. Such adaptation is how initially uncomfortable jeans eventually have a perfectly comfortable fit. But conversely our clothes shape our bodies. I am not speaking only of the way corsets have remodeled the female torso or how women's feet have been reshaped or painfully disfigured by shoes that are too narrow and pointed or that have excessively high heels—not to mention feet horribly deformed by the Chinese fashion for foot-binding which allegedly originated with a Tang Emperor's passion for a dancing concubine whose feet were clad in tightly wrapped white silk to take the comely shape of a crescent moon. We need also to consider the ways our clothing shapes our somatic habits, because the purposive body is not simply a bundle of bones and flesh but a complex of postural and behavioral dispositions that guide our actions without our needing to think about them explicitly. Women develop different habits of walking if they typically walk in high heels and tight short skirts; their manner of sitting is also affected by a habit of wearing dresses or skirts with a high hem line. Cowboys wearing chaps and spurs will also develop a different way of walking. Men accustomed to tight fitting collars and ties and dress suits are likely to move more stiffly, formally, and carefully. This is not simply because of physical constraints; clothes also have a social meaning as they are associated with certain attitudes that wearers of those clothes spontaneously adopt through prior experience in wearing those clothes. Studies have shown that people behave differently when they are wearing their professional outfits (such as a physician's white coat or a police uniform) even if they are off-duty and engaged in non-professional activities. As clothes are made to fit the bodies and movements of men and women, so the bodily behavior of those men and women are conversely made (through training or implicit learning) to fit the meanings of those clothes.

People's bodies and movements vary with different historical periods, different social classes and cultures, different ages and genders, and different professions. The fashion designer must choose the body for which he wants to design. Loos explains broad historical changes in shoe fashion in terms of changes in the feet of those for whom the shoemaker designed his patterns. "What shape of foot should he use as his standard?" Loos asks and promptly answers, "the shape of the foot of the socially most prominent class." Thus, "in the Middle Ages [when] the knights were socially dominant" (and had smaller feet because they were mostly riding), this meant that "the small foot was modern" and most fashionable; and craftsmen therefore emphasized this by "lengthening it with the turned up toe." In the Renaissance when city burghers grew more prominent and city walking gave them wider feet, so shoe fashion became wider, only to shrink again in the dominant court society of the seventeenth and eighteenth centuries (which reveled in the leisurely luxury of sedan chairs and the elegance of slender shoes with high heels for dainty feet), and then again to change its shape for the feet of the busy, speedily walking city dwellers of Loos' turn of the century times, "lengthening it" to accommodate a bigger "big toe," enlarged "since it is used more powerfully to push off" in fast walking (Loos 2011: 45–6). By Loos's logic we could explain the contemporary fashion for sneakers and athletic gear (such as Lululemon Athletica) as a recognition that in late-capitalist consumer society, the large and widely diverse class of people who consume youth culture and associate themselves with vigorous activity and fitness would constitute a commercially dominant class that the fashion designer would want to please.[7]

Through the spread of democratic ideas, technological inventions, and global consumerist forces, Western society and culture have grown very different and more complex than what Simmel and Loos saw in the early twentieth century. The markets for which designers design and sell their wares are considerably more diverse because more sectors have more buying power, while class structures and identities are far more vague and fluid. But many of Simmel's and Loos' insights remain. So does the question of the fit model. Who should be chosen as the somatic model to determine a garment's ultimate design and pattern? If today's answer is an average-sized person, the practical question remains: "Average in which context, average for which group (social, age, ethnic, etc.)?" We can no longer appeal to a particularly prominent social class to fix the norm for average size. A purely logical procedure of compiling a huge database of men's bodily dimensions and then computing a mathematical average of them does not seem feasible or reasonable since real bodies are not like mathematical averages; and the designer is designing not for any average but the average of the retail clients he imagines as his market. The fit model must be more than a collection of measurements; he is a sentient soma whose movements, feelings, and reactions in wearing the garment help the designer to determine how well the garment will look and feel when worn in real life. Designers therefore cherish their best fit models as treasures of crucial somaesthetic input, often concealing their models' identity as part of their design trade secrets.

The fit model is himself a product of fitting, embodying the fit between, on the one hand, the average or median size of the designer's size spread for producing the given garment and, on the other, the ideal body for determining how the garment will look and feel best for the designer's desired clientele. That is why the fit model size for fashion lines aiming at young, wealthy, urban customers is always smaller than for fashion lines aimed at lower-class, middle-aged, middle-America. A closing paradox emerges. We clients of clothing fashion think that we choose our designers, but they have already chosen us, which is why we prefer their clothes. This match of designer and client's desires (aided by the manipulative magic of advertising's image making) is often a better fit than our clothes, unless one is lucky enough to resemble the fit model of a fashion company one admires. But such admiration may arise because its designs fit one so well. The many fits of fashion that weave together opposites in dramatic, dynamic balance are themselves recursively and reciprocally fitted and joined to create a complex and tightly woven fabric of interests, values, strategies, positions, and stylized forms that give fashion a compelling grip on us, even if we discern the arbitrary triviality of its particular fleeting expressions.

3. Theoretical appendix: On somaesthetics

While most philosophers are probably unfamiliar with the crucial fashion function of the fit model, most devotees of fashion are likely unacquainted with the relatively new concept of somaesthetics. Here is a brief explanation. Somaesthetics is an interdisciplinary field of research, rooted in philosophical theory, but offering an integrative conceptual framework and a menu of methodologies not only for better understanding our somatic experience, but also for improving the quality of our bodily perception, performance, and presentation. It is based on the premise that such heightened somatic awareness and mastery offers significant benefits for many aspects of life, including the diverse arts of design (among which fashion finds its place). Somaesthetics emerged from pragmatist aesthetics and from the idea of philosophy as an art of living. Once we recognize the central role of the body (as a living, sentient, perceiving, dynamic soma) in the creation and appreciation of art, then it is logical to explore how we can improve our use of the body or soma to enhance our artistic capacities and pleasures. Not only art's creation and appreciation would be enhanced through this heightening of somatic consciousness, but also the attractive shaping of our lives as an art of living could be enriched by greater perceptual awareness of aesthetic meanings, feelings, and potentials in our everyday conduct of life. Moreover, if we take seriously the idea of the art of living, then, since we live through the soma (not only physically but also emotionally and perceptually), it makes sense to improve the medium of our lives through careful, critical somatic attention and amelioration.

Somasthetics is thus devoted to the critical study and meliorative cultivation of the experience and use of the living body (or soma) as a site of sensory appreciation (aesthesis) and creative self-stylization. An ameliorative discipline of both theory and practice, somaesthetics seeks to enrich not only our discursive knowledge of the body but also our lived somatic experience and performance; it aims to improve the meaning, understanding, efficacy, and beauty of our movements and of the environments to which our actions contribute and from which they also derive their energies and significance. To pursue these aims, somaesthetics is concerned with a wide diversity of knowledge forms, discourses, social practices and institutions, cultural traditions and values, and bodily disciplines that structure (or could improve) such somatic understanding and cultivation. It is therefore an interdisciplinary project, in which theory and practice are closely connected and reciprocally nourish each other. It is not limited to one theoretical field, academic or professional vocabulary, cultural ideology, or particular set of bodily disciplines. Rather it aims to provide an overarching theoretical structure and a set of basic and versatile conceptual tools to enable a more fruitful interaction and integration of the very diverse forms of somatic knowledge currently being practiced and pursued.

There is an impressive, even overwhelming abundance of discourse about the body in many disciplines of contemporary theory and commercial enterprise. But such somatic discourse typically lacks two important features. First, a structuring overview or architectonic that could integrate their very different discourses into a more productively coherent or interrelated field. The second feature lacking in most academic discourse on embodiment is a clear pragmatic orientation—something that the individual can clearly employ or apply to his or her life in terms of disciplines of improved somatic practice. Somaesthetics offers a way to address both these deficiencies.

Somaesthetics consists of three branches that overlap to some extent.[8] The first, *analytic somaesthetics*, is an essentially descriptive and theoretical enterprise devoted to explaining the nature of our bodily perceptions and practices and their function in our knowledge and construction of the world. Besides the traditional topics in philosophy of mind, ontology, and epistemology that relate to the mind–body issue and the role of somatic factors in consciousness and action, analytic somaesthetics also includes genealogical, sociological, and cultural analyses of embodiment, including the body's role in sustaining social and political power. Such studies, most famously advanced by Simone de Beauvoir, Michel Foucault, and Pierre Bourdieu, show how the body is both shaped by power and employed as an instrument to maintain it—how bodily norms of health, skill, and beauty, and even our categories of sex and gender, are constructed to reflect and sustain social forces.

In contrast to analytic somaesthetics, whose logic is essentially descriptive, *pragmatic somaesthetics* has a distinctly normative, often prescriptive, character because it involves proposing specific methods of somatic improvement or engaging in their comparison, explanation, and critique. Since the viability of any proposed method will depend on certain facts about the body (whether ontological, physiological, or social), this pragmatic dimension presupposes the analytic dimension. However, it transcends analysis not only by evaluating the facts analysis describes but also by proposing methods to improve certain facts by remaking the body and the environing social habits and frameworks that shape it. A vast and complex array of pragmatic disciplines have been designed to improve our experience and use of our bodies: various diets, forms of grooming and decoration, martial and erotic arts, yoga, massage, aerobics, bodybuilding, calisthenics, and modern psychosomatic disciplines such as the Alexander Technique and the Feldenkrais Method.

These different methodologies or practices can be classified in different ways. We can distinguish between practices that are holistic or more atomistic. While the latter focus on individual body parts or surfaces—styling the hair, painting the nails, shortening the nose or enlarging the breasts through surgery—the former practices are emphatically oriented toward the whole body, indeed the entire person, as an integrated whole. Hatha yoga, taijiquan, and the Feldenkrais Method, for example, comprise systems of integrated somatic postures and movements to develop the harmonious functioning and energy of the body as a unified whole. Penetrating beneath skin surfaces and muscle fiber to realign our bones and better organize the neural pathways through which we move, feel, and think, these practices insist that improved somatic harmony is both a contributory instrument and a beneficial by-product of heightened mental awareness and psychic balance.

Such disciplines refuse to divide body from mind in seeking the enlightened betterment of the soma (or body–mind) of the whole person.

Somatic practices can also be classified in terms of being directed primarily at the individual practitioner herself, or instead primarily at others. A massage therapist or a surgeon standardly works on others, but in doing taijiquan or bodybuilding, one is working more on one's own body. The distinction between self-directed and other-directed somatic practices cannot be rigidly exclusive since many practices are both. Applying cosmetic make-up is frequently done to oneself and to others; and erotic arts display a simultaneous interest in both one's own experiential pleasures and one's partner's by maneuvering the bodies of both self and other. Moreover, just as self-directed disciplines (like dieting or bodybuilding) often seem motivated by a desire to please others, so other-directed practices like massage may have their own self-oriented pleasures.

Despite these complexities (which reflect the deep interdependence of self and other), the distinction between self-directed and other-directed body disciplines is useful for resisting the common presumption that to focus on the body implies a retreat from the social. That presumption is surely wrong because not only is the body shaped by the social; it also contributes to the social. We can share our bodies and bodily pleasures as much as we share our minds, and they can be as public as our thoughts. Our bodies are visible social markers of our values, affiliations, and tastes. Somatic self-stylization generates an enormous commercial market that feeds the cosmetic, fashion, dieting, exercise, and plastic surgery industries, along with the advertising industry that supports them by stimulating our desire to stylize ourselves somatically. As I mentioned earlier, this desire typically takes the paradoxical form of wanting to fit in yet also to stand out as distinctive. In other words, self-styling involves conforming in some way to the norms of some social taste group (even if it be a subculture that resists mainstream taste) yet not allowing such conformity to group style to preclude one's own individual expression. Moreover, it is crucial to remember that caring for one's own body is essential to caring properly for others, since all helpful action requires bodily means. *Practical somaesthetics* is the third branch of somaesthetics. It involves not the conceptual or theoretical study of methods of somatic improvement but their actual bodily practice. For example, practical somaesthetics is not a matter of reading or writing about yoga or taijiquan, but actually doing their exercises or movements.

Along with the three branches of somaesthetics, there are also three dimensions. Somatic disciplines or practices can be classified as to whether their major orientation is toward external appearance or inner experience. Representational somaesthetics (such as cosmetics and clothing fashion) are primarily concerned more with the body's surface forms, while experiential disciplines (such as yoga) aim more at making us feel better in both senses of that ambiguous phrase: to make the quality of our somatic experience more satisfying and also to make it more acutely perceptive. The distinction between representational and experiential somaesthetics is one of dominant tendency rather than a rigid dichotomy. Most somatic practices have both representational and experiential dimensions (and rewards), because there is a basic complementarity of representation and experience, outer and inner. How we look influences how we feel, and vice versa. Practices such as dieting or bodybuilding that are initially pursued for representational ends often produce inner feelings that are then sought for their own experiential sake. Just as somatic disciplines of inner experience often use representational cues (such as focusing one's attention on a body part or using imaginative visualizations), so representational disciplines such as bodybuilding use experiential clues to serve their ends of external form, helping to distinguish, for example, the kind of pain that builds muscle from the pain that indicates injury. We can see this interrelation of inner and outer also in the field of fashion. We not only want to look good in our clothes, we also want to feel good in them; but looking good can make us feel good, while feeling good in the clothes reciprocally can make us look better in them. This interdependence can perhaps best be seen through negative examples. A suit whose fabric makes us feel uncomfortably hot and itchy will also make us look less attractive by the sweat and discomfort that we visibly display.

A third dimension of somaesthetics can be distinguished for disciplines that focus primarily on building strength or performative skill where the dominant

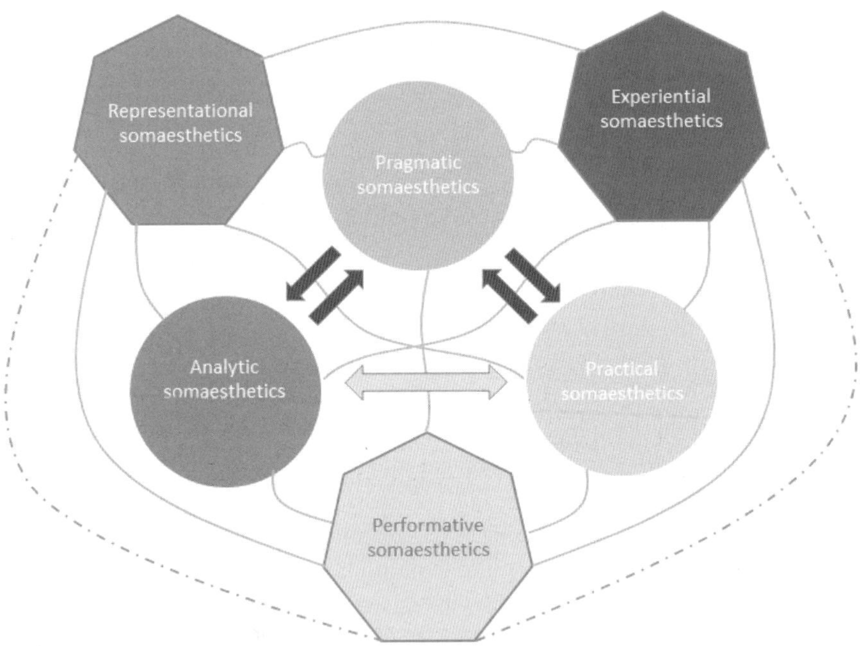

FIGURE 4.1 Different branches and dimensions of somaesthetics and of their interrelations.

concern is not how one looks or feels but on how well one performs or scores according to defined standards of excellence. Practices such as weightlifting, athletics, and martial arts can be seen as belonging to this category, which could be called "performative somaesthetics." To the extent that these disciplines aim either at the external exhibition of performance or at one's inner feeling of power and skill, they might be associated with the representational or experiential categories. However, they seem to suggest a distinctive dimension of their own. To provide an overview of the three branches and dimensions, I present the diagram on the previous page. The broken line indicates the relations between the three dimensions, the solid lines signify the relations between the three branches and the three dimensions, and the arrows symbolize the relations between the three branches.

Notes

1 A Perry Ellis spokesman says the half-inch shoulder pleat is an "aesthetic" design element "that is also functional," creating added comfort because "it provides a little more fabric for your arm along the shoulder seam" (http://www.wsj.com/articles/SB121987040660577371) (accessed May 17, 2015).

2 While most companies specializing in average men's sizes have fit models averaging around 5′10, companies that specialize in "Bigs" or "Talls" will have as their fit model an average of about 6′2. Other dimensions are also important, such as chest, shoulder, and waist sizes.

3 There is a complexity of feeling in such cases, which somaesthetic analysis recognizes and clarifies. Besides the feeling of the clothing felt by the wearer (which includes how it feels on the skin in terms of texture, weight, heat, and constraint of movement), there is also the feeling that a non-wearer gets either in touching the fabric or sensing its texture through visual imagination. Besides being appreciated visually and in terms of touch, the somaesthetics perception of fashion includes smell (not only the fragrance of colognes or perfumes that serve as fashion accessories but also the scents of leather) and also hearing (as with the sounds of noisy jewelry). For a detailed analysis of the multisensory aspects of somatic style, see my chapter "Somatic Style," in Shusterman 2012 (ch. 14).

4 In upper-class groups with a long tradition of affluence and prestige, we sometimes find a form of fashion that is intentionally unfashionable in the sense of conservatively refusing to follow the latest fashion. This attitude displays their prestige at being above the need to show their value and style through trendy clothes, because to follow trendy taste suggests that their own style or taste is not intrinsic or authentic, but instead depends on changing with the times. During my studies at Oxford in the late 1970s, I encountered a number of such upper-class students of such taste in fashion, along with clothing shops that catered to them.

5 In fashion, Loos remarks, "beauty is not part of the equation." Instead, he argues, one should simply be well-dressed, which simply "means to be correctly dressed," according to the most modern, sensible fashion; and this, for Loos, is typically a style that reflects practical concerns of unpretentious simplicity. Hence, "in order to be well-dressed one should not be conspicuous" in one's attire (Loos 2011: 29–30).

6 The *New York Times* reports the 1980s revival in 2009, while fashion media note the 1960s revival for 2013–14, and the 1970s revival in 2015 (http://www.nytimes.com/2009/08/20/fashion/20EIGHTIES.html?_r=0; http://www.fashionising.com/trends/b--1960s-fashion-7918.html; http://www.fashionising.com/trends/b--1970s-fashion-4506.html) (accessed May 17, 2015).

7 The Lululemon website describes its company's products in clearly athletic terms: "We make technical athletic apparel for yoga, running, dancing, and most other sweaty pursuits" (http://info.lululemon.com/about/?mnid=mn;education;about-us) (accessed May 17, 2015).

8 For a more detailed analysis of the structure and aims of somaesthetics, see Shusterman 2008.

Bibliography

Loos, A. (2011), *Why a Man Should be Well-Dressed*, trans. M.E. Troy, Wien: Metro Verlag

Plessner, H. (1981), "Macht und menschliche Natur. Ein Versuch zur Anthropologie der geschichtlichen Weltansicht" (1931), in G. Dux, O. Marquard and E. Ströker (eds), *Gesammelte Schriften*, vol. 5, Frankfurt a.M.: Suhrkamp

Shusterman, R. (2008), *Body Consciousness: A Philosophy of Mindfulness and Somaesthetics*, Cambridge: Cambridge University Press

Shusterman, R. (2012), *Thinking Through the Body: Essays in Somaesthetics*, Cambridge: Cambridge University Press

Simmel, G. (1997), "The Philosophy of Fashion" (1905), trans. M. Ritter and D. Frisby, in D. Frisby and M. Featherstone (eds), *Simmel On Culture: Selected Writings*, 187–205, London-Thousand Oaks-New Delhi: Sage Publications

5 ON FASHION CRITICISM

Lars Svendsen

This essay is about what fashion criticism is and should be like, and it is not in itself an example of what I understand as fashion criticism. It could be described as a meta-critique of fashion, i.e., a critique of fashion criticism. The field of fashion needs serious criticism if it wants to be taken seriously as a proper aesthetic practice. Fashion aims for being something more than just another commodity. It has not attained the same recognition as other forms of art, and this is partly due to a manifest lack of the sort of serious criticism that can be found in visual arts, music, literature, film, etc. In literature and the arts, the existence of negative criticism is accepted. The mentality is rather different in the world of fashion, which needs to accept negative criticism as a natural part of the reception of a collection. The competence of a fashion critic differs from that of a fashion theorist, just as art criticism differs from art theory. Fashion criticism places itself somewhere in the continuum between fashion reportage and fashion theory. Proper criticism has five major components: evaluation, description, comparison, contextualization, and interpretation. The key feature of criticism is evaluation. Fashion criticism will often be reviews, but we also need more elaborate essays in which critics develop ideas in greater depth and can dwell on the role of fashion in our lives. Fashion criticism will then move in the direction of fashion philosophy.

1. Art and fashion

When we look at the history of fashion, we see that designers of clothes had little social prestige until the second half of the nineteenth century. It seems almost incredible to us, in a fashion world where so much hinges on the designers' names, that the names of dressmakers simply were not disclosed up until that point. The dressmakers were in effect nameless. However, the dressmaker wanted to become a designer, something more akin to an artist. It is especially in this context that fashion criticism becomes crucial.

In the separation of art from craft in the eighteenth century, the tailors were left sitting on the craft side. Clothes were placed in an extra-artistic sphere—where they since have remained, for the most part. Ever since *haute couture* was introduced around 1860, fashion has aspired to be recognized as fully fledged art. This was clearly the case with Frederick Worth and Paul Poiret. Worth introduced the "emancipation" of the fashion designer as a simple craftsman, completely subject to the wishes of the customer, to being a "free creator" who, in accordance with the Romantic view of art, created works on the basis of his or her own subjectivity (Troy 2003).

Worth initiated the practice of fashion designers "signing" their clothes, as did artists, by inserting a tag. In fact, the freedom of the fashion designer was rather restricted, as the creations had to appeal to the aesthetic preferences of the customer—and the customer would not pay for "unwearable" clothes. This meant that the creations were not allowed to remove themselves too far from any style that was prevalent at the time. Even when trying to cater to the taste of the customers, most of what the designers created was rejected. Usually, merely 10 percent of an ordinary collection was met with approval by customers (cf. Lipovetsky 1994: 80).

Despite this, Worth initiated the struggle for the clothes designer to be recognized as an artist on a par with other artists. He consciously dressed "artistically," collected art and antiques, and managed to get such recognized photographers as Felix Nadar to take his portrait. The same urge to achieve artistic recognition by collecting art, organizing art exhibitions, etc., was typical to an even greater degree of Paul Poiret. In 1913, Poiret categorically stated: "I am an artist, not a dressmaker." He also began giving his creations names such as "Magyar" or "Byzantium," instead of the numbers that had been customary, in order to add an extra symbolic dimension to the garments.

Fashion designers have never managed to gain full recognition as artists, but they continue to strive so to do. One of the most striking examples of this urge was the emergence of "conceptual clothes" in the 1980s. A great number of fashion designers have used strategies that are normally associated more with contemporary art rather than the world of fashion, by creating clothes that are better suited to exhibitions in galleries and museums than for actual wear. Several of the largest fashion houses sponsor museums of contemporary art, in order to gain closer ties with the art world. They have even on occasion been rewarded with exhibitions at precisely these institutions, which have a quasi-magical ability to transform ordinary objects into something higher: "art." The fashion houses want access to art institutions because these institutions possess heavy symbolic values one would like to see "migrate" to fashion. In the twentieth century, art and fashion were like two neighbors who sometimes happily get along and at other times cannot stand the sight of each other. Or it would perhaps be more precise to say that there has been an asymmetry in this neighborliness, since fashion has always wanted to be loved by art, while art has been more ambivalent, sometimes embracing fashion only to reject it again.

In spite of these efforts, fashion has not attained the same recognition as other forms of art. An important reason for this is that there are traditions for serious criticism within the visual arts, music, literature, film, etc., while this to a large extent is absent from fashion. In serious newspapers, much space is devoted to substantial review and analysis of the arts, but one usually searches in vain for something similar on fashion. One could be tempted to say that fashion criticism has made little or no progress since French symbolist poet Stéphane Mallarmé published the limited-edition magazine *La Dernière Mode* in 1874. In contemporary magazines and newspapers there is, of course, the occasional piece on a major trend, such as eco-fashion, or a portrait of a famous designer, but one rarely sees careful analysis and evaluation of a collection along the same lines as the arts.

2. Between art and capital

The fashion writer should not be seen as the servant of the designer, even though this is the most common role in current fashion writing. There is a mutual dependence between the designer and the writer, as fashion writing is crucial for the establishment and validation of a designer while the designers provide the writers a subject matter. Fashion writers play a crucial role in "creating the 'creators,'" as Pierre Bourdieu (1993a; 1993b) puts it. And they should challenge designers, making them push themselves further.

Bourdieu points out that one of the main tasks of critics and journalists is to produce a *belief* in the objects in the fields they write about—something that in turn strengthens their own position. This can clearly be observed in writings on a great variety of objects, ranging from sports to politics. It is clearly present in fashion journalism as well. However, in fashion journalism this task seems to dominate to such an extent that there is little room for any sort of criticism, and that in turn deprives these writings of most of their credibility. The links between the fashion press and the industry are so close that it is difficult to consider the fashion press as much more than an extension of the fashion houses.

Fashion has always found itself in a space between art and capital, where it has often embraced the artistic side in order to tone down its financial side. However, the commercial aspects of fashion tend to suppress the possibility of genuine criticism. Fashion journalism is to a great extent regarded as an extended branch of the fashion company's marketing department, rather than as an activity with a distinct task and integrity. This attitude has been made especially clear in those cases in which journalists have been banned from future shows after writing reviews with even a hint of negative criticism. For instance, Cathy Horyn has been banned from shows by Armani, Gucci, Dolce & Gabbana, Helmut Lang, and Oscar de la Renta. This would be unheard of in virtually all the other arts.

In literature and the arts, negative criticism is accepted. Authors and artists might not be happy with negative criticism, but it is accepted that the possibility of negative criticism goes with the territory. It would be unimaginable that a publisher like HarperCollins or Penguin would threaten to pull their advertisements from *New York Review of Books* or *Times Literary Supplement* if one of their authors were given a bad review—or that they would refuse to send review copies in the future. Similarly, there is no way Larry Gagosian or Barbara Gladstone would threaten to pull their ads from *Artforum* if one of their artists were completely thrashed in a review there, and neither would they deny the critic access to future exhibitions. The mentality is quite different in the world of fashion, which needs to mature and accept negative criticism as a natural part of the reception of a collection.

In any discipline—be it painting, fiction, or cinema—most of what is produced at any time, will be bad. The same is naturally the case for fashion. No painter, author, or director produces only masterpieces—and neither does any fashion designer. What is more, even masterpieces tend to have their flaws—sometimes these flaws are in fact what make a certain piece interesting. However, when you read fashion writing in magazines and newspapers, you could be led to believe that there are nothing but masterpieces in the realm of fashion.

Yet, without any negative criticism, positive criticism will carry no weight. Praise is meaningful only if there is also a possibility for blame. In other words, if you never reject something because it fails aesthetically or in some other sense, then your positive reviews will fail to have any substance whatsoever.

Fashion magazines are moreover designed in such a way that it is often quite difficult to distinguish between editorial material, artistic contributions, and advertising. The amount of advertising has increased dramatically and now takes up about three times as many pages as the editorial material in a normal edition of *Vogue*, yet it is presented in such a way that it can be difficult to spot that it is actually advertising.

We know that the economy of the typical fashion magazine is such that the majority of the income stems from advertising, not cover price or subscriptions. Hence, one could argue that the primary customer is not the reader, but the advertiser. This clashes with the task of the fashion critic, whose loyalty must primarily be towards his or her own judgment, and then towards the reading public, not towards the advertiser.

So much fashion journalism should be categorized as advertorials, i.e., as advertisements disguised as genuine articles. Is a fashion magazine nothing but a vehicle for advertisements, a medium which only aims to provide a friendly editorial environment for advertisements, such that the publisher can make the largest possible profit? If so, I doubt that it can ever be a medium for fashion criticism, because such criticism can exist only if it is granted a certain independence from the instrumental interests of the advertisers. Fashion criticism must be granted autonomy.

When I published a book on fashion in Norwegian, many fashion journalists were outraged by my comments on fashion journalism. My favorite reply was from a fashion journalist who had been named "fashion journalist of the year" in Norway: "It is not true that we are uncritical. I once wrote a critical review of a Diesel-collection." Of course, that reply made my point even more forcefully. Could you imagine the following reply from a leading literary critic: "It is not true that I am uncritical. I once wrote a critical review of a novel by Dan Brown"? It simply would not happen.

3. Fashion criticism and fashion theory

The competence of a fashion critic differs from that of a fashion theorist, just as art criticism differs from art theory. Sometimes a person can do both things successfully, but I think that is quite rare (an example would be Arthur Danto, who was not only one of the world's leading art theorists, but also wrote excellent art criticism for *The Nation*—though, one should note how different his theoretical and his critical writings are, almost as if they were written by different persons). As for me, I am primarily a theorist, not a critic. Even though I have written and lectured extensively on art, I have deliberately stayed away from writing art criticism. And I believe that I would be a terrible fashion critic, so I have no intention of going down that road. This essay is therefore about what fashion criticism is and should be, and why most fashion criticism falls short of being an example of proper criticism. I am writing a meta-critique of fashion criticism, i.e., a critique of fashion criticism.

Fashion theory itself is very much in its infancy, and is no way near the level of sophistication and diversity found in art theory. As a consequence, fashion criticism cannot at present receive the same kind of support from fashion theory as art criticism receives from art theory. Much of what is written under the label "fashion theory" is of little relevance for the fashion critic who is mainly concerned with the aesthetic aspects of fashion. A lot of fashion theory is just cultural studies and gender theory applied to clothes. I am not saying that there is anything wrong with cultural studies and gender theory as such, but only that they will often be of limited relevance to the fashion criticism more narrowly understood. Fashion criticism cannot simply utilize the conceptual tools and methods of art criticism, but it can, of course, learn from it. All is not well in the area of art criticism, either, but that would have to be the theme for a different essay. I will just mention that in contemporary art criticism, few critics have a well-developed understanding of color, techniques, and materials. It is tempting to say that they have *read* too much and *seen* too little. Fashion criticism must not make the same mistake. A fashion critic must expose him- or herself to vast amounts of fashion, and in the process learn how to *see*. This visual competence is of crucial importance for the task of drawing the relevant comparisons.

There are few educational possibilities for fashion critics, at least nothing comparable to those available for art critics. And there are not too many forerunners who can serve as examples for future fashion critics, but if I were to mention a few, Holly Brubach, Suzy Menkes, Cathy Horyn, Robyn Givhan, Tim Blanks, and Colin McDowell would be on the top of my list. They make clear judgments, their writings are well informed, and you can gain real insight from reading them. Of course, there are large areas of overlap between fashion theory, fashion criticism, and fashion reportage, but there are also significant differences. I would place fashion criticism somewhere in the continuum between fashion reportage and fashion theory. Some of it will be closer to reportage and some closer to theory.

Now, that the question concerning the definition and understanding of fashion criticism (and, in concrete terms, the possibility of practicing it in a more appropriate way than it usually happens) represents a very relevant problem for fashion theory is also confirmed by the widespread diffusion of debates on this aspect today. Outstanding samples of this debate that may be mentioned here are a special issue of "Fashion Projects" (Granata 2014) dedicated to the theme *Fashion Criticism*, and the book by Peter McNeil and Sanda Miller *Fashion Writing and Criticism*. As the authors of this book correctly notice, "we are surrounded by criticism, including the critique of fashion," but "the quality of writing about fashion [is] uneven": if criticism as we mean it today first "emerged through literature and the fine arts," since then it has "expanded to such an extent that we are expected today to be critical of our restaurant meals, our bathroom fittings and our sartorial fashions, although in the strict sense of the word, the remit of criticism is generally accepted to be the art world." The real question, however, is still: "What does the critic do? How do we acquire the skill set to be active critics? In other words, who are the critics, how do we 'become' critics, and what qualities are required to act as a critic? Above all, how do we recognize quality fashion criticism and why is it so narrowly focused and subjective at the moment?" According to McNeil and Miller, "we are accustomed to reading fashion journalism that amounts to no more than excited description and personal opinion, much of it being media-led accolades or 'badmouthing,'" but this "would not be tolerated within the fine arts, literature, the theatre or film." So the question remains: "How might we develop a proper critical vocabulary for fashion writing, which transcends this level and will enable us to understand, assess and above all make value judgements about something as changeable as fashion?" (McNeil and Miller 2014: 3). McNeil and Miller argue that what is essential today—that is, in an age in which sometimes the critic is threatened to "disappear under the weight of blogs and tweets"; an age in which "the world wide web has revolutionized fashion, democratizing its sacred halls, making parades freely available for the first time in history, spreading the word instantaneously about any and every new trend, and delivering to our 'in box' any combination of blog, website or fashion film"—is making it clear that "criticism is not simply 'opinion.'" Indeed, their book "repudiates the idea that we can simply go to the world wide web in order to write about fashion today," and they conclude by claiming that, "in a world obsessed with the image, there is more need than ever before for skilful interpretation and artful comment on these images—in words." (McNeil and Miller 2014: 4, 6, 137).

4. Evaluation, description, comparison, contextualization, and interpretation

Proper criticism has five major components: evaluation, description, comparison, contextualization, and interpretation. The key feature of criticism is evaluation. The aim of criticism is to state as clearly as possible what is of value in a creation. However, evaluation as such is not sufficient to qualify as proper criticism. Simply to make judgments without providing some critical standard and fairly explicit reasons, will not do. The words "criticism" and "critique" are among the most misunderstood in the English language (and their equivalents are just as misunderstood in other languages). For instance, being just "bitchy" is not the same as being properly "critical." Mere negativity is so often confused with genuine criticism. Unjustified negativity is no improvement over unjustified positivity. So let's get clear about the real meaning of "criticism."

The words "criticism" and "critique" stem from the Greek word *krinein*, which means to judge or decide. Further meanings are to separate, distinguish, discriminate, determine, etc. Along the same lines, the Greek word *kritikos* referred to a jury member who rendered a verdict. Criticism is a practice aiming at passing judgments about objects, distinguishing between what is good and what is bad. It must be emphasized that criticism can be positive as well as negative.

Of course, one might argue that there is little reason for a critic to write about what he or she regards as aesthetic failures. After all, one cannot write about everything, and an important part of the critic's work consists in the selection of what is important enough to be written about. So why not just select the good stuff and disregard the failures? The answer is simply that we need critical treatments of both, and that we can often learn just as much—often more—from failures than from a success.

As already indicated, I believe that the most essential aspect of all criticism—be it of literature, cinema, painting, or fashion—is evaluation. This is far from uncontroversial and a matter of great debate in, for instance, current art criticism. However, I will just presuppose such a view of criticism here (for a more extensive defense of this position, see Carroll 2009). What is more: Proper criticism consists of evaluations supported by reasons. This is a quite strong demand. It means that someone who simply claims that this is good and that is bad, but who does not support this claim with explicit reasons, will fail to qualify as a proper critic. Other crucial components of criticism are: description, comparison, contextualization, and interpretation.

Description is about telling readers what a creation is like and how the various parts fit together. How do color, cut, pattern, and texture work together? It lays a foundation for the other aspects of criticism. Comparisons consist in pointing out similarities and differences in relation to other creations. Contextualization is about placing the creation within a framework of the designer's previous work, his or her inspirations, and the wider cultural surroundings. Interpretation attempts to answer the question: What is the meaning or significance of this? This aspect will clearly vary a lot, for the simple reason that some creations are richer in terms of interpretative content than others.

Haute couture might be the most tempting object for the fashion critic, because it seems to provide a richer object in terms of content and originality, but I believe that it is at least as important to let the ready-to-wear be subjected to critical scrutiny, because it is the sort of clothing that actually plays a role in people's lives. One could even say that the more the garments from a given designer are actually *worn*, the less likely is that designer to be an object of serious criticism. Menswear is also far more neglected than women's fashion, even though it is an equally important and fascinating topic. Some creations are simply intended to be beautiful, which is fine, but this leaves relatively little work to do for the interpreter. Other creations are intended to express a richer content, and may not even aim for beauty at all.

At the end of the day, I see these other components as servants of the task of evaluation, as providing the critic with a foundation upon which reasoned evaluation can be built. Evaluation addresses the coherence of the creation and whether it manages to realize the intentions of the designer. Are those intentions significant? Is the creation aesthetically successful?

A fashion critic should know an awful lot of fashion history, and point out significant convergences and breaks. If you looked at the fall collections in 2009, there might at first sight not seem to be any particularly striking similarities between Rick Owen's fur hats, Dries van Nooten's graphical motives, Marc Jacobs' jackets, and the broad shoulders and large suits from Chloe. Of course, there was more than a hint of the 1980s there, but we can be more specific than that. They were all clearly influenced by the now largely forgotten designer Per Spook, but none of them explicitly acknowledged this influence. And when you recognized the influence from Spook, it changed how you viewed their collections, not diminishing them, but you began to grasp certain stylistic connections that were not clearly present for you before. Pointing out features like this is a crucial part of the job of the fashion critic.

5. Critical practice

Fashion criticism should be rigorous, clearly stated, and historically informed. It should neither oversimplify (as current fashion criticism often does) nor be unnecessarily obscure (as current art criticism often is). It should look for vitality and boldness, and distinguish the original from the derivative. It should track a designer's development—or point out standstill or regression—and attempt to figure out what led the designer to make these specific aesthetic choices, elaborate on the techniques and materials that have been used—and finally pass judgment. As already mentioned, a proper judgment is something more than *mere* opinion—it is a *reasoned* or *justified* opinion which aims for broader validity. Criticism can never be completely objective. It must necessarily to a great extent be subjective, saying as much about the critic as about the object under scrutiny. Which is why writing criticism necessarily means exposing yourself. Writing criticism is about struggling to come to terms with what you do not yet know exactly how to deal with, to pass judgment, to expose yourself, knowing that you expose yourself, putting your prestige and your very identity at risk. As Pierre Bourdieu formulated it: "Taste classifies, and it classifies the classifier" (Bourdieu 1984: 6). This is a truth that holds for all of us, but it is especially acute in the case of the critic, whose judgment is at the greatest public scrutiny. Writing real criticism is about putting yourself on the line every single time.

What about disagreements between critics? They should be welcomed. It is never a good sign when too many people agree about too much. It almost always means that we are thinking too little. There *should* be disagreements between critics. Two critics can certainly disagree about the relative merits of two designers, such as for instance Alexandre Herchcovitch and Phoebe Philo. However, one should also note that there will usually be a high degree of convergence between critics in their judgments. One might prefer Herchcovitch and the other Philo, and even find a certain collection plain tasteless, but it would be highly surprising if one of them argued that Herchcovitch or Philo is a designer with virtually no aesthetic merit. Would a serious critic pass such a judgment? There will be disagreements, but disagreements are possible only against a much larger background of agreement.

Genuine criticism should be incorruptible in the sense that it bears no responsibilities towards the designer or fashion house, but only towards aesthetic standards and the reading public. Or to put it differently: the fashion critic should be an outsider, and not a PR agent for the fashion industry. This might seem to clash with another task for the fashion writer, which I have briefly touched upon earlier: the task of critics and journalists to produce a *belief* in the objects in the fields they write about. However, I believe that these two tasks do not clash at all. On the contrary, if you are to produce *belief* in your field, you must be *believable*, and you will not be believable if you are in effect nothing more than a cheerleader for the fashion industry. If you take fashion seriously, and want others to do the same, then you should be all the more concerned with subjecting fashion to proper, independent criticism.

According to the view presented here, criticism is an extremely demanding activity, but who said that it should be easy? It is to work as a proper critic in newspapers and magazines, but one should not forget that it is also a privilege because one is given the opportunity to have influence on the public mind.

Consumers depend on critics to help them navigate through the vast ocean of fashion. This need is greater than ever before because there is a wider array of fashion available now than at any previous time in history. Critics should guide the readers, help them understand the merits and the faults of the objects that confront them, and assist them in the appreciation of new aesthetic ideas.

The fashion critic should be able to explain to readers *why* one judges a garment or a collection to be a success or a failure, helping the reader to *see* these things and gain a greater awareness in their own relation to fashion. It is to some extent to teach readers and consumers the art of criticism, enabling them to make their own informed judgments, which can be supported by reasons. It should help the reader to go beneath the surface, if there is anything there, and ultimately to understand the relevance of these artifacts for our lives. And fashion critics are entitled to demand an effort from the readers. Some might fear that the sort of fashion criticism I promote here, might stifle the creativity and playfulness of fashion. I believe that these fears are unfounded, as criticism in the realm of art and literature hardly has such an effect there.

Does fashion criticism have relevance? I believe that the answer is an unequivocal "Yes." One obvious reason for this is simply the vast influence of fashion on our lives. I would say that fashion plays a far more significant role in contemporary culture than the fine arts. Which makes it all the more urgent to develop critical tools for coming to terms with it.

We need fashion reviews, as they help us recognize the merits and weaknesses of designers and trends, but we also need longer essays in which critics develop ideas in greater depth and can dwell on the role of fashion in our lives. In that sense, fashion criticism will move in the direction of fashion philosophy. It becomes a question of *thinking fashion*. So, what do we mean by thinking? In my opinion, Hannah Arendt is on the right track.

For Arendt, thought is a positively "destructive" activity that undermines habits and rules. As she points out: "All thinking demands a *stop*-and-think" (Arendt 1977, vol. 1: 78). Thinking interrupts our activities and tears us out of the frictionless functionality that is so characteristic of our day-to-day lives. We can also call this manner of thought "reflection," and in reflection we can impose a certain distance between our activities and ourselves. "Thinking deals with invisibles, with representations of things that are absent; judging always concerns particulars and things close at hand. But the two are interrelated" (Arendt 1977, vol. 1: 193). Thinking is clearly tied to judgment. It is in making judgments that thinking is first realized in the world, but such interpretations can only be made if they are brought about by thought. The goal of thought is to return to the world that was the point of a given thought's departure, and this goal implies that thinking must be *critical*—and being critical is nothing more than exercising the ability to make distinctions. The goal of thought, therefore, is not to produce abstract knowledge, but rather to give us the ability to judge, to make distinctions. Which is what fashion criticism should do.

Bibliography

Arendt, H. (1977), *The Life of the Mind*, ed. by M. McCarthy, 2 vols, New York: Harcourt Brace Jovanovich

Bourdieu, P. (1984), *Distinction: A Social Critique of the Judgment of Taste* (1979), trans. R. Nice, Cambridge (MA): Harvard University Press

Bourdieu, P. (1993a), "Haute Couture and Haute Culture", in *Sociology in Question*, trans. R. Nice, 132–8, London-Thousand Oaks-New Delhi: Sage Publications

Bourdieu, P. (1993b), "But Who Created the 'Creators'?", in *Sociology in Question*, trans. R. Nice, 139–48, London-Thousand Oaks-New Delhi: Sage Publications

Carroll, N. (2009), *On Criticism*, London: Routledge

Granata, F., ed. (2014), *On Fashion Criticism* (Special Issue), *Fashion Projects: On Fashion, Art, and Visual Culture*, 4. Available online: http://www.fashionprojects.org/?p=4532 (accessed January 16, 2016)

Lipovetsky, G. (1994), *The Empire of Fashion: Dressing Modern Democracy* (1987), trans. C. Porter, Princeton (NJ): Princeton University Press

McNeil, P. and S. Miller (2014), *Fashion Writing and Criticism: History, Theory, Practice*, London-New York: Bloomsbury

Troy, N.J. (2003), *Couture Culture: A Study in Modern Art and Fashion*, Cambridge (MA)-London: The MIT Press

6 THOUGHT WITHOUT CONCEPT: CAROL CHRISTIAN POELL'S PARADOXICAL AESTHETICS

Christian Michel

O folle Aragne, sì vedea io te
già mezza ragna, trista in su li stracci
de l'opera che mal per te si fé.

DANTE. *Divina Commedia (Purgatorio, Canto XII)*

1. From Carol Christian Poell to C.C.P.

Carol Christian Poell is an Austrian designer who holes up in a studio in Milan's Naviglio district where he unperturbedly designs collections that he displays to the public only when he pleases.

Carol Christian Poell was born in Linz in 1966. After having been trained as a men's and a ladies' tailor in Vienna (Michelbeurn), he studied fashion design at the Domus Academy in Milan. It was there that he founded the production and distribution company C.C.P. Srl together with his partner Sergio Simone. After the first presentation of his men's collection in 1995, he showed his work uniquely through performances that thus set himself apart from the fashion world. As a result he became closely associated with the contemporary art scene, notably through his numerous references to *Wiener Aktionismus*, the issues and actions of which he queries and which, among others, are a central reference in his work. Since 2004, his work has not been presented to the public other than through diverse temporary spaces (abandoned warehouses, industrial factories, slaughterhouses, etc.). The distribution network for his garments and accessories, which are extravagant in terms of production technology, include less than forty retailers worldwide.

Carol Christian Poell has retired from the fashion scene and now shuns the public eye—a single fifteen-year-old stolen picture is the last known image of him. This restrictive policy equally applies to the diffusion of the images of his collections, which are held under a strict embargo. Nevertheless, his influence and fame are inversely related to his media visibility. Secret but influent, underground yet cult, Carol Christian Poell is the designer other designers know and praise. His peers admire his work which is both demanding and puzzling, both experimental and disturbing.

Carol Christian Poell is, above all, an extraordinary creator of fabrics. He develops, from the very first step of their production, 90 percent of the fabrics he uses, in close collaboration with Italian or Japanese weavers, according to extremely compelling demands. He has invented some astonishing materials, such as transparent leathers, or a rubber-like substance into which he "dips" his shoes, boots, or sneakers' upper surface, creating stalactites under their soles. He also "object-dyes" his leathers, using all the original imperfections of the skins (kangaroo, calf, horse, bison, deer, donkey, etc.). He even makes coats out of human hair or fiberglass. His innovations are also formal, and Carol Christian Poell revisits menswear classics by altering the sartorial cuts, in order to create both an extremely lanky and slightly awkward silhouette, which paradoxically emphasizes both masculine and feminine characteristics at the same time. Finally, his work can be seen as conceptual as it is not simply a matter of clothes, it is also a research into the essence and definition of clothing itself. All the garments he makes reveal the process of their construction. In this regard, his work is a work of virtuosity, which mostly revolves around technical thinking. Contrary to other designers, Carol Christian Poell's primary concern is not to dress the human body: his clothes are, above all, objects and bodies per se. Half-garments, half-objects (creatures) Poell's creations redefine the shape of the body in a simultaneous attempt to cancel and recreate its anatomy.

2. Catastrophe

Carol Christian Poell's work is a conceptual interrogation on the nature of the garment, it is also an examination of the source of its identity, notably by the attention lavished upon singular structural points, what René Thom calls "catastrophic points," points where a sudden change appears on a surface (*kata-strophê* meaning etymologically "change of form"):

> There is a milieu which is the place of any kind of process, and one distinguishes two kind of points, regular points and catastrophic points. Regular points are these where the local phenomenological analysis doesn't decipher any singular accident; some visible variations can happen, but these variations are continuous. On the contrary, there are some points where the phenomenological analysis reveals brutal and discontinuous accidents, in particular some visible discontinuities, and this is what I have named catastrophic points.
>
> **THOM** 1988: 32[1]

By analogy with the human body—and Carol Christian Poell's work shows that the garment is not only what covers the body, but a body in itself—stitches are like tendons, whose function it is to hold the anatomical segments together. "Segment," the word has to be understood according to its etymology ("What is separated") and to its biological definition ("The segment is a part of an organ distinct from the whole, though maintaining a continuous relation with it"). It is, however, an autonomous unity, what Aristotle calls a "flexion" (*kampsis*: cf. *Metaphysics*: V, 6, 1016a 9–19): a part separated from the whole, yet remaining a continuation of the whole. Hence the segment can be seen as having a double relation: between *whole* and *part*, between *continuity* and *discontinuity*

3. Seams

A minimal definition of a garment could be: different pieces of fabric sewn together to cover the human body. The specificity of Carol Christian Poell's work is that each and every constituting element of a garment—fabrics; stitches; shapes; relation to the human body—is interrogated in its structure, in its function, in its meaning. The work with these different elements cannot be distinguished from a reflection on them. Among these elements, the treatment of the seam displays a great conceptual inventiveness. In a garment, stitches play a major role, since they are part of its structural unity (making the heterogeneous a continuous unity) and its dynamical function, since they are an essential component of the garment's articulations, allowing it to follow the human body's movements. Last but not least, stitches play an important role in preserving the garment's integrity: they are on one hand what ensures its solidity, but on the other hand they sometimes have to break, especially when an unexpected and unusual tension may cause the tearing of the fabric. Stitches are a paradoxical element: they are at the same time strong and weak parts. Strong enough to make the garment last as long as possible, weak enough to be able to break in case of urgency. Carol Christian Poell enhances both functions that intrinsically define the stitch: solidity, frailty.

Let us now examine the different types of stitches that Carol Christian Poell has developed throughout the years and which have their own characteristics:

taped-seam, *scar-stitch*, *overlock-seam*, *invisible-seam*, *chain-seam*, sorted by their order of appearance in his work.

The *taped-seam* is a regular seam that is reinforced with a transparent tape (technically: "thermosolder taped"). Traditionally, this kind of tape helps rendering the garment waterproof; visually, it highlights—exhibits—the seam, which is usually a hidden part of the garment, concealed by the lining. There is another seam, or better said, an evolution of the *taped-seam*, that appeared later: the *meltlock-seam*, where the seam is overmelted with a transparent tape, thicker though than the *taped-seam*. Carol Christian Poell has now removed the lining from most of his jackets since 2003, which makes the tape on the inside, and the seam that it covers, twice visible: because the lining no longer hides it, because the tape underlines it, making it visually more significant. The tape is used like a joint in architecture—a part of the structure, which simultaneously unites and separates. Let us note, while we are dwelling on the subject, that the Poellian garment is like a work still showing the traces of its own construction, defining itself as the palimpsestic memory of its own history.

Let us notice that the highlighting function of the seam has also been carried by the bright yellow seam (technically called "contrast overlock-seam") that Carol Christian Poell used for example in SS 2006 ("U-Turn" collection) on the inside of the garments.

Scar-stitch and *overlock-seam* ("Visible Overlock Seam") share common features: both are overcast seams that give the seam the visual aspect of a scar—as

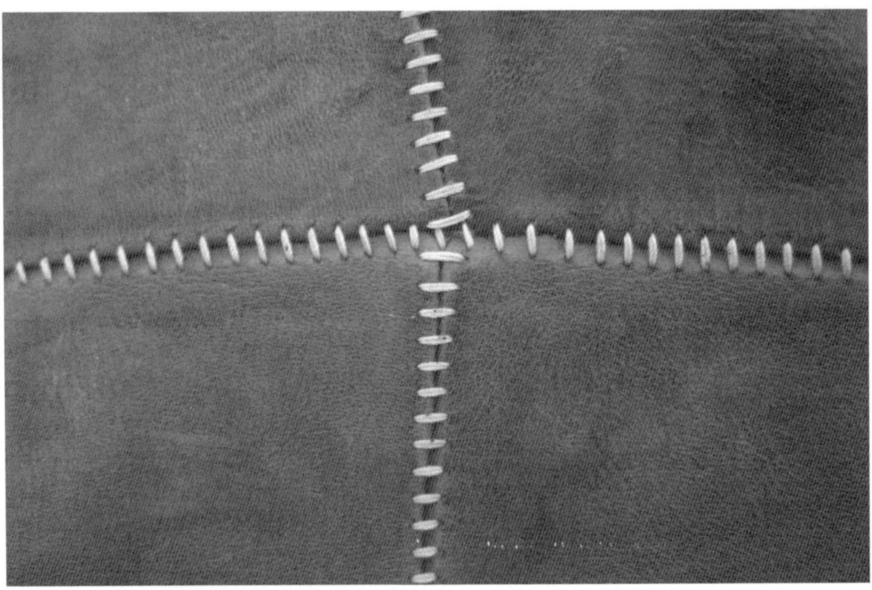

FIGURE 6.1 Overlock-seam.

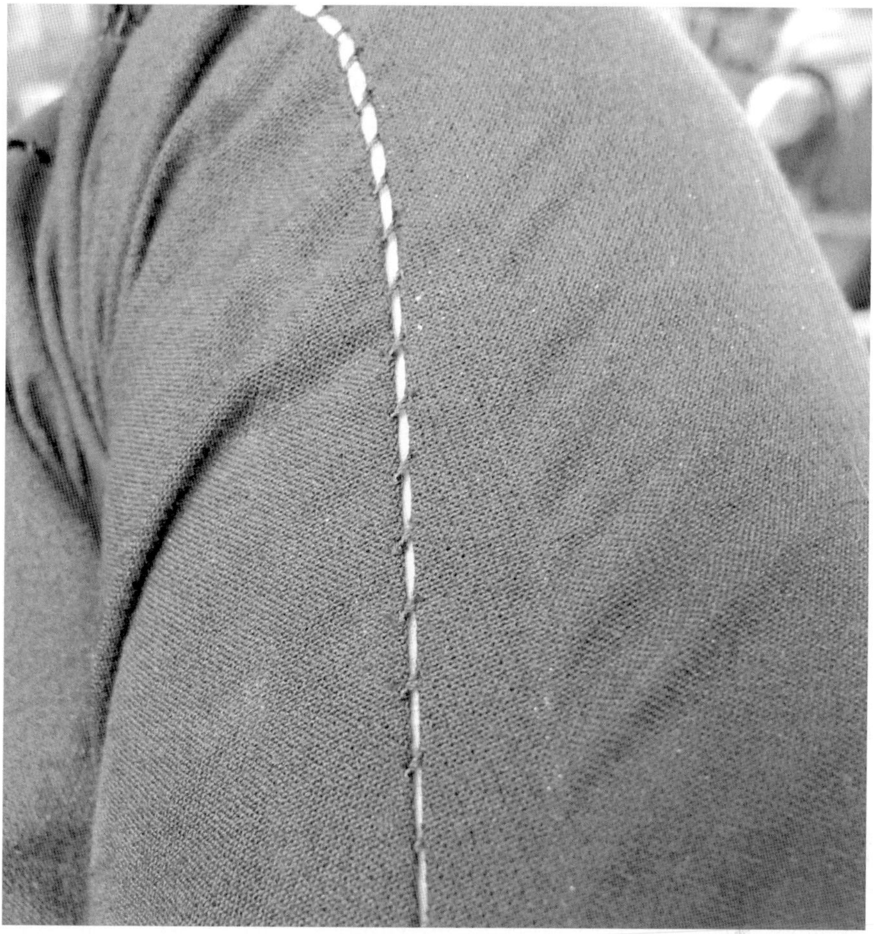

FIGURE 6.2 Chain-seam.

it is obvious by its name *scar-stitch*. They are sewn on the inside of the garment but also visible on the outside, on its visible part. *Overlock* differs though from the *scar-stitch* by the gauge of the thread, heavier for the overlock, and the stance between the dots, broader. The *meltlock-seam* is used to reinforce the inside of the *overlock*.

The *invisible-seam* and the *chain-seam* differ from the previous stitches, where the pieces of fabric are assembled edge to edge. In contrast, both these seams leave a gap between the fabrics that are no longer jointed, forming an open split. Their difference lies in their make-up and their visual effect. While the *chain-seam* is a regular cotton thread, the *invisible-seam* consists of a nylon thread, which is translucent—almost *invisible*—and flexible. When the pieces of fabric sewed by the *invisible-seam* are not under tension, their edges join together, the seam is closed, the split invisible. When the body induces some tension, the edges can work loose, without the seam breaking, revealing the flesh beneath which was formerly hidden by the garment—hence its technical name: "open seam with glued on seam-allowances." In contrast to this, the *chain-seam* is made out of a rigid thread—*chain*—that leaves the seam constantly open, though the visual effect is at its maximum when the seams are under tension.

4. Articulations

These different forms define a constellation that can be identified by a limited collection of oppositions: interior vs. exterior; concealed vs. revealed; flexible vs. rigid; continuous vs. discontinuous.

Seen historically, the succession of the five seams presents a dialectical progression, but not in the Hegelian meaning. Seams are usually hidden, concealed, invisible, since they are an element of structure, a means and not an end. Firstly, Carol Christian Poell makes the seam visible by underlining it (*taped-seam*), even though it stays partly concealed, since it appears only on the inside of the garment. At this stage, its visibility is in an evasive mode. Then, the seam becomes clearly visible on the outside of the garment (*scar-stitch*; *overlock*), as if it had been turned inside out. And even more visible with the *overlock*. The third stage is the inversion of the previous stage, its antithesis: the seam becomes invisible, while the seam puckers open. Fourth, and last step, is the synthesis between visual significance and invisibility: the thread of the *invisible-seam* becomes once again a cotton thread, hence more visible than the *invisible-seam* but less so than the first ones, due to the loose zigzag type of the *invisible-* and *chain-seam* sewing. Carol Christian Poell explores the whole range of possibilities: at both ends, the *taped-seam*, which is half visible, and the *chain-seam*, half invisible; in between, the *overlock* which is completely visible while the *invisible-seam* is almost invisible. This tension between hiding and revealing, visibility and invisibility, is a major characteristic of Carol Christian Poell's work: turning the garment inside out, designing reversible garments, not only because it is a technical challenge, but because it brings the unseen/unknown to light, the inside to the outside, the structure to the surface. As such, there is a constant effort to draw the wearer's (and the viewer's) attention to the structure of the garment, and its architectonic lines, by disturbing his *a priori* conception of what it should look like.

There is yet another possible interpretation, that no longer insists on the continuous evolution, but rather on the paradigmatic change introduced by the *invisible-seam* and the *chain-seam*. Here the major step is topologic. While the *taped-seam* is on the inside of the garment and the *scar-stitch/overlock* on the outside, the *invisible* and *chain-seams* are neither on the inside, nor on the outside: they are literally *in-between*. This time, the third form is not only a synthesis but it also surpasses—or sublates—the previous seams, now in the Hegelian meaning:

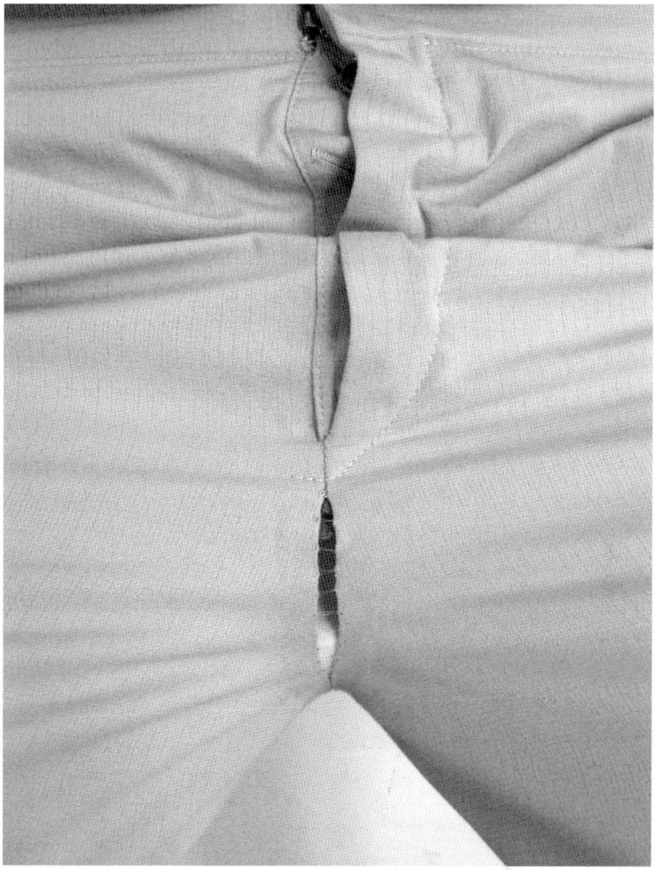

FIGURE 6.3 Invisible-seam.

they create a new topological space, which extends still further the opposition between under and upper, inside and outside, recto and verso. As Hegel observes:

> "To sublate" has a twofold meaning in the language: on the one hand it means to preserve, to maintain, and equally it also means to cause, to cease, to put an end to. Even "to preserve" includes a negative element, namely, that something is removed from its immediacy and so from an existence which is open to external influences, in order to preserve it.
>
> **HEGEL** 2013: 80[2]

Is Carol Christian Poell's work thoughtful? We have already noticed that Poell's work focuses on the catastrophic—i.e. significative—parts of the garment. Opposed to any ornamental, decorative, or folkloric play with the garment, Poell proposes a reflection on its structure, not to say its infrastructure—a possible legacy of his former training in traditional tailoring. Contrary to designers who favor superstructure over infrastructure, by analogy with the famous Marx quote from *Zur Kritik der politischen Ökonomie* (1859), and who could be called formalist or baroque, Poell gives priority to infrastructure over superstructure, since the material and its fabrication take precedence over its form. In Marx's own words:

> The totality of these relations of production constitutes the economic structure of society, the real foundation, on which arises a legal and political superstructure, and to which correspond definite forms of social consciousness. The mode of production of material life conditions the general process of social, political, and intellectual life.
>
> **MARX AND ENGELS** 1971: 9[3]

Fabric is not only first, it is the ground, the "foundation" on which arises an aesthetical superstructure that determines ("conditions") different possibilities, but within a limited range. What is more, his investigation is simultaneously systematic, organized, and exhaustive. With reference to this, should we focus now on the remaining couples of opposites (continuous vs. discontinuous; flexible vs. rigid), the five seams can be seen to be deployed in the four categories, showing that all the logical possibilities implied are fully explored:

- continuous and rigid: taped-seam
- discontinuous and rigid: chain-seam
- discontinuous and flexible: invisible-seam
- continuous and flexible: invisible-seam.

One can note two specificities. Firstly, that *scar-stitch* and *overlock* are missing since they are not easily featured amongst these categories. They could belong to the continuous and the rigid, but they are not as rigid as the *taped-seam*. Neither are they as flexible as the *invisible-* or *chain-seam*. Nevertheless, the *scar-stitch* is more rigid that the *overlock*, due to the short stance between dots. This leads to the conclusion that the two seams, that have so far been considered as an homogenous category, actually belong to different ones:

- continuous and rigid: taped-seam; *scar-stitch*
- discontinuous and rigid: chain-seam; *overlock*
- discontinuous and flexible: invisible-seam
- continuous and flexible: invisible-seam.

The use of the *meltlock-seam* to reinforce the *overlock-seam* on the inside undoes nevertheless the previous distinction, making the *overlock* as stiff as the *scar-stitch*.

One should hence distinguish two types of *overlock*: the soft version (without *meltlock-seam*), and the stiff version (reinforced on the inside with the *meltlock-seam*, technically called "Visible Meltlock Seam").

The second point is that the *invisible-seam*, which is the most complex seam amongst the four, belongs to two different categories: discontinuous and flexible; continuous and flexible. It shows that Carol Christian Poell's thoughts are not only thorough, but also inventive, since the *invisible-seam* features structural characteristics that could have been displayed in two different seams. His thoughts are not only systematic, but also economical—Ockhamist: "*Numquam ponenda est pluralitas sine necessitate*," "Plurality is never to be posited without necessity" (*Quaestiones et decisiones in quattuor libros Sententiarum Petri Lombardi*, 1495, i, dist. 27, qu. 2, K).

It also helps to define the way Carol Christian Poell draws attention to the garment's singularities: through the invention of paradoxical features, like the *invisible-seam*, which is a seam without seam, and a seam that looks like a tear. Revealing the flesh underneath, the *invisible-seam*, like the *chain-seam*, also contributes to the feminization, or demasculinization of the garment, since they allow the skin, or the underwear, to show through the opening in the seams.

5. Wound, scar, life, and death

Systematic, thorough, and inventive, Carol Christian Poell's thoughts are also meaningful, as can be seen in the tension between continuity and discontinuity. While the sewing, as a rule, aims to erase the discontinuity between assembled sections, the *overlock* and the *scar-stitch*, whose name evokes fabric and skin, preserve, and even expose, the discontinuity of which they are the vestigial trace. The same goes for the *taped-seam*, even though the tape reconstitutes the continuity. On the other hand, the other types of sewing accentuate discontinuity to the prejudice of continuity, and define the garment as a frail surface, constantly on the verge of tearing, breaking, dismembering. *Invisible-* and *chain-seams* can pucker open due to the tensions induced by body movement. However, the *chain-seam* being stiffer than the *invisible-seam* will, in the end, inevitably wear out and break.

Seam, as scar, is a complex form. A scar is, of course, the trace of a wound, but whose edges have been rejoined. Although the seam is a discontinuity, it is of a kind that establishes a *second species* continuity, and is the expression of a vital force. Seam like scar is the sign and the proof that healing has prevailed over decay, reunification over disjunction, continuity over discontinuity. Stitching, as any other form of weaving, thus struggles against death, which is the fundamental discontinuity, as told in the story of Isis sewing Osiris' body back together or, on the other hand, as shown in Arachne's reaction to Athena destroying her tapestry. And so Carol Christian Poell proposes, through his art, a formal and material transposition of the struggle opposing vital forces and deadly forces, between life and death, which constitutes the main theme of his work, and which is revealed through the tension between continuity and discontinuity. This tension echoes the different types of materials that he uses. On the one hand, he object-dyes pieces of leather that do not hide the fact that they are the skin of a dead animal that often bears the traces of the violence they have suffered; on the other hand, he develops new fabrics (over 90 percent are exclusive productions) in a close relationship with the mills. Vegetable opposes the animal, just as weaving (which is a creation of a new fabric) opposes tanning (which is eternization of a dead hide).

In this respect, it may be appropriate to make a distinction between two sorts of seams: those where continuity prevails over discontinuity (*taped-seam*) and those where discontinuity prevails over continuity (*invisible-seam*, *chain-seam*, etc.). But the forms invented by Carol Christian Poell do not easily lend themselves to unambiguous reductions: the *invisible-seam*, one of the forms which appears to be on the point of breaking, is also a flexible seam, in opposition to the rigidity of the parts it articulates, allowing looseness, liberty of motion, and thus, *in fine*, related to life. This tension between continuity and discontinuity, unity and fragmentation, life and death finds its most emblematic embodiment in the "one piece" garments from the "Dead End" collection (2010), where this tension is illustrated as a constitutive of sewing.

The asymmetrical double scar's pattern is indeed used to signify, in an apparently paradoxical way, the fundamentally continuous nature of the piece of cloth used. If the two scars converged together—if they re-established a continuity between themselves—then the garment would be discontinuous. It is because of the preserved discontinuity between the two scars that the garment is continuous. And so, the discontinuity of the double scar reveals the continuity of the garment. The same tension can also be observed in the beautiful shoulder of the 2009 high-collar coat (another example, in the following collection: OM/2340, "Dead End" collection, 2010), previously seen on the FW 2007–08 fishtail coat (GM/2319, "Disjointed" collection), in which the front part of the shoulder is built as a traditional tailored shoulder—discontinuous—and the rear part as a raglan sleeve—continuous.

To steer clear of the temptation to interpret Poell's work as macabre, it would be more appropriate to define it as the scene of a tension, irresolute and Heraclitean, between the mortiferous and the vital forces which coexist at least as much as they confront each other, and where the former engenders the latter: "And it is the same thing in us that is quick and dead, awake and asleep, young and old; the former are shifted and become the latter, and the latter in turn are shifted and become the former" (Heraclitus of Ephesus, 88), "ταὐτό τ΄ ἔνι ζῶν καὶ τεθνηκὸς καὶ [τὸ] ἐγρηγορὸς καὶ τὸ καθεῦδον καὶ νέον καὶ γηραιόν· τάδε γὰρ μετὰ-πεσόντα ἐκεῖνά ἐστι κἀκεῖνα πάλιν μεταπεσόντα ταῦτα."

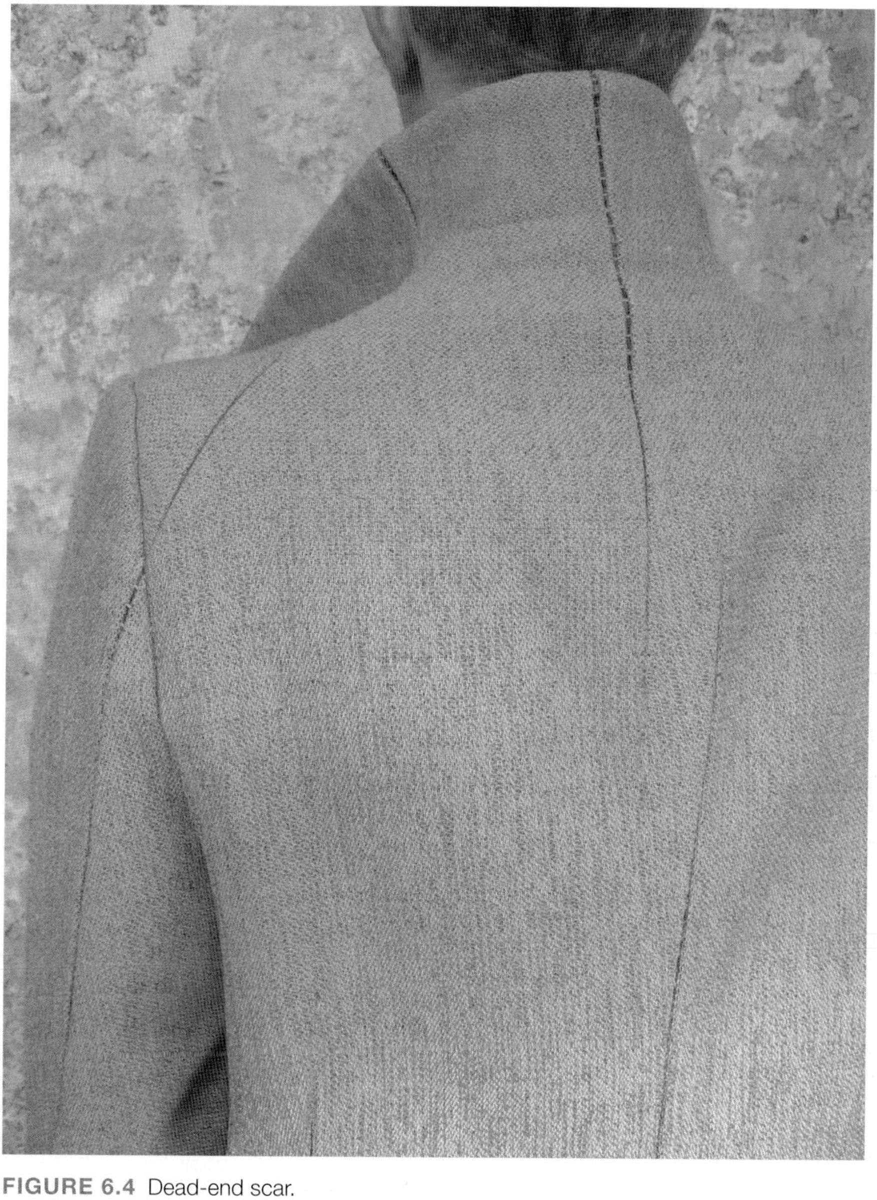

FIGURE 6.4 Dead-end scar.

This is what defines the Poell garment as essentially paradoxical. And thus one is able to propose an explanation to the contradictory feelings and emotions experienced by wearers of Carol Christian Poell creations: an impression of confidence and omnipotence, as the garment is a shell, but, at the same time, induces a feeling of fragility and anxiety, for it is constantly menaced by loss.

6. Nazism/Actionism/Poellism

Poell claimed in an interview that he would like to work with human skin in the same way he does with those of animals (see Poell 2008). But he adds, not without humor, that he has yet to receive the necessary authorizations. This claim is both strange and shocking. It transgresses a double taboo, ontological and historical. Ontological because the human being is not an animal, at least according to the dominant humanist philosophical conceptions still prevailing at the beginning of the twenty-first century. Historical because the use of human skin as material evokes the darkest hour of European history. If we attempt to go beyond the provocative aspect we can, nevertheless, make sense of this desire. A garment is, according to Poell, like a second skin. It is therefore not surprising that proximity can be inversed, if only phantasmatically, to become identity, personifying the metaphoric.

Going back to this statement, which evokes so explicitly the mental image of reducing a human being, once dead, to the state of an object, takes the form, in European imagination, of the figure of Ilse Koch and more largely the Nazi genocide. However, it can also be found in Kafka's short novel where the servant gets rid of Gregor's corpse by throwing it away in the garbage can. Another reference to the extermination of the Jews in Europe can be found incarnate in the human hair sleeveless coat (Fe-Male, FW 2000–01, "Trilogy of Monotypologies III") or the human hair tie (SS 2006, "U-Turn"). Poell therefore poses, as Adorno did before him but in his own way, the question of creation after Auschwitz. And his answer—like his clothing—is not comfortable.

Some of the forms that are characteristic of his collections unquestionably evoke the Nazi uniform. One can note the high and pinched waist of the formal jacket, also present in uniform jackets where the taper is further accentuated by the belt. The shape of the overlock leather jacket is reminiscent of the "pilot jacket," the vest worn by aviators, but its proximity with the vest worn by flying ace Erich Hartmann is striking: same collar and inelastic waist in both jackets, in contrast to the more classical pilot jackets.

These citations of Nazism can only be fully understood if we relate Poell's thought process to the larger concept of the European avant-garde of the 1960s and 1970s, driven by the first post-war generation, notably the Viennese Actionists.

Various references to Actionism can be found in Poell's work, paying homage through direct citation or re-writing. Direct citation: the red latex circle seen on the ground of the 2009 collection presentation recalls the red circle of the blood-splattered participants of the *Orgien Mysterien Theater* performance, held in Napoli (Hermann Nitsch: April 10, 1974). Homage: the razor, one of the Actionists' favorite tools, notably used by Günter Brus during the *Selbstverstummelung*, but also by Rudolf Schwarzkogler, is presented as a pendant by Poell. Re-writing: a founding act of Actionism was a performance held on June 1, 1962 by Otto Muehl, Hermann Nitsch, and Adolf Frohner, all three of them entombed in an atelier-cave

(*Einmauerung*) where they created a series of works, notable among them the "7. Malaktion" composed by Hermann Nitsch with blood and red paint spread on a canvas using brushes and sponges. On the door, a manifesto asking, among other things, the public to liberate the imprisoned artist. Forty years later Poell presents the "Traditional Escape" collection (SS 2002) during a performance which saw models escaping through the window of the Milanese studio. The two performances are like mirror images of one another, "Traditional Escape" answering *Einmauerung*: the Actionists imprison themselves, the models escape; Actionists are shut in a cave, models escape by a first-floor window; Actionists violate then crucify a lamb before splitting open its head with an ax; models wear horse leather jackets.

More often than not the places chosen by Poell to present his collections are eminently Actionist: a refrigerated room ("Best Before" presentation: October 14–16, 2000), a disused abattoir ("Three Refrigerated Cells": June 28, 2000), a dog pound ("Public Freedom": January 17, 2001), or the disaffected bathroom of "00" (2008).

Generally speaking, there are numerous similarities between Poell's aesthetics and that of the Viennese Actionists. They hold in common a sense of provocation; the primacy of the grotesque and the carnivalesque reversal of values; the use of the body and skin as artistic material; the staging of a tormented body; deconstruction of stereotypical representations of the body through expressionist distortions of proportions; sacrificial relationship to animals and use of their blood, etc.

Certain forms are also shared by both Poell and Actionism such as the scar (see Günter Brus, "Self-Painting 1," 1964). In *Wiener Spaziergang* (July 5, 1965), Günter Brus covers himself in white paint, his body vertically divided by a long black painted scar which echoes in ulterior, more radical performance where he actually cuts himself (series of *Selbstverstummelung* and *Zerreissprobe*: for example, "Resistance Challenge": June 19, 1970).

This reference gives us a clear picture of the nature of Poell's stitchings, that are as much scars as incisions. Indeed, if all stitches are strictly speaking scars, in the sense that they join together two different, discontinuous parts, certain stitches, notably the *invisible-seam* and *chain-seam*, when open due to tension, present a dynamic emergence of incisions into the garment.

As to the Actionist fascination for disembowelment and the exhibition of entrails, it finds a more abstract and subtle transposition in Poell's unlined jackets, pieces that reveal, even flout the interior of the jacket, normally hidden from our eyes. In this sense, Poellian aesthetics is, like that of the Actionists, obscene—a play on this word that can be found in the 2008 collection video: "Off Scene."

If Poell can be considered an inheritor or follower of Actionism transplanted to Italian soil, as was Hermann Nitsch before him, it is important to point out that he belongs to another generation (he was born in 1966). Even though his thinking may be inspired by the preoccupations of the Actionists, he cannot be assimilated with them nor, *a fortiori*, be reduced to them. Poell is not Franko B., who repeats without creating. The Actionists' intention was to literally provoke post-war Austrian society, which was still in denial of its responsibility in the Shoah (myth of the *Anschluss*), unlike their German neighbors. What is the purpose of Actionist interventions? They reveal the hidden side of Nazism that Austria so enthusiastically embraced before disavowing its passion. Decorum: prestigious uniforms, majestic parades, cult of strength and beauty. The other side of the coin: death camps, corpses ejecting their bodily fluids in the gas chambers and piles of disarticulated corpses that Actionists evoke in their performances. However, Actionists only bring to the fore terror and disgust, whereas Poell tackles fascination as well. In this way his work, while politically incorrect, is psychologically sound and shows greater artistic complexity than his Actionist forebears.

Fascination is perceptible in those designs that show evidence of the plastic perfection and severe classical proportions prompted by Nazi aesthetics. On the other hand, Poell reveals the hidden side of this fascination; repulsion and what this surface perfection hides: extermination, terror, agony, to which the leather (skin) garments bear witness: scarified bodies, desiccated skin, soiled colors. However, no matter what kind of treatment he inflicts on leather hides, he would never, unlike Yves Klein, go as far as burning them.

His clothing always bears the trace, as was mentioned earlier, of the animal's suffering but it is also the tomb of the human beings that Nazism attempted to relegate to the rank of animals. In this respect, the type of leathers used by Poell are not irrelevant: pig, horse, kangaroo, donkey. They are all animals that entertain a relation of proximity with the human being, be it by their nature (the pig's digestive tract is similar to our own, which explains the Jewish and Muslim taboo regarding its consumption) or by the popular and cultural representations associated with them. As to bison leather, introduced in the 2010 collection, it might be an allusion to the Indian genocide, another mass murder.

In Kafka's novel, the father does not want to know what happened to his son's body, discarded like garbage by the maid. Gregor will thus be robbed of a tomb and epitaph. Against the effacement of those who have disappeared, Kafka writes *Die Verwandlung*. And Poell creates garments that clothe mourning.

7. Symbolism in the time of paranoia

Poell's work systematically associates opposing characteristics: the garment is both skin and armor, supple and rigid; stitching is continuous and discontinuous, shapes masculine and feminine, designs anatomical and anti-anatomical; his aesthetics is classical and baroque; his garments provoke fascination and repulsion, etc. These opposing characteristics are not to be found on different clothing but coexist in the same garment. The Poellian aesthetics is not so much contradictory as paradoxical. His work is defined by the tension between antagonistic and incompatible positions that are however closely associated in the mode of conflict (paradox, ambiguity) or appeased tension (oxymora, irony). In this sense, discomfort and worry, effects mentioned previously, must be recognized as the very basis of his research rather than its mere consequences.

Once again the correspondence with Kafka is striking; the latter making generic and fictional indecision the center of his short story: Gregor is both human and insect; the story is both realistic and fantastic, etc. Both artists share an ultimate conviction: the refusal of metaphor that even prompted the Prague writer to say he despaired for literature.

No citations, immediate historical references or, *a fortiori*, folkloric ones can be found in Poell's work. Symmetrically the choice of materials, exclusive and surprisingly original, focalizes attention on the tangible dimension of clothing, the most literal, inducing the risk of blindness—or fetishism.

Parallel to that, Poell's work is founded on an attempt at demetaphorization or rather concretization of the metaphor. The garment, according to Poell, is not only a second skin, it is skin; stitching is not only *like* a scar or incision, it *is* scar and incision—and the human being, a potential corpse. One might point out that leather is skin. Yes and no. On the one hand, it is a skin but a skin that has been transformed, that has lost many of its initial characteristics. On the other hand, a leather garment is only wear/bear-able on the strict condition that its initial nature as a skin, bloody and animal, be forgotten or, at least, hidden. In this way, the Poellian aesthetics succumbs to a literalistic impulse, taking the metaphor at face value. Once again, like Kafka who responded to his father calling his friend Isaak Lowy a vermin (*Ungeziefer*) by creating a character literally transformed into a vermin. But his work is not, for this reason, devoid of signification, absurd or unfathomable, as literalism is not a negation of the symbolic. Abolishing the space between symbol and object is always secondary, that recognizes the power of the symbol but attempts to limit its proliferation.

Nevertheless, the dream of a phantasmatic abolition of the distance between sign and flesh persists. In this way the underlying dynamic of his work, that takes the word at face value, is undoubtedly psychotic, as is also indicated by the collection's title: "Paranoid" (SS 2007). Did not Freud, another famous Austrian, declare that an artist is no more than a successful psychotic, because he finds a way to share his own private delirium with a large audience?

8. Work of art?

The question as to the artistic dimension of Carol Christian Poell's work is doubly unfounded. Firstly it implies an axiological perspective that adds little to the critical debate. Secondly it clashes with the very nature of the object, that belongs to the category of applied arts, hybrid by nature, between hand-crafted object and work of art. It can be noted, however, that there is a surprisingly enduring tropism in Poellian clothing, which can easily emancipate itself of its wearer to attain the status of an autonomous object.

This question finds a relative pertinence if one removes it from the point of view of nature to that of interpretation. Poell's work is rich with multiple forms, often contradictory, hence complex, that resist comprehension and interpretation. In addition to this, they are polysemous, as illustrated by the stitching. Yet, beyond the variety and richness of the forms, which are the mark of creativity, Poell's work is remarkably coherent, in diachronicity as in synchronicity, forever proposing different answers to the same old questions, according to the logic of an organic body of work. In this sense his work challenges the fashion system, defined as perpetual renewal and fascination of the ephemeral. If stitches play, in Poell's work, a major role and are an object of investigation, his thoughts deserve to be qualified as true thoughts, since his works bears the trace of an investigation that (1) explores all the logical possibilities of a form or a technique, (2) displays them logically and articulates them together, and (3) gives the form/technique both an aesthetical and ontological meaning, as it is shown in the tension of continuity and discontinuity. Let us note, while we are dwelling on the subject, that our definition is more Aristotelian than Husserlian or Fregeian, i.e., based on the existence of logical underlying principles rather than defined by the mere existence of an object of thought. His thoughts are not conceptual though, they are not worded nor verbalized, but incarnated, embodied in the garment, and possibly revealed by the analysis, which is not a translation, nevertheless, as garments are not a proper language (contrary to what structuralists like Roland Barthes (1990), in particular in his 1967 *Fashion System*, may have suggested).

Finally, his work bears the print of his ponderings on the very nature of his objective: clothing, of which the singularities are not only worked on but also questioned, even problematized. Aesthetic inventions are indissoluble from conceptual developments without actually being abstract; like any authentic artist or artisan Poell thinks *materially*.

More than a designer or a stylist, Carol Christian Poell is a tailor who gives birth to new forms by transforming matter. And the material he works on is not fabric or leather but the human body itself, whose representations are reinvented, taking new and unseen forms.

Notes

1 "On a un milieu qui est le siège d'un processus de quelque nature que ce soit, et l'on distingue deux types de points, les points réguliers et les points catastrophiques. Les

points réguliers sont les points où l'analyse phénoménologique locale ne décèle aucun accident particulier; il peut y avoir des variations observables, mais ces variations sont continues. Au contraire, il y a des points où l'analyse phénoménologique révèle des accidents brutaux et discontinus, en particulier des discontinuités observables et c'est ce que j'ai appelé les points catastrophiques."

2 "Aufheben hat in der Sprache den gedoppelten Sinn, daß es soviel als aufbewahren, erhalten bedeutet und zugleich soviel als aufhören lassen, ein Ende machen. Das Aufbewahren selbst schließt schon das Negative in sich, daß etwas seiner Unmittelbarkeit und damit einem den äußerlichen Einwirkungen offenen Dasein entnommen wird, um es zu erhalten."

3 "Die Gesamtheit dieser Produktionsverhältnisse bildet die ökonomische Struktur der Gesellschaft, die reale Basis, worauf sich ein juristischer und politischer Überbau erhebt, und welcher bestimmte gesellschaftliche Bewußtseinsformen entsprechen."

Bibliography

Barthes, R. (1990), *The Fashion System* (1967), trans. M. Ward and R. Howard, Berkeley: University of California Press

Hegel, G.W.F. (2013), *Wissenschaft der Logik. Erster Band* (1812), Berlin: Hoffenberg

Marx, K. and F. Engels (1971), *Werke*, vol. 13, Berlin: Dietz Verlag

Poell, C.C. (2008), "Menschenhaut zu Leder verarbeitern", *ART. Das Kunstmagazin*, November 18, 2008. Available online: http://www.art-magazin.de/design/12500/carol_christian_poell_junges_design?p=2 (accessed August 10, 2015)

Thom, R. (1988), "Exposé introductif", in J. Petitot (ed.), *Logos et théorie des catastrophes. À partir de l'œuvre de René Thom* (Actes du colloque international de 1982 à Cerisy-la-Salle), 32, Genève: Patino

7 CAPRICES OF FASHION IN CULTURE AND BIOLOGY: CHARLES DARWIN'S AESTHETICS OF "ORNAMENT"

Winfried Menninghaus

In the second part of his 1871 book *The Descent of Man, and Selection in Relation to Sex*, Darwin consistently used key concepts of philosophical aesthetics. This applies not only to the term "beauty"—which has a broader use far beyond philosophical aesthetics—but also to the more distinctive ciphers of eighteenth-century anthropological aesthetics such as "taste for the beautiful" (Darwin 1981: 108) and "sense of beauty" (Darwin 1981: 63). In keeping with this tradition, Darwin emphasized the positive aesthetic appeal of "novelty," "exaggeration," and "variety" (Darwin 1981: 230–1, 351, 354). Furthermore, he explicitly referred to the eighteenth-century discourse on "ornament," and he did so in keeping with the special role "capricious" types of ornament—such as the arabesque and the grotesque—had in this context. In a striking terminological move, Darwin applied the terms "ornament," "caprice," "capriciousness," and also "fashion" directly to natural bodies (Darwin 1981: 230–1, 339–40, 352). The term "caprice" as used by Darwin has a considerable tradition in British eighteenth-century aesthetics. Their German equivalents are *Laune*, *Marotte*, *Tick*, and *Manier* (Strasser 1976; Menninghaus 1995: 26–45). Kant's definition of an aesthetically "capricious manner (*launichte Manier*)" (Kant 1907: 335–6) is part of the tradition that informed Darwin's use of the term.

Evolutionary biology tends to avoid this terminology, as though it were an awkward reminder of pre-scientific ways of writing that gave free rein to loose metaphors. For decades, such concepts have simply been absent from interpretations of Darwin's ideas. The wide array of association-laden terms used by Darwin ended up being reduced to "physical attractiveness" alone (ironically, this term, too, is very rich in contemporary cultural semantics and by no means scientifically "clean"). This essay places particular emphasis on the aesthetic and cultural semantics Darwin's concept of a "sense of beauty" refers to. Specifically, it addresses five key aspects, with a special focus on the third and the fifth:

1. The historical configuration of biology and aesthetics which Darwin continued and transformed.
2. The historical semantics of "beauty" Darwin draws upon.
3. His very special recourse to the aesthetics of ornament from the later eighteenth century to his own time.
4. His references to the mid-nineteenth-century significance of fashion.
5. His reformulation, and simultaneous "deconstruction," of the classical ideal of the human body.

In principle, cultural semantics plays two opposite roles in the sciences: it both enables and limits scientific cognition. My focus will be on how Darwin's use of cultural semantics rendered his novel biological insights even more striking and rich in meaning rather than merely disturbing them. Furthermore, Darwin's evolutionary aesthetics will be shown to shed a new light on the philosophical aesthetics it draws upon.

1. Biology and aesthetics

In most Western languages, the predicate "beautiful" has long been equally applied to natural phenomena ranging from landscapes to sexual bodies, and to cultural artifacts and practices, thus suggesting a shared core meaning or at least an analogy between the two. Plato's concept of *éros* for the beautiful covers the whole spectrum from sexual to highly intellectual charms (Plato, *Symposium*: 206b–d). The notion of the "vividness" or "liveliness" of representations has been a thematic desideratum of poetics at least since the Renaissance (Fehrenbach 2003a; 2003b); eighteenth-century aesthetics associated this notion directly with the contemporary biological discourse on "life" (Avanessian et al. 2009). Kant's theory of the aesthetic "furthering of the feeling of life" (Kant 1907: § 23), and his definition of both "aesthetic pleasure" and of "life" itself as processes of self-perpetuation and *autopoiesis* (Kant 1907: §§ 10, 12, 64–5), bear striking witness to the considerable affinities between biology and aesthetics (cf. Bierbrodt 2000; Müller-Sievers 1997; Zuckert 2007). While eighteenth- and early nineteenth-century aesthetics had been shaped and transformed by their overlap with biological discourses, Darwin performed a complementary bridging of the gap: he transformed biological thought through numerous references to discourses in aesthetics. His biological theory of "beauty" is thus by no means a curiosity on the margins of an otherwise biology-free discourse. On the contrary, his aesthetics sits squarely within the tradition of historical and philosophical aesthetics precisely because its arguments are grounded in biology.

2. Beauty as autonomous expenditure

Darwin kept thinking about "beauty" for several decades chiefly because it seemed to challenge his theory of natural selection. Bodily features such as decorative feathers, horns, antlers, etc., are "carried to a wonderful extreme" (Darwin 1981: 279) in numerous species: they have become so large, or have taken on such a form, as to be mostly a hindrance in the "general conditions of life" (Darwin 1981: 398) and of little use as weapons. Edmund Burke's *A Philosophical Enquiry Into the Origin of Our Ideas of the Sublime and the Beautiful* (1757) seems to have guided Darwin's inquiry into "beauty" and "taste" very directly. Burke's treatise, which Darwin explicitly referred to on several occasions (Darwin 1974a: 274; 1974b: 332, 341), had already tackled Darwin's evolutionary master-example, the "extreme beauty" of the peacock's ornament. He even couched his discussion in Darwin's terms, underlining how the peacock's beauty conflicts with natural "fitness," and highlighting that bodily forms perceived as beautiful cannot simply be explained in terms of being "well-adapted" to the requirements of survival (Burke 1986: 95, 106).

In Darwin's view, selection for beautiful ornaments follows a logic of ongoing self-reinforcement, of favoring difference for the sake of difference—a principle, incidentally, the discovery of which Darwin credited to Alexander von Humboldt (Darwin 1981: 351). Formulations such as "mere novelty, or change for the sake of change" (Darwin 1981: 230), "beauty for beauty's sake" or "mere variety" (Darwin 1981: 230), dramatically underline the much-discussed "autonomy" or "self-legislative" quality of aesthetic preferences *vis-à-vis* pragmatic considerations. Darwin even went far beyond the more edifying versions of "aesthetic autonomy." He conceived of beauty first of all as scandalous excess, as potentially self-destructive luxury—we might almost say with Bataille: as sovereign expenditure (Bataille 1988).

However, on deeper reflection, even Kant and idealist aesthetics ascribed a special function to the very purposelessness of the beautiful. Darwin likewise arrived at a functional explanation: though mostly handicaps in the "general conditions of life," aesthetic ornaments provide competitive advantages in the highly specialized context of sexual courtship. The distinction between natural and sexual selection allowed Darwin to decouple the conflicting characteristics of aesthetic purposelessness and aesthetic functionality by relegating them to two different contexts. The extravagant ornament's relative indifference to important practical goals—such as securing food and self-defense—accounts for its "autonomy," while its benefits in the highly specific context of sexual choice establish its adaptive function. To be sure, the Kantian "disinterestedness" of the aesthetic judgment is clearly turned on its head in Darwin's theory, as the idealist notion of a purely "intellectual interest" (Kant 1907: § 42) is replaced by a marked sexual interest. At the same time, not only the terms used, but also the figures of thought—above all the interweaving of the self-reinforcing autonomy and functionality of beauty—are without exception borrowed from traditional aesthetics. Darwin did not speak in loose metaphors; he provided a reinterpretation of traditional aesthetics worthy of reconsideration.

3. Darwin's aesthetics of "ornament"

Darwin's reference to ornaments that are "carried to a wonderful extreme" (Darwin 1981: 279) alludes to the debate on extravagant, arabesque-grotesque ornaments, from which classicism sought to set itself apart in the name of moderation and "natural" taste. Rocaille ornaments, of which Figure 7.1 gives a typical example, framed their objects with abundant decorations that could well exceed the actual object of ornamentation in size, displaying a splendor both playfully capricious and glamorous.

Darwin's take on similar ornamental excrescences shaping the appearance of peacocks or birds of paradise implies a clear stance *vis-à-vis* the aesthetic debate about excessive or modest ornamentation. For Darwin, even the hypertrophied ornaments condemned by classicism are anything but "unnatural"; extravagant excrescences and arabesque digressions adorning the body can in fact be found throughout the natural world.[1] Darwin's concept of sexual body "ornaments" likewise connects the discourse of evolutionary biology to a central category of philosophical aesthetics. From at least the time of Karl Philipp Moritz—a novelist, linguist, and psychologist who also wrote several very dense treatises on aesthetics—and Kant, ornaments were considered the epitome of "purposeless" and "meaningless" beauty. Arabesques, ornamental tendrils, and decorative edgings of every kind figured here as accessories, as *parerga* (Menninghaus 1995: 94–118). In this context, Kant explicitly referred to the beauty of "foliage serving as framings" (Kant 1907: § 16). When applied to natural bodies, such a sharp distinction between the ornamental addition and the ornamented object—which, incidentally, marks Darwin's concept of ornament as a genuinely modern one—produced a deliberate

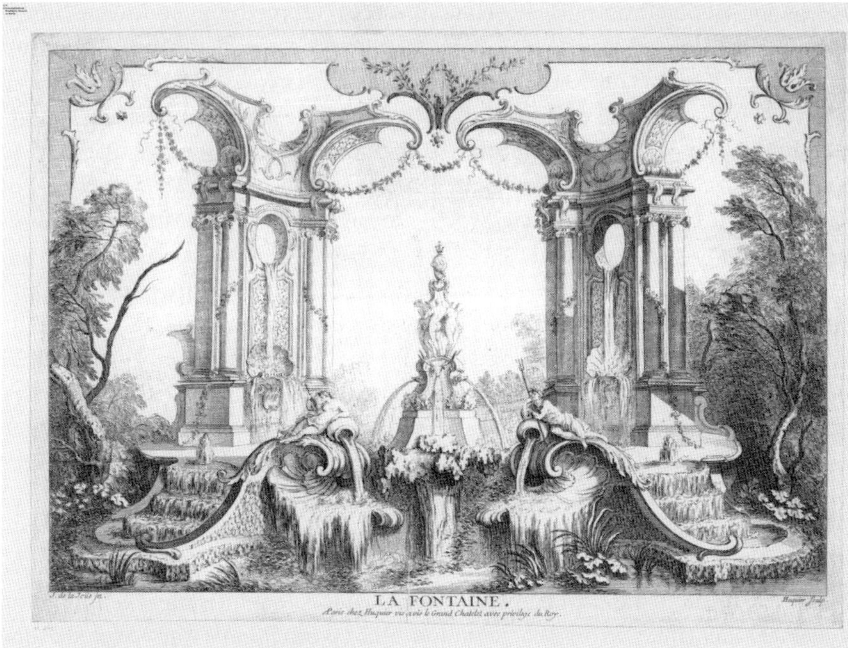

FIGURE 7.1 J. de Lajoüe Jn. and G. Huquier (1735). La Fontaine—A Paris chez Huquier vis a vis le Grand Chatelet avec privilege du Roy.

sense of alienation, a rupturing of these bodies' integral wholeness. Darwin even had the gall to conceive of certain parts of the body—without any qualification—in terms of ornaments literally added by evolution to a previously unadorned body. The agent of this ornamentation is no longer a Creator God, whose act of creation went beyond practical wisdom by also bestowing beauty upon the world. Instead, it is acts of sexual selection by the opposite sex that have rendered specific "ornaments" hereditary and reinforced them over long periods of time. Darwin is the first and perhaps only author in the history of aesthetics to conceive of the beautiful body—rather than merely the grotesque counterpart of the beautiful body, as Bakhtin did (1984)—through strict application of the tools provided by the aesthetics of ornament, the grotesque, and arabesque. This perspective strongly subverts holistic theories of form and implies a radical partialization of the aesthetic objects of desire.

The poetics of *caprice* emphasized the unmotivated, arbitrary, random, and even partly absurd nature of a phenomenon that is nonetheless compelling in its inherent lavishness. Whimsical preferences for extravagant feather headdresses are ultimately just as erratic as are the whimsical *caprices* to which the pink bottoms of some ape species owe their existence (Darwin 1977: 207). As with a whimsical caprice, or hobby horse, there is undoubtedly something endearing about this phenomenon. Yet this does nothing to cancel out the element of the absurd and off-beat, or even the downright crazy in more extreme cases. Darwin had all of this in mind when he discussed the peacock's tail—and ultimately every sex-related aesthetic preference found in the natural world. The beings that hold to these structurally capricious preferences must surely be a bit crazy. Otherwise, at least in Darwin's view, entire species would not have taken even the most outlandish body ornaments to such extremes.

With respect to literature, Darwin's diagnosis of (sexual) nature's *capriciousness* resonates not insignificantly with the poetics of capricious digressions characteristic of Lawrence Sterne's *Tristram Shandy* (1759–67), Denis Diderot's *Jacques le fataliste et son maître* [*Jacques the Fatalist*] (written 1773–5), and several literary "arabesques" of German Romanticism. Sterne's novel announces itself as portraying the *Life and Opinions* of its protagonist. However, the novel persistently disrupts the narrative trajectory the reader expects to be offered by taking multiple, self-proliferating, and complexly interwoven detours. These digressions capriciously consume several hundred pages before the protagonist is even born. The narrative art of German Romanticism employs similar devices that interrupt the unfolding of a linear narrative, or drama plot, and add layers upon layers of arabesque digressions (Oesterle 1984: 119–34; Menninghaus 1995: 94–190). In both cases, paratexts and digressive elaborations consume so much space and (reading) time that the (presumed) narrative core of the resulting works of art appears to be stretched and postponed to the point of falling apart. Darwin applied to natural bodies literally the same categories which had been inventively adapted by historical literary aesthetics in order to grasp the provocative productions of Laurence Sterne (1713–68), Ludwig Tieck (1773–1853) or E.T.A. Hoffmann (1776–1822).

Pushing the resonances between Darwin's concept of capriciously ornamented biological body fashions and cultural phenomena even further, stock certificates (see Figure 7.2) were among the most striking nineteenth-century phenomena that were designed in a highly capricious and arabesque fashion of visual display (Busch 1985). Through their ornamental design features stock certificates lived up to the aesthetic feat performed by the peacock's tail. The underlying mechanism is very much the same: like peacocks, stocks enhance their *promise of value and performance*, and hence their *desirability*, through excessive visual ornamentation.

Both evolutionary biology and philosophical aesthetics have widely disregarded the apparently consistent and transformative use Darwin made of various traditions of eighteenth- and nineteenth-century aesthetics for the purpose of conceptualizing his model of sexual selection. The dense *cultural* semantics of the terms he adopted contribute significantly to the wealth of nuances in Darwin's book, and to its trans-disciplinary stature.

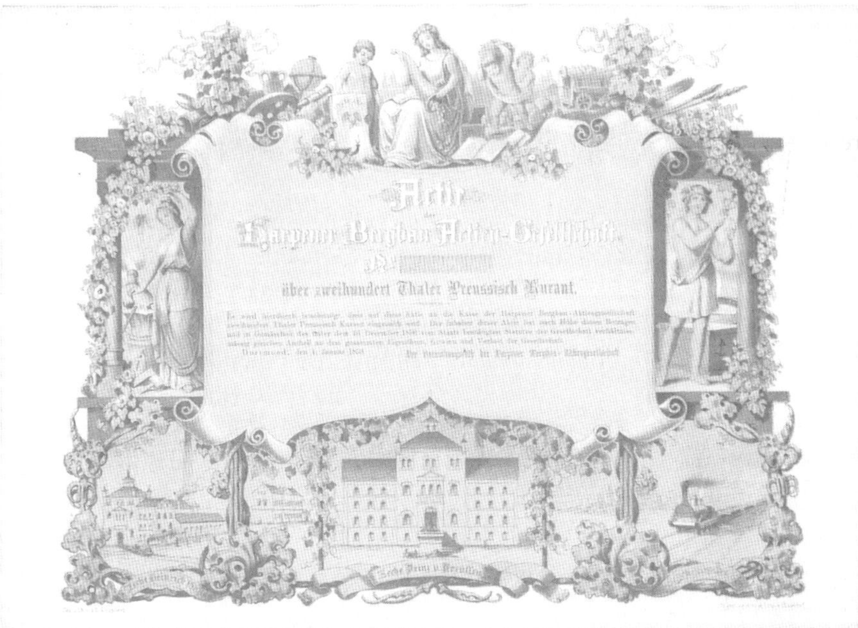

FIGURE 7.2 Johann Baptist Sonderland (1805–78). Stock Certificate Harpener Bergbau AG.

4. The time of fashion

Darwin viewed the "caprices" of cultural "fashions" (Darwin 1981: 64, 230–1, 339–40, 352) as an extension of, and substitute for, the sexually selected caprices that shaped the natural bodies of sexual organisms. Fashion is the runaway *cultural* process of the apparently "capricious" emergence and (re)enforcement of aesthetic preferences. It radically increases the rate of the evolutionary race for ornamental sex differences for their own sake. Fashion transforms the (seemingly) arbitrary emergence, spread, and eventual stabilization of desired characteristics—a process that takes thousands of generations in biological evolution—into phenomena of ever-shorter duration; it enjoys a far greater degree of freedom with respect to the human physical constitution and has an unfailing capacity to surprise with capricious inversions. With fashion, we find the peacock-like Darwinian caprices of (sexual) nature in evidence at every turn.

Historical documents support the idea that the surprising parallel between clothing fashion and biological evolution struck many of Darwin's contemporaries as utterly persuasive. In 1872, Darwin's relative George H. Darwin published an article on "Development in Dress" that began with the following bold hypothesis:

"The development in dress presents a strong analogy to that of organisms, as explained by the modern theories of evolution" (G.H. Darwin 1872: 410).[2] The article distinguished dress features that can be conceived of as "natural selection"-style adaptations to novel pragmatic requirements of the environment from other dress features that suggest an analogy with the "sexual selection" paradigm:

> Besides the general adaptation of dress [. . .] there is another influence which has perhaps a still more important bearing on the development of dress, and that is fashion. The love of novelty, and the extraordinary tendency which men have to exaggerate any peculiarity, for the time being considered a mark of good station in life, or handsome in itself, give rise I suppose to fashion.
>
> **G.H. DARWIN** 1872: 410

The detailed chapter on "Badges and Costumes" in Herbert Spencer's book *Ceremonial Institutions* (Spencer 1879: 174–92) continued this blending of evolutionary biology and fashion theory in a consistent and novel way. Thus, on the one hand, Darwin's reasoning about the "taste for the beautiful" drew on a philosophical tradition that was itself informed by biology. On the other hand, it involved a complementary transfer in which the highly cultural phenomenon of clothing fashions served as a viable and persuasive analog to processes of biological evolution.

According to the philosopher and cultural critic Walter Benjamin, the nineteenth century was the first century of fashion, in that only then did the mass production of objects solely marketed for ever-more-fleeting fashions emerge (Benjamin 1982: 113, 127, 576, 582). In this sense, Darwin's theory of beauty as "fashion" is deeply anchored in its immediate cultural context. Thus, while the semantics of ornamentation and caprice found in Darwin's aesthetics incorporates nuances dating back to the aesthetics of the late eighteenth century and the romantic capriccios of the early nineteenth century, Darwin can simultaneously be considered as a (yet to be acknowledged) theorist of fashion—and hence, of a phenomenon that acquired novel significance particularly in Darwin's own time. Remarkably, he did not shy away from using concepts that had a strong historical and cultural flavor to portray ancient evolutionary processes in a rhetorically pointed fashion.

This almost suggests another parallel with Benjamin, this time with respect to representational strategy. By theorizing the sexual ornaments of natural bodies in terms of a recent and even contemporary cultural aesthetics, Darwin's thought produces something akin to "dialectical images" (Benjamin 1982: 495, 578–80, 592). The origin of these images lie in the very period covered by Benjamin's history of the nineteenth century. And they have a similar aim: to enhance our understanding of the fashions which have shaped us—and which we now are.

5. The human fashion of naked skin

Darwin's reflections on the aesthetic evolution of the human body are generally out of synch with the paradigms of contemporary research on physical attractiveness. Furthermore, the key feature Darwin focused on is barely mentioned by today's researchers in the field, despite the fact that the basic theoretical assumptions informing current research essentially draw on Darwin's general concept of *sexual choice*. Darwin made no reference to waist-to-hip-ratios, baby face patterns, body mass indices, or any of the other body features highly prized by today's cult of beauty. Only one "ornament" interested him with respect to the human body—yet he considered this one crucial. This very "ornament" is usually not even considered to be one; rather, it is taken to be the non-ornamented baseline of the human body. I am referring to what replaced our non-human ancestors' hairy covering, that is, the strange phenomenon of naked skin (Darwin 1981: 375–82). By singling out naked skin, Darwin focused on what is unquestionably the most striking difference between the overall appearances of humans and apes.

For Darwin, naked skin does not mean the absence of clothing and thus the resulting display of sexual organs. Rather, he viewed it as the prime bodily ornament of the human species. Unlike almost all other forms of sexual ornament observed by Darwin, this ornament applies to the *whole body* rather than being an *addendum* here or there. Darwin's "narrative" of naked skin took the apes as its consistent point of reference. Though obviously lacking this characteristic, for an evolutionary account to be possible apes must have had some kind of feature from which the hypothetical human preference for bare skin could take off. Darwin identified the hairless areas around the (female) genitals of many apes and on the face of the mandrill, which function as sexual signals, as the evolutionary point of departure for the development of naked skin in humans (Darwin 1981: 291–3).[3] Guided over a very long period of time by a preference for regions of hairless skin, sexual selection increasingly amplified this feature of ape attractiveness. Despite practical disadvantages—such as the loss of a thermal and mechanical body protection—Darwin credited this process with being powerful enough to bring about near-total denudation, particularly of the female body (Darwin 1981: 291–3). As a result, a "capricious" taste for areas of naked skin that we essentially share with many apes has been pushed to the point of producing a whole body version of what used to be the sexually alluring hairless spots on the apes' bodies—and by implication an almost entirely sexualized human body surface.

In addition to the spectacular expansion of the ape's hairless "hot spots," the aesthetics of the human body involves a direct inversion of the attributes *hairless vs. hairy*. While in many ape species it is above all, if not exclusively, the genital-erogenous zones that are depilated, it is on these very areas that evolution has added hair on the human body. Furthermore, the relative depilation of the human body is reinforced by the contrast with a particularly hair-rich scalp, which has generated an entire spectrum of a novel hair aesthetics (color, sheen, texture, fragrance, movement) on an otherwise largely depilated body (Etcoff 1999: 120–9). Both phenomena are particularly well-established as secondary female sexual characteristics. The switch from the often garish color signals on the apes' depilated hot spots to the discretely toned color continuum typical of human skin can also be understood as a directional evolutionary break with "ape fashion." Faced with the task of transforming the "chimpanzee look" into a new body fashion by pushing some originally minimal differences ever further, a top designer could scarcely have done better than the process of sexual selection did through ongoing aesthetic distancing as Darwin describes it. In a fashion both capricious and inherently consistent, this continuous exaggeration of differences appears to have been based solely on multiple dimensions of the binary distinction *hairy vs. hairless.*

The denudation of the skin shares with the stag's extravagant antlers and the excessive plumage of many birds an aesthetic sovereignty *vis-à-vis* considerations of "fitness," at least with regard to thermal and mechanical protection. Darwin did not claim that the human skin, whether before or after denudation, served no other biological functions. His speculations are not, therefore, incompatible with alternative explanations of naked skin based on natural selection.[4] Darwin is exclusively trying to make the case that "to a certain extent" (Darwin 1981: 376)—a very cautious way to put it—the extreme mutation of the almost entirely hair-covered ape into the almost entirely "naked" human being has been *in part* an aesthetic runaway process driven by preferences for very special appealing looks. In this sense, the process by which the ape became naked is analogous to tendencies of cultural fashions to push a preferred feature to increasingly extreme levels, an example being the fashion for short skirts, which, by virtue of its own momentum, tends to rapidly lead to complete exposure of the legs.

With respect to most of its parameters, human beauty is in fact defined through the reinforcement of differences from apes. Differentiation of this kind, based solely on ornamentation, has often been observed, particularly among closely related species: "in many taxa of arthropods and vertebrates closely related species differ most in secondary sexual characters" (Lande 1987: 84). Darwin's observation that, "to our taste, many monkeys are far from beautiful" (Darwin 1981: 310) thus corresponds to a general rule of fashion-related distancing among closely related species. On an evolutionary scale, this phenomenon promotes the avoidance of hybrid mating and thus encourages species isolation. Differences in appearance arising from sexual selection are therefore particularly relevant to the differentiation of previously identical organisms into distinct species (Gould and Gould 1989). In fact, many species of insect can be distinguished solely by their sexual ornaments, including bizarre penile fashions (Eberhard 1985), while a number of bird species can be distinguished only in light of their sexually favored coloring.

To put it differently, differences of fashion or aesthetics, particularly among closely related creatures, quite literally make many species what they are.

Evolutionary theory is thus able to explain Edmund Burke's remark that "there are few animals which seem to have less beauty in the eyes of all mankind [than monkeys]" (Burke 1986: 105), and to likewise shed a light on why in Goethe's *Elective Affinities* apes are described—in an only seemingly paradoxical fashion—as "human-like" and at the same time aesthetically "repulsive" (Goethe 1987: 236). What is at stake here is the aesthetic rejection of one's own earlier body fashion, which is now seen as radically "uncool"—just as Benjamin identified one's own parents' choice of clothing as every generation's "most powerful anti-aphrodisiac" (Benjamin 1982: 113).

Darwin's view of aesthetic preferences turned into biological body traits defined the skin as the opposite of a "naked fact": as a highly unlikely distinguishing feature that was literally "selected" by human beings, and that, as a form of comprehensive nakedness applying to the entire body, is unknown among other primates. The very few species that show similarly naked skin—such as the naked mole rat or cats and dogs that were bred to be (largely) devoid of hair—typically strike us as being very ugly and even somewhat uncanny. This aversion seems to highlight the significance that we place on our naked skin. Obviously, we jealously want to monopolize this feature, and find every "mimicry" or, to be more precise, every parallel in other species appalling.

Naked skin is thus not only an absence of protective hairs or feathers, but an alternative form of bodily *clothing* selected over many generations. In this respect it is analogous to the most elaborate ornaments of fur and plumage, though it functions "rhetorically," to use Quintilian's terms, via *detractio* (detraction) rather than *additio* (addition) (Quintilian 1953: VIII 5, IX). And there is a second key aspect to this. Precisely because naked skin is the only ornament defined first and foremost through absences—through the lack of feathers, hair, and fur—it is itself able to function as the setting for further additions and ornamental markings of every kind. In this sense, naked skin is a superb feat of sexual selection. Having come about through the polarizing reinforcement of ape preferences for select hairless spots, it offers a uniquely flexible canvas for the application and display of ever-new and ever-varied fashionable addenda that are intentionally and culturally produced. No one has gone as far as Darwin did in conceiving of the human body as an organ of fashion.

Independently of Darwin's evolutionary reasoning, the classical aesthetics of sculpture had arrived at a similar conclusion. It considered it essential that the human body be depicted unclothed, and indeed less for the sake of displaying sexual features than because the curvature and surface features of skin define humans as human in a striking way. We are, as Desmond Morris strikingly put it (1967), *The Naked Ape*. To forego this feature in the art of sculpture would amount to nothing less than denying our outer appearance its primary ornament. At the same time, the provocative, utterly non-classical starting point of the mandrill and ape's rear ends, as well as the analogy with the elaborate plumage of peacocks and other birds, also furnished Darwin's new foundation for the classical aesthetics of sculpture with an anti-classical turn towards the arabesque and grotesque. From a comparative and functional perspective, the smooth continuum of human skin that classical aesthetics rightly celebrated as a hallmark of the human being (Menninghaus 2003: 52) thus became readable as an utterly crazy fashion. This fashion is equivalent to the most grotesque ornaments found in the animal kingdom and the world of art; indeed, it takes these ornaments to an extreme and ultimately outdoes them. In other words, Darwin opened up a completely novel perspective on the much-discussed beauty of the human body: he suggests reading it as a garish arabesque or grotesque in the sense of the historical aesthetics of ornament.

Far from merely making use of the historical semantics of traditional aesthetics, Darwin's thought has the potential to change and reconfigure this semantics itself. It is conceivable that certain representational techniques of the *Jugendstil* (*Art Nouveau*), which fuse the beautiful human body with motifs of arabesque decoration may represent a historical continuation of Darwin's dual perspective on the human body. Reading Darwin from the perspective of philosophical and historical aesthetics thus discloses aspects of his thought completely absent from the reception of his theory of beauty within the fields of both evolutionary biology and empirical psychology.

(translated from German by Alex Skinner)

Notes

1 For other aspects of the grotesque in Darwin's thought, see Beer (1985: 81), and Bown (1999).

2 I owe the reference to this text to Julia Voss.

3 For the complex relationship between female and male sexual ornaments in apes and monkeys see Wickler 1967: 69–147.

4 For an overview about the various explanations of the naked skin see Morris (1967: 42–8), and Rantala (2007).

Bibliography

Avanessian, A., W. Menninghaus and J. Völker, eds (2009), *Vita aesthetica: Szenarien ästhetischer Lebendigkeit*, Zürich-Berlin: Diaphanes

Bakhtin, M.M. (1984), *Rabelais and His World*, trans. H. Iswolsky, Bloomington: Indiana University Press

Bataille, G. (1988), *The College of Sociology 1937–39*, trans. B. Wing, ed. by D. Hollier, Minneapolis: University of Minnesota Press

Beer, G. (1985), *Darwin's Plots: Evolutionary Narrative in Darwin, George Eliot, and Nineteenth-Century Fiction*, London: Ark Paperbacks

Benjamin, W. (1982), *Das Passagen-Werk* (1927–40), in R. Tiedemann and H. Schweppenhäuser (eds), *Gesammelte Schriften*, vol. 5 (1+2), Frankfurt a.M.: Suhrkamp
Bierbrodt, J. (2000), *Naturwissenschaft und Ästhetik, 1750–1810*, Würzburg: Königshausen & Neumann
Bown, N. (1999), "Entangled Banks: Robert Browning, Richard Dadd and the Darwinian Grotesque", in C. Trodd, P. Barlow and D. Amigoni (eds), *Victorian Culture and the Idea of the Grotesque*, 119–39, Aldershot: Ashgate
Burke, E. (1986), *A Philosophical Enquiry Into the Origin of Our Ideas of the Sublime and the Beautiful* (1757), ed. by J.T. Boulton, London: University of Notre Dame Press
Busch, W. (1985), *Die notwendige Arabeske. Wirklichkeitsaneignung und Stilisierung in der deutschen Kunst des 19. Jahrhunderts*, Berlin: Gebr. Mann Verlag
Darwin, C. (1974a), "M Notebook", in H.E. Gruber (ed.), *Darwin on Man: A Psychological Study of Scientific Creativity*, together with Darwin's early and unpublished notebooks transcribed and annotated by P.H. Barrett, 266–97, New York: E.P. Dutton
Darwin, C. (1974b), "N Notebook", in H.E. Gruber (ed.), *Darwin on Man: A Psychological Study of Scientific Creativity*, together with Darwin's early and unpublished notebooks transcribed and annotated by P.H. Barrett, 329–51, New York: E.P. Dutton
Darwin, C. (1977), "Sexual Selection in Relation to Monkeys" (1876), in P.H. Barrett (ed.), *The Collected Papers of Charles Darwin*, 207–11, Chicago: Chicago University Press
Darwin, C. (1981), *The Descent of Man, and Selection in Relation to Sex* (1871), Princeton (NJ): Princeton University Press
Darwin, G.H. (1872), "Development in Dress", *Macmillan Magazine*, 26: 410–6
Eberhard, W.G. (1985), *Sexual Selection and Animal Genitalia*, Cambridge (MA)-London: Harvard University Press
Etcoff, N. (1999), *Survival of the Prettiest: The Science of Beauty*, New York: Doubleday
Fehrenbach, F. (2003a), "Lebendigkeit", in U. Pfisterer (ed.), *Metzlers Lexikon Kunstwissenschaft. Ideen, Methoden, Begriffe*, 222–7, Stuttgart: Metzler
Fehrenbach, F. (2003b), "Calor nativus—Color vitale. Prolegomena zu einer Ästhetik des 'Lebendigen Bildes' in der frühen Neuzeit", in U. Pfisterer and M. Seidel (eds), *Visuelle Topoi. Erfindung und tradiertes Wissen in den Künsten der italienischen Renaissance*, 151–70, München-Berlin: Deutscher Kunstverlag
Goethe, J.W. von (1987), *Wahlverwandtschaften* (1809–92), in *Goethes Werke*, vol. 20, im Auftrage der Großherzogin Sophie von Sachsen, Weimar: Böhlau (reprint München: dtv, 1987)
Gould, J.L. and C.G. Gould, eds (1989), *Sexual Selection*, Scientific American Library: New York
Kant, I. (1907), *Kritik der Urtheilskraft* (1790), in *Kant's Gesammelte Schriften*, vol. 5, ed. by Königlich Preußische Akademie der Wissenschaften, Berlin: Georg Reimer
Lande, R. (1987), "Genetic Correlations Between the Sexes in the Evolution of Sexual Dimorphism and Mating Preferences", in J.W. Bradbury and M.B. Andersson (eds), *Sexual Selection: Testing the Alternatives*, 83–95, Chichester: Wiley
Menninghaus, W. (1995), *Lob des Unsinns. Über Kant, Tieck und Blaubart*, Frankfurt a.M.: Suhrkamp
Menninghaus, W. (2003), *Disgust: Theory and History of a Strong Sensation*, trans. H. Eiland and J. Golb, Albany: SUNY Press
Morris, D. (1967), *The Naked Ape: A Zoologist's Study of the Human Animal*, London: Cape
Müller-Sievers, H. (1997), *Self-Generation: Biology, Philosophy, and Literature around 1800*, Stanford: Stanford University Press

Oesterle, G. (1984), "Vorbegriffe zu einer Theorie der Ornamente: Kontroverse Formprobleme zwischen Aufklärung, Klassizismus und Romantik am Beispiel der Arabeske", in H. Beck, P.C. Bol and E. Mack-Gérard (eds), *Ideal und Wirklichkeit der bildenden Kunst im späten 18. Jahrhundert*, 119–39, Berlin: Gebr. Mann Verlag

Plato (2008), *Symposium,* trans. B. Jowett, The Project Gutenberg EBook (http://www.gutenberg.org)

Quintilian, M.F. (1953), *Institutio oratoria*, trans. H.E. Butler, in T.E. Page and E. Capps (eds), *The Institutio Oratoria of Quintilian*, Cambridge (MA)-London: Harvard University Press-Heinemann

Rantala, M.J. (2007), "Evolution of Nakedness in Homo Sapiens", *Journal of Zoology*, 273: 1–7

Spencer, H. (1879), *Ceremonial Institutions: Principles of Sociology*, vol. 4, London: Williams and Norgate

Strasser, I. (1976), *Bedeutungswandel und strukturelle Semantik. "Marotte, Laune, Tick" im literarischen Deutsch der Gegenwart und der Frühen Goethezeit*, Wien: Verlag Karl M. Halosar

Wickler, W. (1967), "Socio-Sexual Signals and Their Intra-Specific Imitation Among Primates", in D. Morris (ed.), *Primate Ethology*, 69–147, London: Weidenfeld & Nicolson

Zuckert, R. (2007), *Kant on Beauty and Biology: An Interpretation of the "Critique of Judgment"*, Cambridge: Cambridge University Press

8 FASHIONABLE PROTEUS: ESSAY ON THE EUPHORIA OF FASHION FOR FASHION'S SAKE IN AN AGE OF SHALLOWNESS

César Moreno-Márquez

1. Fashion/s. Fashion for fashion's sake

A *philosophical* understanding of fashion requires that we not be blinded by its strange combination of shine and trifle that pertains to the mundane pluralism of its expressions, "innovations" or "anecdotes" (whatever is in style in each moment), which precisely seem to best (and insufficiently) express what we understand as *fashion/s*. If we say "table" or "car" we are not necessarily prompted to think of many tables or cars, nor of their transformations. It is as if the unit of the *eidos* keeps us close to it, infusing us with indifference towards its cases or examples. However, when we say "fashion" we are required to think of *transformations-and-plurality*, because they are part of the content of the general concept of fashion, whatever that content may be—and, above all, as in our case, when it comes to dressing. In other words, we could say that "fashion" is similar to a collective noun.

It is commonly through the *diachrony* of fashions and the growing *synchrony* in its diversity, but also *in spite* of the diachrony and synchrony, that "fashion" can be understood. This "fashion" always appears in *the styles* (be it this or that style, from whatever *the season* may be): for such is its dynamism and its "charm," its distinctive sign and its frailty, but also its emblem or its way of being, linked to transitory adhesions, not making any firm compromises, and being refractory to the phrase "till death do us part." And, nevertheless, fashion, despite its infinite hustle, is always true to itself: *fashion* or *being-relatively-fashionable* or *being-in-style*. I am referring to its stimulus, its always expectant desire, its community, and its time. The establishing of the relationship between fashion and the styles is a difficult task, one that does not pretend to pit the styles that *go out of style* and fashion, which never goes out of style, against each other, but rather to ponder about them in their articulation. Clearly, we require a considerable amount of discipline that, mostly, philosophy must teach us to use. Fashion is an *emergence*, a *type of phenomenologization* in dressing, or an *irruptive-force* that we can only understand when we don't fall victim to the manifestations that fleetingly consolidate and determine it. This is demanding work, for it is up to the fashions to seduce, involve, repel, or entertain us with their oddity. Only through a philosophical discipline of delimitation could its infinite modification and its blatant capability for transformation be observed. And not necessarily as defects, but as what *essentially* constitutes the truth about what fashion generates and the content of its unity ("fashion").

It will therefore be understood that these arguments explain the importance of responding to fashion *for its sake*, as the basis of the contemporary *consummate fashion* (cf. Lipovetsky 1994), and that they justify the attempt to find the *anthropological* expression that could best correspond to it. The philosophical interest of the "for its own sake" would help us purify the phenomenon bringing together its *idea* and its *force*. More so than in any other age (cf. Moreno 2012), we are capable of comprehending the power of the consummate fashion, in a moment where "Fashion" has freed itself from any temptation of *uniformity* (Lipovetsky 1994: 235) and that celebrates the synchrony of many different tendencies. It is in this *being-for-the-sake-of-it* that we can appreciate the creative and destructive power of fashion, its potential for *creativity* and its *voraciousness*: what is *to come* is used/consumed and becomes *passing*, but only as a medium that favors the *more-to-come*, *what-will-come-again*: fashion is always triumphant,[1] as excess of what is renewed for the *next season*.

2. Fashionable Proteus. From nudity to fashion

If it were possible to *build* (*create*) a favorable subjectivity for fashion, one that was knowledgeable and an adequate user of such, it should indeed not only be able to judge its play of *mundane* meanings for the clothing, which provides it with reasonable and common appearances, frequently related to its circumstance. Even before and even more than this, the "subject" of fashion as such should be especially receptive to the *play of meanings* in regards to becoming dressed, precisely the same in response to a *non-significant nudity* which may *simply* be covered in clothing, assuredly, but also decide to be-in-style. What this represents to the other is an "expense," an excess, a luxury of creative nonsense, a joy in the transiency which are alien to the immediate *mere use*, whether it be circumstantial or pragmatic for the clothing. The non-significance of the nudity allows for daily clothing and for the transformations towards mere "clothes," but also towards the "Everything looks good" and the "Why not?" (Moreno 2004), which—so to speak—appear in fashion's imaginary emblem.[2] Perhaps we may only truly understand it in our momentarily postmodern, liquid, Protean, hypercommunicative age that has become empty yet at the same time saturated (cf. Lipovetsky 1994 and Gergen 1991). Fashion denies belief to the utilitarian plot (and penury) of the world. This is one of the bases of its potential *eroticisms* (cf. Squicciarino 1986: especially chap. 5, which deals with "Outfits and Sex-Appeal"). Ultimately, it may even be said that the fashionable Proteus is more naked than it might seem when he simply is naked and only demands clothes with which to cover himself. The person subject to fashion is with complacency, *implicitly* nude from head to toes, and may *amusingly* receive whatever it may be. While clothing requires bodies and world (Barthes 1984), it seems as if fashion appeals to a nudity transformed into a sort of *mannequin/model*.[3]

Therefore, fashion for fashion's sake requires a protagonist, one which we believe can be found in the *fashionable Proteus* as an anthropological quintessential expression of transformation, of versatility, and capacity to assume the formality of the *diversity* and *transformations* of fashion *in itself*. I believe it would not be too daring to look back to the late fifteenth century, when Pico della Mirandola wrote his *Oratio de Hominis Dignitate* (On the Dignity of Man), and linked the humanist assertion of man with the figure of *Proteus*. Upon assessing some of the qualities of human beings that would make them the reason of *unbounded admiration*, Pico maintains that the marvel of man would not be located in the said qualities, neither—for example—in the venerable Platonic motive of the dominance of reason over passion but instead, in the *versatile* and *fickle* nature of human beings, in being a "creature of an indeterminate image, without a visage proper to yourself" (Pico della Mirandola 1988: 5). Even though his myth has been left far in the past, what remains of him is the emblem that represents the *mutation* and the absence of a fixed or unmovable essence such as the traits of dignity (liberty) of human beings. Only his acclaimed nudity, his being *stripped-of-any-mundane-features*, would be up to the standard of man and of the confidence deposited in his freedom. A man may be whatever he may wish, nothing would be forbidden to him in the Garden of Eden of possibilities, if well he may decide to rise to goodness or descend to evilness (see Moreno 1993).

It is not possible to deal with the mythical figure of Proteus and extensively discuss it here. Such is not my purpose, rather it is simply to utilize this figure to ponder about our human condition and our circumstance in an age as of today, at the dawn of the twenty-first century, and how fashion allows us to think of the said condition and circumstance in a *certain* and *concrete* way. Human modifications cling on to possibilities of transformation and *autopoiesis*, thus requiring, in all necessary conditions, maps to serve as guides and charts by means of which to build (Geertz 1973: 45, 49), as well as incentives and possibilities for excitement, and the *motivating* memory of its own *capacity of change*, *creativity*, and *playfulness*, amidst and against the seriousness of culture, withdrawing energy from the volubility and contingency in benefit of human creativity, and of joy for the future and the community. Force of change in exchange for almost nothing at all, change for and to continue changing; change because it pleases us to do so: only in exchange for the attraction of the *in-another-way* (from one to one's self, from one's self to others, and from others to one's self), eternally against the *tedious*.

For this reason it is necessary that we maintain *formal* reasoning. In regards to the fashionable Proteus and fashion for fashion's sake, the attraction is not that of the *content* of the style, but rather the *pure significance* of "being-in-style." We must not reject the fact that at the end of the fifteenth century the link between the human being and the Protean condition gained importance. Before the "serious" advent of what we call "modernity," in the transit that leads to it we can lucidly observe the possibility of *being Protean*, which, nonetheless, would not be explored *philosophically*. After the discomforting and skeptic sixteenth century, almost all of the efforts went to focus, in regards to the *image of the human being*, in the possibilities that *rationality* (especially scientific rationality) and *cogitative interiority* would bring. The breakaway from the past and the eagerness for the future became very serious. Presumably what we call "fashion"—projected in the sense of dressing—would not have a positive ending from the new history of *rigor*, *authenticity*, and *interiority*. In one of the memorable passages of his *Meditations*, Descartes (2008: 23) referred to the disturbing possibility that the hats and capes that we see on the streets could conceal specters or artificial men; men that we would otherwise judge true men according to their thoughts. The (exterior) body and the (questionable) appearances must be overcome. Therefore, who could care not just about the *clothes*, but also about their eclosion and their entertainment as *fashion*? The outfits become mere exteriority, gaining the contempt of *cogito* and reason, those of which demand interior truths (*In interiore homine habitat veritas*) of *intellective* and *jury* dominance of what's real. Time must go by in order for the outfits to become *sufficiently exterior* thanks to the style and so that it could free itself from the dialectic complex of the expression (expression of the interior *cogito*) and from what's useful/reasonable[4] and serviceable/social.

The humanist Pico had thought of humans as Protean beings, but at a profound and very morally committed level. They would symbolically link themselves, they would choose or they would be exposed to intense transformations; even if they were angelic or beastly (!), and profound. However, the fashionable Proteus that we've conceived is *epidermic*, he *surfs* through transformations and diversities, and becomes *liquid* (Zygmunt Bauman). Only then—in the now—will we be able to understand what fashion means.

With all certainty, philosophy's apparent contempt towards the subject of "fashion" is due to the *contingent* and *frivolous* variability of the contents that are implied by fashion, whatever the style may be. It seemed to appear that philosophy—while betraying its *will of concept* in a way—was more interested in the *styles* than in *fashion*, perhaps because they are easier to criticize while fashion presents a much more disturbing dimension. However, I have already indicated that what truly results as philosophically interesting are not the styles as expressions of a *hermeneutically relevant* variability, but rather all of the *strength* of fashion for fashion's sake, which reveals a radical way of *being in the world* and a way of guiding our experience. All the while styles exhibit the preferences of the fashionable Proteus (for they are provisional attempts of reducing the *complexity* and the excess of *euphoria* of the significants cf. Barthes 1984: 286–7): fashion exhibits his Self.

The burden of fashion when it comes to dressing resides in that it refers to the *external* aspect of the Proteus. Nevertheless, after considering everything, wouldn't it be easy to think that the metamorphosis be only *superficial*? Isn't it perfect that it be that way? Where fashion in dressing has its weakness is also where its strength emerges, as well as its success and its exemplary evidence, which is in many ways beneficial and therapeutic. The place granted by society to fashion in our culture, which is freed from demands and lacks sense (while it is also freed from being a *covering mask*), makes fashion in dressing not just a theoretic model, but the most popular and ostensible form of what we call "fashion," something which is able to easily introduce itself into the *reflexivity* of people and society. It is easy, extremely dynamic, comfortably recyclable, low cost, doesn't demand any reasons (it is one of the most joyfully despotic), and is favored by an accommodating contingency that is shareable and "socializing," and allows effective slips in the social fabric and in diverse circumstances.

Past beyond the Lipovetsky/Maffesoli controversy of the 1980s, it is clear that the fashionable Proteus is as pleased in Lipovetsky's "process of personalization" (Lipovetsky 1983: *passim*) as in Maffesoli's "relational person" (Maffesoli 1987; see also Maffesoli 1996). In any case, it is not in the horizon of the identity and of its strong demands (*pedestal*-identity, *bunker*-identity), where the fashionable Proteus would feel comfortable. And yet it is also not about the destruction or the masking of the identity. Fashion is not affected by the Cartesian inquietude regarding whether or not there would be *real* men and women under the hats and capes. It is the *play of appearances* that the hats and capes provides that constitutes fashion's strength and what concerns the fashionable Proteus. The Protean *Self* (cf. Lifton 1993) is relaxed, versatile, and swift, and it is not worried in disposing of a firm nor oppressive identity, but rather in being able to enjoy the pleasure of a *sympathizing* and *relational savoir-être*. Be it for better or for worse, fashion doesn't demand an interior, identical, authentic, real, and rational *cogito*, but rather a ductile, circumstantial, grouped *cogito* that is not against its body and its appearances, and not only with regards to itself, but also regarding what it can ask or expect from others. It doesn't ask for truth or reason, just for *enjoyment*, *playfulness*, and *participation*. Of course it also doesn't look for entanglements or hermeneutic wisdom, nor does it necessarily want to become held up in balancing the *consequences* of whichever style (there are so many "moral" and "aesthetic" arguments in this regard!), *innocently* yielding the criteria simply to "for one's pleasure" and to *acceptance* (adaptation). It is not necessary to assume any other necessity superior to the excitement of the "It's what's in right now!" or the "It's what everyone's wearing!"

After all, for the fashionable Proteus all of fashion's charm or *glamor* is concentrated in the purity of being-in-style. This is the only certainty: the care for and the eroticism of fashion. Everything else is secondary. And so to add: doesn't it take a certain merit to want to *live up to the times*, to *participate*, and to (want) to *be liked*, showing that we haven't "thrown in the towel" when it comes to our social identity? It is for this reason that in our growingly reflexive and formal postmodernist society, what's truly fashionable, more so than any style, is just the mere fact of being-in-style.

3. On multiple fashions (diachrony and synchrony)

The epochal advent of the *fashionable Proteus*—and not only its expansive possibilities in the fashion industry in a world of advanced capitalism; not even the *Homo democraticus*—has made a viable and spectacular synchrony of the diverse styles, which coexist favoring the experience of "fashion" as opposed to "the styles" without having to appeal to the passing of time. If it is true that fashion used to be

1 *what goes out of style*, now, still being such, it is also true that a style is also
2 *a choice* at the heart of *fashion*.

A new style doesn't just "appear" when another style fades away; instead different styles can coexist relatively and simultaneously. In the short run, even if the transformation is maintained "by seasons" that bring whatever is new, styles no longer simply *arrive*, rather they *coexist*, and they are chosen; something which requires much more *intervening* on the part of the user in order to *reduce their complexity* (Luhmann 1995).

There is no doubt that this is a great feat. Every day it becomes more difficult to accuse fashion of that *uniformity* that used to be (and can be) one of its main moral charges. This does not necessarily mean that it is not there—it must be—but rather that since there are many "tendencies" that share the same present, the possibility for monopolistic uniformity is deactivated. Old critiques are no longer so relevant in the sense that styles put bodies and souls at the same level in a sort of soft "totalitarianism." Thus—and this is what becomes decisive—neither is it necessary for the style to go out of style, nor that it be in absolute majority. In this sense, the gratifying diversification of its immense territory and, at the same time, its *complexity* and *freedom* when it comes down to choosing have never been greater. It was an indisputable success for Lipovetsky when he spoke in the 1980s of the postmodern subject as a narcissist and immersed in an *à la carte* consumption (cf. Lipovetsky 1983). It is always, once again, the *great fashion* of the fashionable Proteus which prevails over this becoming in the successiveness of time and the *synchronic* plurality. In exchange for the dispersion of participation or gravity centers, the *soft* cohesive force that fashion entails (Lipovetsky) is weakened. In any case, never would the space of fashion have been more plural, kaleidoscopic, or democratic. There is not another proper meta-story than that of the fashionable Proteus and the being-in-style capable of *indiscreetly* absorbing the styles in favor of fashion in itself. The extreme pluralism is combined with the acceleration in the changes that *fast fashion* causes. The fact that everyone believes that they are or can be fashionable is the key to the paradise for production and consumerism. Proteus effusively waves to Narcissus and to democracy, trying to "keep Procusto in line."

4. Fashion show (*haute couture*) and street fashion

We can find this fashionable Proteus in many types of expressions, of which we must highlight two prototypical *settings:* in that of the common, shared, popular, democratic, and day-to-day space of the street, through the expression of *street fashion,* which is massively connected to the *prêt-à-porter* (ready-to-wear) and energized by *fast fashion;* and also in the ultra-exclusive *fashion show* of the *haute couture* which is brimming with creativity, aesthetic exoticism, eccentricity, and luxury.

Indeed: two possibilities or modalities of the *phenomenologization* of the clothing-fashion permanently remind us of the infinity-of-fashion: the fashion show of the *haute couture* and the street fashion under the aegis of the fast fashion. The first supposes a certain culmination of fashion's own madness as an "abstract," absolute, and mesmerizing eclosion of *nonsense.* Momentarily freed from the world, taking shelter in its bubble of immanency, fashion which has still not reached the street, nor commerce, nor the user, and which has still not let itself be participating in the *daily life* nor be persecuted by the diverse constraints, is more

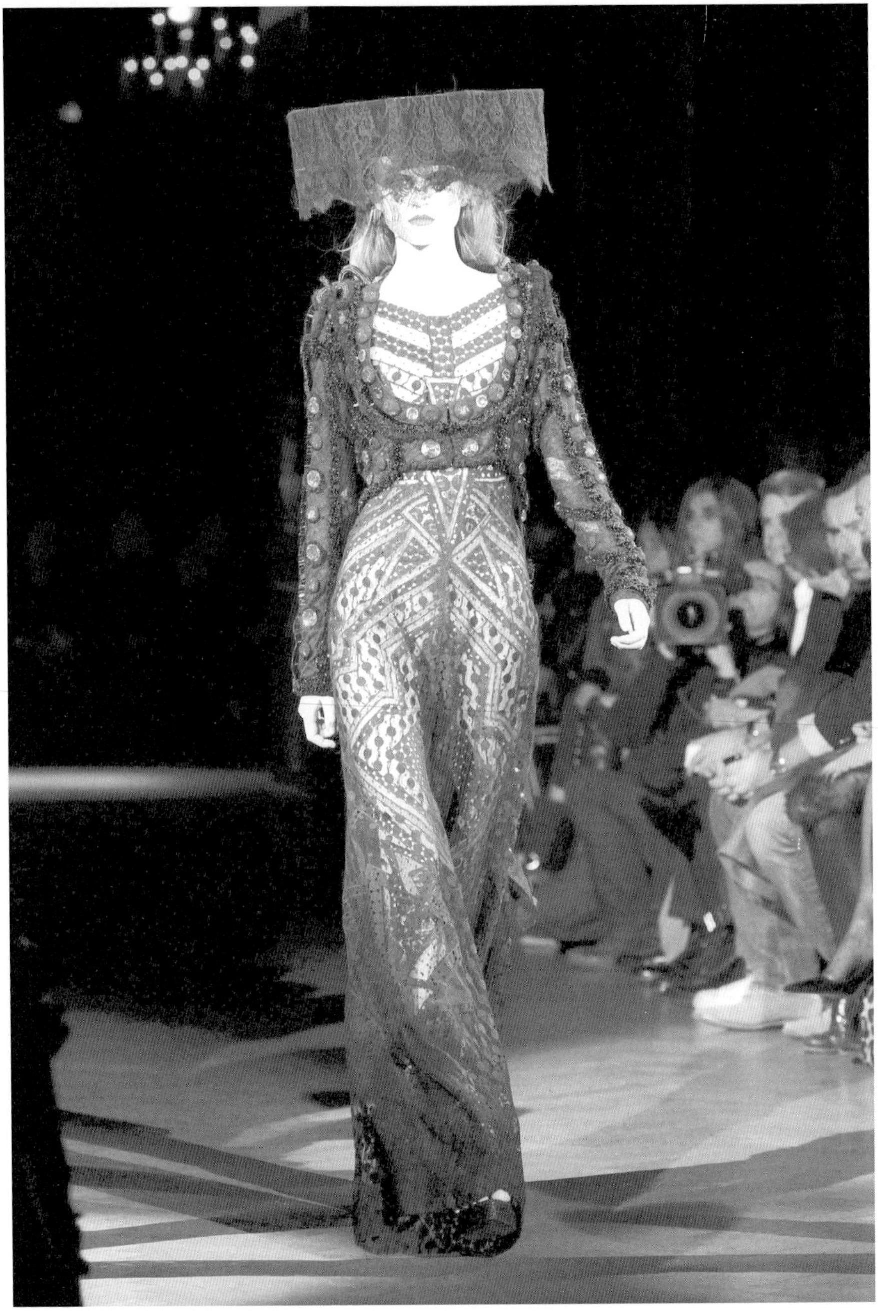

FIGURE 8.1 Paris Fashion Week Haute Couture S/S 2010—Givenchy.

free and sovereign than any other fashion up close to the "standard" of users will ever be. It is not dependent of possible *interchanges* that will expose or alienate it inasmuch as being exposed to be sold or used, needing only to throw itself into a crazy exuberance of its infinite variations, luxuries, and excessive forms, of a *sexless* and *limitless* eroticism, without waiting for the endorsement of any majority, perhaps being able to aspire to indirectly create *tendency*. It is the moment that fashion reserves itself to become truth as unreality, as excessive expenditure or rigorous luxury. A true stimulus and ideal inspiration, paroxysmal and hypercreativity of desire. It is difficult to imagine the fashionable Proteus being happier, more sophisticated, and more creative than in this area of pure design, without ever even demanding to be like others or to form a group. Rather, it has to do with the privilege of the "exclusive." In this aspect, for the *haute couture* what we normally understand as fashion is a cruel rival, reduced to consumerism, commerce, and the majority. And nevertheless, the moment of *haute couture* indulges fashion because it reminds it of the power of *pure clothing* from which fashion, in all truth, is sustained and which it betrays constantly. Jean Baudrillard has expressed this perfectly, citing *Vogue*:

> Couturiers are the last adventurers of the modern world. They cultivate the *acte gratuit*. "Why *haute couture?*" a few detractors may think. "Why champagne?" Again: "Neither practice nor logic can justify the extravagant adventure of clothes. Superfluous and therefore necessary, the world is once more the province of religion." Potlatch, religion, indeed the ritual enchantment of expression, like that of costume and animal dances: everything is good for exalting fashion against the economic, like a transgression into a play-act sociality.
>
> **BAUDRILLARD** 1993: 94

Much more differently than the eminently contemplative space of the fashion show of the *haute couture* is the participative, day-to-day space, indeterminately fluctuating between artifice and spontaneity, of the street fashion or of the street style, which accomplishes at a street level, the dream of non-exclusiveness (Proteus as an individualized, eccentric narcissist), but rather of the participation and democracy of dressing. A perfect complement to the stimulating and creative eccentricity of the runway. All the while the "fashion" of the fashion show of high couture ousts all except a very limited minority, all have access to the street fashion (Rifkin 2000): an *open bar* for being-in-style. With an extraordinary diversity, it offers users thousands of examples so that when they imitate them they may feel they are in-style. Its best alliance is with the fast fashion, a recent discovery in the world of design, production, and distribution of fashion which looks for consumption parting from the latest tendencies, being able to renew itself at a greater speed than the seasons allow.

The fashionable Proteus is as happy with the fashion show of the *haute couture* as he is with the street fashion, in which in exchange for less sophistication, but thanks to a great number of combinations, the spectacle is immense. After all, what better public space than the street for the *spread* of fashion? (Calefato 2002: 178) It's enough to look and think: "I like that outfit," "it goes great with everything," "that person has a good taste" . . . so that it may be incorporated into the desire to be-in-style (in this regard, see Girard 1966).

This all goes to make the Proteus try out *what may-be-an-outfit* and the power of human transformation. In between these spaces nothing would have tested better than, even if this idea doesn't seem intuitive as we previously said, *nudity* which welcomes everything, without putting any limits: nudity without meaning, as a possible maximum bearer. From it emerges not only dressing in accord to the necessity of the existing (protection, modesty, sociability, etc.), but also the luxury of an excessive diversity. A naked body that is not due to indigence or helplessness, but rather the contrary: empty and, at the same time, full, shared by the *inter-visibility*, a body of each and every one, in every case mine and everyone else's.

Such is the glorious *depthless surface* of fashion and, in spite of the possible doubts with Cartesian resonances, incredible *appearance* and *transparency* of the styles. *There is nothing to hide.* The *no-meaning* frees the appearances without barely any restrictions, and turns them innocent in just the right measure so that they will satisfy fashion, only fashion, for being fashion.

5. Just now. Living up to the times

Even though the synchrony in the plurality of the fashions has advanced much in the last few years as a legitimate, explicit, and desirable possibility in many ways, it is still impossible to conceive fashion without taking into account its singular style of *temporality*. In the future of "what's to come" the style will necessarily become a fleeting *present* (for use and enjoyment), with its own *letting-go*. In contrast to production, which has a projective and planning component, use opens only pseudo-projectively, for it must do so with a great dose of *waiting*, *interrogation*, and even *patience*.

Lived much more intensely and rapidly than any other fashion, fashion in clothing supposes an *expectation turned to a future* where we know what is to come, but with an *undetermined* content of which the designers have a few key points that the majority is unaware of. "The new" doesn't depend so much on the content, but on the own temporal qualification of the what's-to-come, where even the "retro" can be new (Girard 1966: 186). The novelty is *always* marked by the *sense* of "living-up-to-the-times." In no other expression of fashion will it be better captured as a *transit* as it happens with the fashion of dressing, is accomplished season after season, faster each time thanks to the fast fashion, with which the experience of "obsolescence" and of the *demodé* are fueled. Over a decade ago Marinetti's futuristic race car surpassed Baudelaire's melancholic "passerby-clouds"

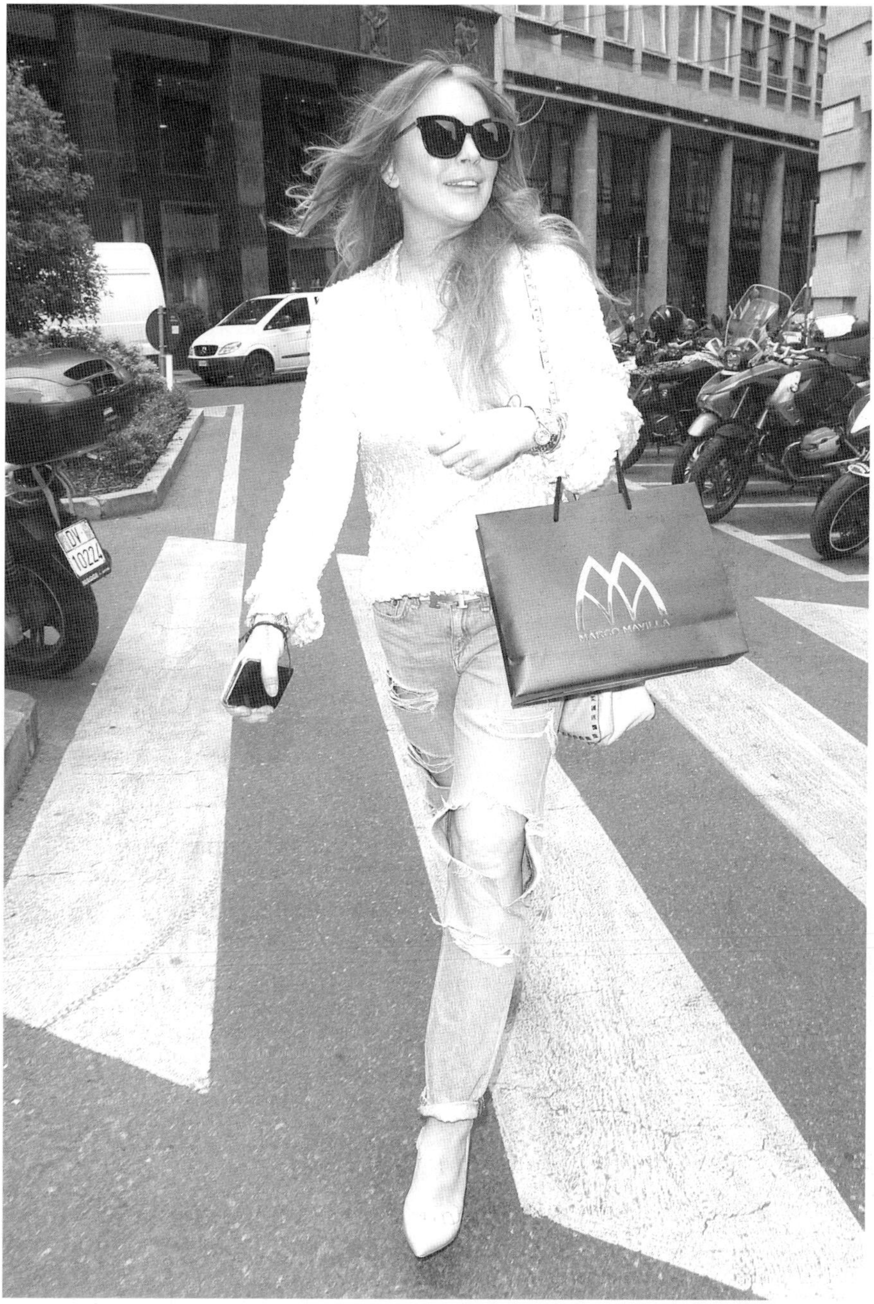

FIGURE 8.2 Lindsay Lohan shopping in Milan.

in this experience of transit, which in regards to our topic is not the passing of time, but rather the passing of fashion. The new season will make us think that the time for change has come, the propitious moment for *change of clothing*. And yet, paradoxically, when it comes to dressing fashion is not in truth "progressive" in a strict sense. It has to do with always wearing-the-latest, but this wearing-the-latest only *varies* and *diversifies,* it doesn't properly advance towards anything.

So incomparably more intense is the experience of *welcoming the future* (the next season) than the experience of *letting-go*, that being in style can be considered by users as a sort of *anti-aging* therapy. The fashionable Proteus is pleased in believing: "I am not separate from my *contemporaries* and neither do I want to be," "I am modern," "I like my moment." Being in style composes the expressive aspect of a certain *reconciliation with the present* and the happiness of the *just-now moment*. I am "modernized." Youth and fashion go hand in hand, to the point where only one who truly feels young, or wants to pretend feeling young, goes in style. The fleetingness of fashion, which is *realized by destroying itself* (Fabbri 1987: 22), is festive and vitalist. When all is said and done, fashion will always result victorious, indifferent to its own expressions, allowing us to barter enthusiasm and expectation for neglect and *jovial* forgetfulness. The horrible image of Cronos devouring his babies isn't an adequate one. Next to a lesser and condescending Angel of History (González García 2010), incapable of drama and of tearing things apart, fashion requires an Angel of Victory that will accredit the triumph of the fashion that's to come. The experience of *expiration* with regard to fashion, as well as the connection between death and fashion (Leopardi 1981: 39; Benjamin 2002), are phenomenologically secondary. Only from melancholy or deception could we imagine fashion as a *memento mori*, for in contrast to other goods and luxuries of this world, it, fashion, simply does not aspire to any type of survival.

What is decisive in the future of "the next season" is that, being purely formal, it is *never ending*, always being alive. There is no *end* to be reached, only transits to be *curious-and-enjoy* about. To the extent that it satisfies a quick time, fashion is an *accelerator* (Marquard 1991), a low intensity *superconductor* for the narcissist and Protean life in its wish to "live up to the times" in the wave of the thought: "We are the contemporaries!"

6. The fashionable Proteus as an imitating Narcissus. A sense of community

Fashion is an *anti-aging* therapy, surely, but also an *anti-loneliness* device. It is not solely about the protagonist of fashion feeling accompanied when it comes to deciding/following-someone/something (Simmel 1971: 295–7), but also that the being-in-style becomes a triumphant, or at least "correct," *participation* to the extent that being fashionable resembles "having your team score a victory." It may even be that one is by herself, but if one *believes* that she is in-style, simply with this belief she will form part of a more or less major community. One "joins the winning side."

The consciousness of participation is based, especially in the case of fashion, in a powerful dynamic of *imitation* as well as *contagiousness* where Lipovetsky, based on Tarde, has known how to oppose *tradition as a link*, conceding imitation-in-fashion the power of opening the future (Lipovetsky 1994: 226–7; on this, see also Simmel 1971: particularly 295 *et seq.*). Imitation on the horizon, of course, of an *inter-visibility* in the case of fashion in dressing, be it *inter pares* (street fashion) or, for example, following the diverse figurations of what we could consider as the *major* or *model mutant* (in many cases representing some sector of the *star-system*), that serves as a guide to be imitated. In this way, moving in communities/inter-visibilities the versatile and fickle image of the fashionable Proteus becomes kaleidoscopic, creating influence zones, "lumps" of *visibility-and-influence* at the heart of the immense social everything.

The fashionable Proteus is an *imitating Narcissus* who is enormously pleased by participating in a community that allows an efficient play of reflections in order to make possible a mutant-shared narcissism which, on top of everything, generates powerful currents of attraction and seduction in which the *visual routines* ultimately benefit the fashions that are at first more uncommon or worthy of rejection. Fashion demands a narcissist Proteus, but one that is sufficiently socialized, willing to join "frequencies" of *soft unanimity* that allow for a sense of community at the same time that, due to their "superficiality," can let free or not compromise other more relevant and "responsible" dimensions of the person.

Simmel perfectly recognized the great double tie that fashion maintains: on the one hand, *with the community*, and on the other, *with each individual* (Simmel 1971: *passim*). In this way, it perfectly satisfies the spaces that must be reserved for the community, while at the same time it provides the individual with the opportunity for personal interpretations *sui generis* and for deviations from the norm. I previously indicated that the underground dispute between Lipovetsky and Maffesoli must not be sharply resolved. Neither can Lipovetsky whisk away the social and communitarian-*Dionysian* deed of being in style (in fact he becomes obligated to speak strongly of *imitation* . . .), nor can Maffesoli overlook Lipovetsky's analysis concerning individualism and the process of personalization. The fashionable Proteus combines both perspectives. Neither does it have a firm identity in which to jam in its narcissism (it is not a "strong" individual), nor could the imitation block the variability that is introduced in its desire to "personalize" or "modify" itself. What becomes decisive is the exchange. However being in style is not done by simply imitating (we have the *minimal marginal difference* where each user is allowed to add something), but rather by participating, precisely in the measure that the fashionable Proteus also keeps an important caveat for his *distinguishing* narcissism.

Proteus doesn't agree to be one-single-identity-for-his-self. If it transforms in itself, its *Self* is strangely more than just one—this individual—a *changing multitude*: many and diverse. One may certainly change his own, but in all truth, Proteus is a *multitude in transformations*. The *eidos* of fashion is accessed not by the alterations made by one's self, but rather by the *coexisting variations* of many diversities.[5] And in the case of the fashionable Proteus it is manifested as an inter-appearance that proliferates by its lack of meaning and "aesthetic" empathy. Narcissus gives credit to the *ars combinatoria* not only as a reference for production, but also on the level of use-and-enjoyment. If the designer is a specialist in difference (Erner 2004), so are the users who are *connoisseurs*. Narcissus requires the smallest singularizing (these shoes, that belt, this haircut . . .) or marginalizing differences which, in their most positive aspect, suppose that the protagonist has a more or less level of *esprit de finesse* and of *reflexive* knowledge of fashion and of his own personality-style . . . in many cases, a real resourcefulness for creativity, in the horizon of possibilities for *personalization*.

7. Once again fashion for fashion's sake. The fashion-power

The fashionable Proteus plays with, practices, and follows fashion only for fashion's sake, without expecting anything in return, only the enjoyment of fashion in itself. Many other criteria will be left aside: aesthetic, moral, pragmatic, social, etc., not allowing for a misunderstanding between the passion for fashion with anything that is not fashion itself. Who cares who was "under the cape and hat" that so troubled Descartes? No: fashion functions *as fashion* . . . and it may be accompanied by a psychic truth, a moral qualification, but that doesn't necessarily have to be so. In fact, *fashion-power* is shown in that it makes everything that is not necessary to-be-in-style contingent: paradoxically, it encourages submission and, at the same time, it encourages play and infidelity, making its users docile and ductile.

1. In the peripheries (relating, unstable, and moving) of the phenomenon of "fashion" when its protagonist is the fashionable Proteus, we find its most extreme expressions, and therefore most unusual, somewhat exotic, minorities, etc., that nonetheless encase a high level of exemplariness, allowing us to capture the truth of fashion in its most radical level, not just a discolored, devaluated truth (as, for example the truth of the "human being" that could be offered just by our "neighbor"). Let us think, for example, of the *fashion victim*.[6] It seems that the greatest comprehension of fashion *on its own* is presented to whoever was a perfect victim of its despotism, reaching almost the status of a "martyr" or descending to become, depending on the case and the scale of values, an "idiot" or a "sick person." However, the history of fashion is made clear and distinct especially (although not

only, of course) in the altar of the sacrifices that it demands and in the victims that it produces. Let us think of the wigs of the eighteenth century, of the corsets of the nineteenth century, of the high heel shoes of the twentieth century ... Leopardi (1981) and Simmel (1971),[7] amongst others, referred to the sacrifices that fashion demands. The victim easily demonstrates fashion's enormous force of imposition, which makes whatever reasons that are not fashion on its own turn superfluous. If this could please Proteus, it would be because he could feel to be the protagonist and see himself expressed in the *neither/nor* of fashion as such: neither beautiful nor ugly, neither comfortable nor uncomfortable, neither provocative nor demure, neither ... nor ... It is simply own of its own: fashion, and it is the transforming-for-it or in its honor what prevails. It is, in a certain way, a modality of radical *expending* (Bataille)—of money, of excitement, of energy—*at all costs.* In this sense, the fashionable Proteus can display, at least from a certain point of view, a negatively sick or sinister image. The fashion victim is proof of the *a fortiori* of the fashion-power.

2. The case of underwear is especially illustrative in comprehending that the fashion phenomenon is in no doubt a "social" phenomenon and of majority (in different levels) where our *visible* aspect is elucidated, but which, nevertheless, does not require the *effective* public look, but rather mostly an experience of participation in which what becomes decisive is an *introjected virtual other. Fashion-power*'s look (Sartre) collaborates in the *panoptism*. If well it may be true that in order to become infected or to reproduce, fashion requires an *effective inter-visibility*, however, in its minimal refuge it must be able to occur in intimacy. In this sense, the infiltration of the social meaning of fashion contributes in simulating communication (Baudrillard 1993: 94). I feel as one with my contemporaries in the vanguard of the soft avant-garde fashion.

3. We are on a path towards the *euphoria* of the multitude of signifiers for minimal meanings. Ripped jeans or creepers are good examples of styles that many seem to dislike. What is interesting or what they make us think about is not whether we like them or not, but its light-hearted reason of being more than its *sufficient reason*, which is eclipsed or stripped of its relevance.

In regards to clogs, in another exemplary order—I have chosen a random example—an advertising text from a few years ago (the Spanish printed edition of *Marie Claire*, from April 2010) explains that they had a rural origin, in an attempt to isolate the foot from the floors filled with hay and from wet terrains. It is usually associated to the Netherlands, but they first appeared in China. In the 1960s they came to be part of hippie clothing. The Swedish clogs became famous with the arrival of the obsession for anatomic shoes. In the 1990s, they reappeared with the grunge movement ... until they were eventually recovered by Lagerfeld/Chanel. A *philosophical* understanding of fashion consists of going against the current of the pretension in trying to find reasons. They may be there, but they could not qualify fashion *as fashion*, i.e., in its very essence: they could explain it (why such style), but they could not deny that *in extremis*, like the rose of Angelus Silesius, fashion . . . "flourishes just because it does so."

8. Euphoria and the excess of the significant

Towards the end of *The Fashion System*, Roland Barthes states that:

> Compared with *A* ensembles, which are open and alienated, *B* ensembles appear partially pure; they do not in fact experience the "reifying" nomination of the signified [. . .]; they become alienated from the world only by the rhetoric of clothing [. . .] and by the rhetoric of signification [. . .]. In other words, *B* ensembles do not "lie": in them the garment signifies Fashion openly. This purity—or frankness—stems from two conditions. The first is constituted by the extreme disproportion which the denotation of Fashion introduces between the number of its signifiers and that of its signifieds: in *B* ensembles, the signified is positively singular: it is always and everywhere Fashion; the signifiers are quite numerous, they include all variations of the garment, the plethora of Fashion features; here we recognize the economy of an infinite metaphor, which freely varies the signifiers of one and the same signified. Naturally, it is not a matter of indifference that the disproportion be established to the advantage of the signifier: any system which consists of a large number of signifieds for a restricted number of signifiers generates anxiety, since each sign can be read in several ways; on the contrary, any inverse system (with a large number of signifiers and a reduced number of signifieds) is a system which makes for euphoria; and the more a disproportion of this type is accentuated, the more the euphoria is reinforced.
>
> **BARTHES** 1984: 286–7

It is in the fashion of dressing, in what Baudrillard calls *slight signs* where the liberation of the significants and the precariousness of meaning is more scandalous and radical: "The acceleration of the simple play of signifiers in fashion becomes striking, to the point of enchanting us—the enchantment and vertigo of the loss of every system of reference" (Baudrillard 1993: 87).

Fashion turns into *euphoric* experience to the extent in which it seems to break away from whatever meanings may be assigned to it and so far as it, fashion, is always *more* than this, that or the other fashion, but not in a merely *Platonic* sense (as it seemed to be implied at the beginning), rather because, from a more *deconstructive* perspective, "fashion" is a signifier ("it's in style"; "it's fashionable") with a meaning that returns to the signifier itself, and it doesn't really have a true meaning except that it is "fashionable" and that means that "it's in," "it's become common," "it sells well," "it's frequently seen," "it doesn't make much sense but it's fashionable." The signifier is very powerful, efficient, and autoreferential, in direct proportion to the shortage of meanings. It seems necessary that fashion inasmuch as fashion tends to devaluate the meanings, to the extent in which these may *conceal*—as if they were rebelling against their pure formalism—the meaning of fashion on its own (its *emptiness* and its *plethora*) and may distract it from itself, give it meaning and experience . . . which are no longer fashion! But it is true: the excess of the signifier and the penury of meaning *liberate* fashion (cf., in general, Erner 2004: part I): there is nothing to interpret (despite the effort that is often made to extract the "gold" from a meaning); and in this sense, it does not cause distress, according to Barthes. And yet, perhaps we should deny Barthes in the sense that, when exacerbated, euphoria leads to anguish when faced with the growingly relevant question: "what should I wear?" Before, this question would not have made as much sense, back when the synchronic pluralism of the styles was not as intense. Fashion had already previously decided about "what I should wear" (Heidegger 1996: 118–20). However, it is precisely the *synchrony* that has contributed the user's *exigency when deciding*, and the postmodern Narcissus is no longer easily satisfied with prefabricated answers. Thus it is not about the *distress* of the meaning, but rather about the urgency, the pressure, the anxiety to *resolve complexity*.

This doesn't mean that the outfits that fashion is responsible for—and indirectly fashion itself—cannot be understood from its multiple expressiveness. In any case, however, fashion for fashion's sake can only be understood in depth, and not without risks, when it lacks necessity or tends to distance itself from the *principle of sufficient reason*. For fashion, Jean-Luc Marion's *principle of sufficient intuition* (Marion 2002: §§ 19–20) is valid: to take everything that is given, which radicalizes the Husserlian phenomenological *principle of all principles* (Husserl 1982: § 24), only that Marion denies the previous horizon. This is why euphoria and saturation occur together.

This going beyond the pressures of the sufficient reason and of the psychic expressionism, is one of the decisive methods in fashion's rebellion against the modernity that witnessed its birth and philosophically depreciated it.

Only this sort of *arbitrariness* makes fashion be fashion. It is not about an affirmation of the *absurd*, but rather about a going beyond the *pragmatics* and *reasonability* of the meaning. In this respect, even if it is inserted into the daily world-life, fashion is, in its own way, outside of its usual coordinates of meaning so that it may provide daily-life with a *crazy touch*. The fashionable garments leave their *brief reality as outfits* to obtain their *crazy truth* outside of the meaning and the genesis, as pure fashion.

These "minor" metamorphoses that fashions go through are what make the fashionable Proteus *modestly* happy. For example, ripped jeans (to which I already alluded to before) would lose their relevance as fashion from the moment where they became dependent on not having money to buy a new pair of jeans or because they had tore! *Out-reasons*! It is not about fashion garnishing the absurd through the non-significance, but about the fact that thanks to the absurd—from the indirectly reasonable to the (apparently) absurd—fashion shines and its autonomy is strengthened. As in every truly absolute power, it is the *arbitrariness* that is dominant, not the generosity or the demand to *give-reasons*. As in every true power—I will warn at this point—it will prefer *followers* that submit themselves without asking "Why?" It is no wonder that fashion lives its moment of greatest splendor in the moment when we feel that we are leaving modernity behind. It will not even conform to a hedonist or pragmatic reason, nor to a moral or aesthetic reason either! Baudrillard clearly stated:

> It epitomizes everything that the regime of economic abstraction censures. It inverts every categorical imperative. In this sense, it is spontaneously contagious, whereas economic calculation isolates people from one another. Disinvesting signs of all value, it becomes passion again—passion for the artificial. It is the utter absurdity, the formal futility of the sign of fashion, the perfection of a system where nothing is any longer exchanged against the real, it is the arbitrariness of this sign at the same time as its absolute coherence, constrained to a total relativity with other signs, that makes for its contagious virulence and, at the same time, its collective enjoyment. Beyond the rational and the irrational, beyond the beautiful and the ugly, the useful and the useless, it is this immorality in relation to all criteria, the frivolity which at times gives fashion its subversive force [. . .], which always, in contradiction to the economic, makes it a *total social fact*—for which reason we are obliged to revive, as Mauss did for exchange, a total approach.
>
> **BAUDRILLARD** 1993: 93–4

9. On-fashion, off-fashion

Since Pico thought up Proteus until now, in the postmodern refiguration of the fashionable Proteus, there is no doubt that Proteus, with its real and symbolic transformations, has completely infiltrated into the reality and the imaginariness of contemporary culture. The philosophy of existence and existentialism strongly contributed to the criticism of an ontified, static, and closed human nature. It was the golden age for the anthropological concept of *aperture* and for the discussion of human nature. Proteus could have "sponsored" the existential revolution of the twentieth century. Afterwards, more specifically in the second half of the twentieth and the first decade of the twenty-first century, he has been able to keep "sponsoring," beyond the effervescences of May 1968, the new style in the transformation of the contemporary man. In recent times, the new *postmodern Proteus* has found multiple opportunities to look for his own space in an *age of shallowness* in which, in a paradoxical combination, everything has become worthy of enthusiasm and disappointing at the same time (I am thinking of Lipovetsky and his *society of disappointment* or—far from Lipovetsky's ideas—in Claudio Magris (1984) and his harsh criticism of *new innocence*).

I do not believe that it is our task either to reprobate nor to praise the *soft* and superficial culture of merely being-in-style . . . Umberto Eco's essay *Apocalittici e integrati* (1964) has not lost validity. Fashion offers a valuable expressive and symptomatologic material that is not only used for the analysis of the present, but also for the comprehension of our *being in the world* and *being with others*. As it has been abundantly demonstrated, especially by Lipovetsky, fashion is embedded in the most intimate part of our contemporariness, and it is precisely this circumstance that provides the phenomenon of fashion with all of its fascination and its (indirect) restlessness. More specifically, due to the advantages that advanced capitalism provides, fashion in clothing responds with pressure and anxiety to a culture that gives prestige to the exterior/superficial (where the idea of "What you get is what you see ain't nothing more to it" is dominant—except that by now it barely has any replicating criticism) and to change for the sake of it, and can therefore negatively affect the introjection of the model of change that is implied in being-in-style. Proteus risks losing its best and most profound metamorphic possibilities completely. And it would not be a bad thing for it to be this way, many would think, since leading the metamorphism to the most extreme truth would be resultingly disturbing. In such a sense, fashion is a consolation. If the ability to be *exemplary* is reserved for the function, which would correspond to fashion, in order to remember the desire to *show*, *participate*, *seduce*, and *change*, fashion would exceedingly carry out this, as it were, symbolic function and that sort of small release valve that it represents, connected to a certain possibility of dynamism and health.

Nevertheless, for the Proteus the risk resides in—in this and other cultural vectors—in losing "orientation" and assuming without complexes and with nonchalance the non-sense also *outside of fashion's play-area*. It does not have to do with going into the dialectology between the *alignment of fashion* and the *fashion of alignment*, which looks to quickly criticize fashion (fashion as alignment) in the name of authenticity, autonomy, freedom, etc.—being then the critique towards the alleged alignment what actually becomes fashion (cf. König 1985: chap. 30). The problem arises when we indiscriminately and expansively transfer the model "fashion" to everything. I do not believe it to be necessary for us to assume the *new innocence* that Magris criticizes. It is not just about not needing a Descartes that would ask himself about the subjects behind the hats and capes, but rather—and this is what seems more worrisome—that *general meaning* would not be necessary, with everything that it would imply. This is a real danger, to the extent in which fashion depends, as we have already seen, on the non-sense and on its comprehensive, reiterative, joyful, and fun fruition, from season to season. If well it may be that fashion, when bound to its mere reality means a set of possibilities that are generally "nice," if it happened to turn exemplary, paradigmatic … its niceness could become threatening.

For this reason, I believe it is necessary to preserve fashion in its own space, preventing it from becoming idolized and occupying an excessive symbolic space. Even if it were true that fashion is no longer a simply sectorial phenomenon, but that instead penetrates all of postmodernist culture, being fashion in clothing to a good extent the imaginary launching point of that profound penetration, though nonetheless, it is necessary to keep thinking of the possibilities of the *off-fashion* or of a healthy, therapeutic, and liberating indifference.

In accordance with a certain scale of values for our most venerable Western traditions, fashion tends to be associated with a certain "immaturity" of its users (especially the most enthusiastic). We will not go into defending this perspective, which conceals an important prejudice. There is a lucid immaturity (I refer here to certain theses of W. Gombrowicz) and a toxic immaturity, that lets itself be detected in the discomfort of the *devaluation of the experience* of being-in-time and being-with-others that fashion, precisely in its possibility for absolutism, immaturity, and ridicule, can cause, becoming thus its only ludic—and lucid—possibility in a tragicomic assessment.

In the same way that there is a technological *rationality* that is based in *operational efficiency*, there would also be room to talk about a rationality of fashion in which the *elision of meaning* and the experience of *superficiality* becomes an essential key of the *fashion-power* and of the *fashion-machine*. The fashionable Proteus is part of the Protean condition of the existing human being, but there is no doubt that he is susceptible to being programmed, stimulated, and incentivized. The purpose of *building subjects behaviorally* ideal for fashion for fashion's sake does not seem tranquilizing, something that could only be avoided if the Proteus was *also* thought up of and enhanced from the possibility of a strategic disconnection from *off-fashion*, in which the potential criticism of the *life-world* would be indispensable.

To this regard, it would be interesting to create a succinct, but essential, history of the *disappointment of fashion*, in which we would have to give the floor to those who had been its most enthusiastic adepts, where they were let down by the excitement that fashion had one day seemed to promise them. We would have to ask these other fashion victims, more so than merely asking theorists. These fashion victims are much more interesting than the remains that the passing fashions leave in their wake. Otherwise, it is still curious that we are living a profound crisis in the *truth of democracy* (Nancy 2010) and the eclosion of a *consummate fashion* at the same time. Perhaps it may be the case of two phenomena that are independent or, more probably, that have an intimate connection that would be worth exploring.

Notes

1 "A fashion that doesn't prosper and is not effective, is not a fashion" (Fabbri 1987: 21).

2 "Fashion does nothing but segregate, and creates nudity as a *supersign* of the outfit" (Baudrillard 1976: chap. 3, § 4). This text cannot be found in the English edition (cf. Baudrillard 1993: 95).

3 In regards to this point we could think of the models' exhibition of nudity on the runway which concludes with the Robert Altman film *Prêt-à-porter* (1994). Once we have passed the point of nudity, we can expect everything else that's to come. In this regard, cf. Moreno 2007.

4 "In our culture, tethered as it is to the principle of utility, futility plays the role of transgression and violence, and fashion is condemned for having within it the force of the pure sign which signifies nothing. Its sexual provocation is secondary with regard to this principle which denies the grounds of our culture" (Baudrillard 1993: 95).

5 Which would lead us to Husserl. I will leave the reference for those readers who are interested, since it is impossible for me to thoroughly develop here this idea. Cf. Husserl 1973: §§ 86–93. See Moreno 2012.

6 In general, Erner 2004 is a very profitable reading.

7 "Fashion is merely a product of social demands, even though the individual object which it creates or recreates may represent a more or less individual need. This is clearly proved by the fact that very frequently not the slightest reason can be found for the creations of fashion from the standpoint of an objective, aesthetic, or other expediency. While in general our wearing apparel is really adapted to our needs, there is not a trace of expediency in the method by which fashion dictates, for example, whether wide or narrow trousers, colored or black scarfs shall be worn. As a rule the material justification for an action coincides with its general adoption, but in the case of fashion there is a complete separation of the two elements, and there remains for the individual only this general acceptance as the deciding motive to appropriate it. Judging from the ugly and repugnant things that are sometimes in vogue, it would seem as though fashion were desirous of exhibiting its power by getting us to adopt the most atrocious things for its sake alone. The absolute indifference of fashion to the material standards of life is well illustrated by the way in which it recommends something appropriate in one instance, something abstruse in another, and something materially and aesthetically quite indifferent in a third. The only motivations with which fashion is concerned are formal social ones" (Simmel 1971: 297–8).

Bibliography

Barthes, R. (1984), *The Fashion System* (1967), trans. M. Ward and R. Howard, New York: Hill and Wang

Baudrillard, J. (1976), *L'échange symbolique et la mort*, Paris: Gallimard

Baudrillard, J. (1993), *Symbolic Exchange and Death*, trans. I. Hamilton Grant, London-Thousand Oaks-New Delhi: Sage Publications
Benjamin, W. (2002), *The Arcades Project* (1927–40), trans. H. Eiland and K. McLaughlin, Cambridge (MA)-London: Harvard University Press
Calefato, P. (2002), *El sentido del vestir*, Valencia: Engloba
Descartes, R. (2008), *Meditations on First Philosophy with Selections from the Objections and Replies* (1641), Oxford: Oxford University Press
Eco, U. (1964), *Apocalittici e integrati. Comunicazioni di massa e teorie della cultura di massa*, Milano: Bompiani
Erner, G. (2004), *Victimes de la mode? Comment on la crée, pourquoi on la suit*, Paris: Éditions La Découverte
Fabbri, P. (1987), "El engreimiento y el disgusto como fenómeno social y estético", in *Moda y diseño, un desafío cultural: reflexiones sobre el fenómeno de la moda desde la perspectiva de las ciencias sociales, la filosofía y el arte*, ed. by Centro de Promoción de Diseño y Moda, 21–49, Madrid: Centro de Promoción de Diseño y Moda
Geertz, C. (1973), *The Interpretation of Cultures: Selected Essays*, New York: Basic Books
Gergen, K.J. (1991), *The Saturated Self: Dilemmas of Identity in Contemporary Life*, New York: Basic Books-Harper Collins
Girard, R. (1966), *Deceit, Desire and the Novel: Self and Other in Literary Structure*, Baltimore: Johns Hopkins University Press
González García, J.M. (2010): "Walter Benjamin: Ángel de la Victoria y Ángel de la Historia", in J. Beriain and I. Sánchez de la Yncera (eds), *Sagrado/Profano. Nuevos desafíos al proyecto de la modernidad*, 41–64, Madrid: Centro de Investigaciones Sociológicas (CIS). Available online: http://digital.csic.es/bitstream/10261/65424/1/Walter_Benjamin_Academia29.pdf (accessed October 21, 2014)
Heidegger, M. (1996), *Being and Time* (1927), trans. J. Stambaugh, Albany: SUNY Press
Husserl, E. (1973), *Experience and Judgment: Investigations in a Genealogy of Logic* (1939), trans. J.S. Churchill and K. Ameriks, London: Routledge
Husserl, E. (1982), *Ideas Pertaining to a Pure Phenomenology and to a Phenomenological Philosophy. First Book: General Introduction to a Pure Phenomenology* (1913), trans. F. Kersten, Dordrecht: Springer
König, R. (1985), *Menschheit auf dem Laufsteg. Die Mode im Zivilisationsprozeß*, München-Wien: Carl Hanser Verlag
Leopardi, G. (1981), "Dialogo della Moda e della Morte" (1824), in M. Fubini (ed.), *Operette morali, seguite da una scelta dei "Pensieri"*, Torino: Loescher
Lifton, R.J. (1993), *The Protean Self: Human Resilience in an Age of Fragmentation*, New York: Basic Books
Lipovetsky, G. (1983), *L'ère du vide: essais sur l'individualisme contemporain*, Paris: Gallimard
Lipovetsky, G. (1994), *The Empire of Fashion: Dressing Modern Democracy* (1987), trans. C. Porter, Princeton (NJ): Princeton University Press
Luhmann, N. (1995), *Social Systems*, trans. J. Bednarz and D. Baecker, Stanford: Stanford University Press
Maffesoli, M. (1987), "Los juegos de máscaras: moda y tribus en la post-modernidad", in *Moda y diseño, un desafío cultural: reflexiones sobre el fenómeno de la moda desde la perspectiva de las ciencias sociales, la filosofía y el arte*, ed. by Centro de Promoción de Diseño y Moda, 91–114, Madrid: Centro de Promoción de Diseño y Moda
Maffesoli, M. (1996), *The Time of the Tribes: The Decline of Individualism in Mass Society*, London-Thousand Oaks: Sage Publications

Magris, C. (1984), *L'anello di Clarisse. Grande stile e nichilismo nella letteratura moderna*, Torino: Einaudi

Marion, J.-L. (2002), *Being Given: Toward a Phenomenology of Givenness*, trans. J.F. Kosky, Stanford: Stanford University Press

Marquard, O. (1991), *In Defense of the Accidental*, Oxford-New York: Oxford University Press

Moreno, C. (1993), "Intersticio y trascendencia. Posibilidades y dignidad del animal admirable", *ER. Revista de Filosofia*, 16: 43–71

Moreno, C. (2004), "Vértigo de la posibilidad, complejidad y axiología", *Escritos de Filosofía*, 44: 139–62

Moreno, C. (2007), "Sin objeto. Epojé, vanguardia y fenomenología", *Phainomenon*, 14: 307–25

Moreno, C. (2012), "Eidos y periferia. Rutina y trascendencia in extremis en el horizonte de una humanidad proteica e híbrida", *Recerca. Revista de Pensament i anàlisi*, 12: 23–51

Nancy, J.-L. (2010), *The Truth of Democracy*, New York: Fordham University Press

Pico della Mirandola, G. (1988), *On the Dignity of Man* (1486), Indianapolis-Cambridge: Hackett Publishing Company

Prêt-à-porter (1994), [Film] Dir. Robert Altman, USA: Miramax Films

Rifkin, J. (2000), *The Age Of Access: The New Culture of Hypercapitalism, Where All of Life is a Paid-For Experience*, New York: Tarcher-Putnam

Simmel, G. (1971), "Fashion", in *On Individuality and Social Forms*, 295–7, Chicago: The University of Chicago Press

Squicciarino, N. (1986), *Il vestito parla. Considerazione psicosociologiche sulla indumentaria*, Roma: Armando Editore

9 THE FASCINATION OF CONTINGENCY: FASHION AND MODERN SOCIETY

Elena Esposito

1. Modernity as "*âge de mode*"

Fashion is a typically modern phenomenon—in the sense that it only exists in modern society, and in the sense that it expresses in a concentrated way the essence of modernity. This is the assumption underlying the present article, which I will try to illustrate and comment in the following pages. This approach can be surprising, because the public often thinks that fashion existed in all societies, and also because we tend to define modernity on the basis of more "serious" phenomena, like the emergence of scientific rationality or of national states. But fashion, in its apparent frivolity, involves crucial aspects of modern semantics, as the forms of individuality and the relationship with time. The key issue, as we shall see, is the concept of contingency, which in modern times acquires a new and unprecedented significance, illustrated by fashion and its forms.

Why modernity leads to these changes is an enigmatic question, although the concept continues to attract the attention of scholars, especially in the fields of sociology and history of ideas. What we can observe, however, is the gradual dissolution of the ordered setting of traditional semantics and the transition to a different form of order—vastly more flexible, contingent, compatible with components of disorder. The univocal order of the cosmos, as it was reflected in metaphysics and theology, but also in the systems of rhetoric and of various disciplines, gives way to a plurality of orders not always coordinated, with criteria, methods, and priorities that are different and independent from each other.

Sociology connects this transition with the differentiation of society in fields more and more independent of one another, each driven by its own function with its criteria and its priorities (Durkheim 1893; Luhmann 1997: chap. 4). The hierarchical order of traditional societies, reflecting the eternal and indisputable hierarchy of the universe, is now fragmented in all fields in the "heterarchical" order of modern society, with a multiplicity of different hierarchies that coexist and cannot be reduced the one to the other. Politics, science, law, education, religion, the arts, and other areas of society are no longer coordinated, producing, for better or for worse, the enormously higher complexity of modern society: much more variety, but also constant difficulties of coordination. Certainly the diffusion of the printing press also contributed to this increase in variety, making visible for the first time the evolution of texts and the diversity of publics (now anonymous and uncontrollable) and of possible interpretations (Eisenstein 1979).

Fashion addresses this complexity and helps to spread it, providing at the same time the tools to manage it. It is unstable and idiosyncratic, volatile and subjective, shared and idiosyncratic. Fashion bursts as a threatening and often incomprehensible disruptive element in the society and in the semantics of the time, expressing in a concentrated way a completely new attitude, with many consequences. Without taking into account this context, one cannot grasp the scope and presuppositions of fashion, often seen as marginal and essentially frivolous.

Before modernity, actually, fashion did not exist, and there was not even a term to indicate it. Only towards the beginning of the seventeenth century in France the female term "*la mode*" appears in addition to the male "*le mode*," which by no coincidence comes from the modal field (cf. the heading "Mode" in Ritter and Gründer 1984).

Fashion, as we will see, is first of all the recognition and dissemination of a modal notion, contingency, although its appearance was so disruptive because it was not limited to the academic field or to theoretical reflection. The scope of fashion went far beyond the realm of the speculation about the possible and the necessary, and was going to produce a feeling of transience and variability in all areas of life: "le goût, the vivre, la santé et la conscience" (La Bruyère 1992b: XII, 1). Fashion indicated what medicines to use, what kind of food to appreciate, the feelings to experience and how to express them, whether wearing a wig, the shape of the garments and even the attitude towards religion: "tout se règle par la mode" (La Bruyère 1992b: XII, 16).

Not only: also the criteria and categories applied to the world (and to fashion) were affected by fashion: "Even knowledge must follow fashion; and where it is not fashionable one must be able to pretend to be ignorant" (Gracián 1647: n. 120); "Comme la mode fait l'agrément aussi fait-elle la justice" (Pascal 1992: n. 95), and also "for excellence there is a fashion" (Gracián 1647: n. 20).

That in all these areas the rules were not stable anymore was seen as a waiver of rules in general. Fashion changes with time and also leaves a before unthinkable

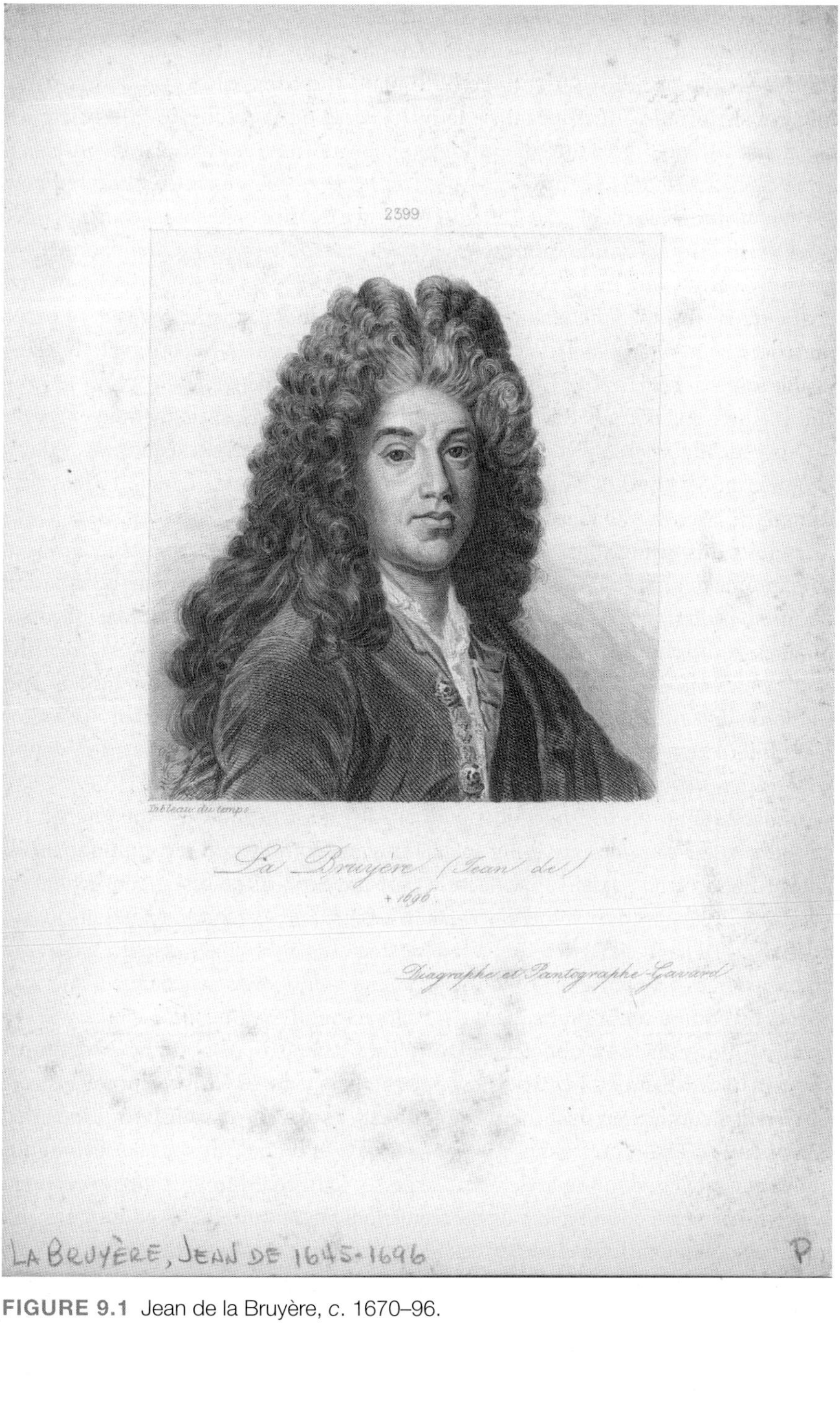

FIGURE 9.1 Jean de la Bruyère, *c*. 1670–96.

space to individual originality, and this appeared initially as the rejection of any kind of order. A pamphlet from 1617 draws from the fact that "chacun se donne cette authorité de s'habiller comme il lui plait" the conclusion that "aujourd'huy tout est confusion, tout est permis à tous" (Godard de Donville 1978: 74–6).

Fashion, therefore, acquired boundless extension, not only because it concerned every area of life and every thought and feeling, but because it also indicated how to regulate life and reflection. Grenaille, writing a treatise on fashion, wants to offer "une description generale de nostre siecle," because its fundamental character is given by variety and change (Grenaille 1642: 1). Indeed, this recently discovered character is supposedly a feature of the world in general, and so the lack of order does not concern only society but assumes cosmic overtones. According to Fitelieu, in the same period, "tout l'Univers se ressent de la Mode" (Fitelieu 1642: 17–18), and this trend is not positive at all. At the beginning of the seventeenth century it was practically a widely accepted commonplace to represent fashion as a deity, daughter of Saturn or change[1]—an image that remains effective for very long and can still be found in Mallarme: "La Mode est la déesse des apparences."

In all fields fashion introduces a radical change, that understandably aroused the concerned attention of the observers of the time, ranging from condemnation to fascination (Grenaille 1642; Fitelieu 1642). Fashion looked like absolute madness,[2] although shared by all and as such inevitable,[3] leading to subvert the order established and confirmed by tradition with a completely new, moody, and unreasonable attitude. Fashion seemed to supplant the interest in what is good or nice, and in general in the pursuit of perfection, with an inexplicable attraction to what is new or different, which is liked as such.[4]

What emerges in this period is a global attitude and not just the interest for clothing or for its role in marking social differences and social recognition. This is what I meant when I said that fashion first appears in the seventeenth century. Obviously an attention for the way of dressing and presenting oneself always existed, as always existed the awareness that this way changes with time and circumstances—already in Rome the style and colors of togas changed, and also the way to drape them (Tertullian, *De Pallio*; Quintilian, *Institutio oratoria*: VIII, 5). This, however, was not yet fashion. They changed responding to external changes—for example, because new materials or new dyeing techniques were discovered—and in any case they changed because of some reason, which appeared convincing. One dressed to show to others his wealth and his sense of belonging, and one changed clothing style because he thought that the new form was more beautiful or more comfortable or more convenient, because he liked it better and knew why. When fashion changes, on the contrary, the reasons why we like the new fashion better are quite mysterious—often there are no reasons at all and this very absence of motives contributes to the fascination of fashion.[5]

The attitude that emerges in the seventeenth century is much more complex and improbable: as we all know by now, fashion is followed not because we think that it is beautiful (fashion is increasingly ostentatiously ugly) or comfortable (the incredible uncomfortableness of fashionable objects was the subject of jokes already in the eighteenth century) or convenient (an unreasonably high price can become an element of attraction). We do not think that fashion complies with external criteria, that have their own logic to which it adapts. Fashion creates and modifies its criteria itself, thereby manifesting its autonomy. The basic distinction of fashion is "in/out," and only the cycle of fashion decides what is "in" and how long—the "why" is not interesting. If we like something because it is beautiful, we can argue our belief and do not expect to change it, unless new reasons or new information come up. If we like something because it is fashionable, on the contrary, our motivation is purely tautological,[6] and we are fully aware of transience: we know that next year we won't like it any more, as last year we liked other things, with no reason, and we know that this evanescence is an essential element.

Since the seventeenth century we live in a "*âge de mode*"[7] of volatile and seemingly capricious orientations, that arose great alarm in all observers of that time. Tradition taught to appreciate stability and *prudentia*, constancy and reasonableness, which were confirmed by the course of time and by experience, and made individuals reliable for the others and for themselves. In the seventeenth century, on the contrary, the opposite attitude becomes popular, looking for novelty and change, inconsistency and unpredictability—an attitude that appeared incomprehensible and dangerous.[8] What can be the state of a society in which individuals, rather than imitating the great models of antiquity (in the sense of classical *imitatio*), praise their own elusive originality, which it is not clear either to the others or to themselves? (cf. La Rochefoucauld 1992: 69, 103) It is quite understandable that the alarmed contemporary observers interpreted the transformations underway as a process of decay and dissolution of the moral and ontological setting of society. How can you understand a society whose orientations hold even and precisely because you know that they will change—like fashion, of which we only know that it will soon be replaced by a different fashion, which will make us dress and think differently? How can you rely on orientations that can always change, because they are based on no undeniable foundation, but only on the variety of times and circumstances? What kind of capricious and unreliable man was emerging?[9]

2. Necessary contingency

What people were observing was the general transition of society from the orientation to the necessary to the orientation to contingency—to principles and criteria that do not hold for everyone at all times and in all circumstances, but hold at a specific time and in a given context, and change with time and situations. This is precisely the sense of *contingency*, observed since ancient times as the condition of something (in logic a sentence) that is neither necessary nor impossible.[10] A contingent state, when it comes about, is there (hence it is not impossible) but could also not be there or be otherwise (it is not necessary). While necessity, impossibility, and logical possibility[11] can be abstractly studied and formalized, regardless of time and of the observer, on contingency you cannot say anything stable and definitive, and that's why it was excluded from the attention of modal logic.[12] To deal with contingency you must go and see the specificity of time and circumstances—but traditionally a local truth appeared unreliable and partial, only belonging (if anything) to the secondary field of opinion.

In pre-modern societies, principles and criteria were set and followed because they were (or were considered) necessary: the beautiful, the right, the true, the good, had to be stable and universal—even if human limitations allow to approach them only in an incomplete and therefore inevitably variable way. In modern society, on the contrary, variability is not only inevitable, it is also appreciated. For the first time novelty and pluralism are not avoided as annoyances, but are even actively sought for (Esposito 2013).

Novelty is always ambiguous and flexible, and even its evaluation as positive or negative changes with time and with the observers. Today's tendency is clearly to prefer the new with respect to the old, but this is not at all obvious; indeed is one of the main oddities of modern society.[13] This does not mean of course that today there are only novelties, but that our society chooses and enhances the aspects of novelty with respect to the aspects of continuity (the old).

In ancient times and in all pre-modern societies, the new was feared and despised. It appeared dangerous and highly demanding. The new was seen primarily as an inconvenience: it makes what is given and familiar look old and outdated, and sets in motion a process of transformation that is always uncertain and risky. Until the new appeared, in fact, what is given was simply what it was, appreciated and accepted according to its qualities. When the new shows up, however, the given automatically becomes old and must be justified, as tradition or as a classic—a laborious process of destabilization.

In traditional societies, the new was feared and despised because it brought instability and unrest. The stability of society and the world was based on sacred texts, which were not questioned and were complete in themselves (Meier 1980: 451; Graus 1987: 156 ff.). The person who claimed to introduce something new was considered reckless and necessarily in error, because in the inherited wisdom there was nothing to add or to correct, unless you wanted to refute divine guidelines; the innovator immediately became a heretic (Spörl 1930: 299 ff.). Montaigne (1991: I, XLIII) still maintained that change should be feared in everything, except in bad things—with the inevitable consequence that the person who looks for novelty pursues something bad, against the good and the right. Novelty was first of all an annoyance to be avoided as much as possible. When something new appeared (as was inevitable—a new tool, a new technique), one tried to neutralize it as merely an apparent novelty, which was already known to the ancients but had been neglected or forgotten over time. It only seemed new because we forgot what existed before or did not recognize it.

Our attitude is quite different: since the sixteenth century, we experience what Luhmann called a "semantic hypertrophy of variation" (Luhmann 1997: 472). Confronted with the bifurcation between the old and the new (they are both always present), we opt decidedly for the new. This is a completely unprecedented attitude: now the new is not just tolerated, but sought after and appreciated—and now we do not only like the new, we like only the new. The feature of novelty becomes almost a prerequisite to appreciate other aspects: apparently only what is new can be liked.[14] Novelty becomes a criterion of value and is prized in all fields: in the arts, in the mass media, but also in science and political debate—and primarily in fashion.

How can we explain this seeming madness, this inexplicable tendency to look for the *périssable* side of things, which is that they are new? (Valéry 1948) The new does not last; it disappears as a novelty at the very moment in which it is understood. The new consumes itself and constantly requires the production of new innovations to replace the ones that have been used and canceled in the very search for and exploitation of the new. The more one renews, the more one must renew: one needs more and more extravagant novelties, and needs them more and more often.

In this frenzy of change, alternative forms of validity emerge, that work even if they are temporary and we know it—indeed they hold precisely for this reason.

There is a move to contingent references in all fields, from science to law to aesthetics—references that could be different, we know it, and that's why we accept them and we orient to them (Luhmann 1992). Scientific truths are presented as strictly controlled but provisional propositions, valid precisely because they will be superseded by the advance of research—they are valid today knowing that in the future they will not be valid anymore, because of the evolution of knowledge which they themselves set in motion. Positive law, the foundation of all our normative systems, does not apply because it reflects natural justice (that nobody knows), but because it is the outcome of a decision (it is "*positum*"), which could have been different and can always be changed in the future, but as long as is valid must be respected. Our laws are no less valid because they could have been different, but are valid because of their flexibility—the other side of the assessment of novelty, which we like also and precisely because it deviates from tradition. Neither an immutable law nor a necessary truth would be plausible in our complex and restless society. The complexity to be managed would be too high for the univocity of a necessary reference.

Contingency has become the foundation of semantics, both in the temporal and in the social sense. For a few centuries our sense of time is no longer guided by the reference to an eternity in which all times are present and the "future things" are as determined as the "past things." The sense of the present is not given by its continuity with the past but rather by the preparation of a future that does not exist yet, of which we only know that it will be different from everything we know (Koselleck 1979). The present and the future will be different from the past, and will be the more different the more we know it and try to act on them. The future is open, thus in a sense contingent in a more radical way than for Aristotle: we do not know how it will come about because it is undetermined in a fundamental sense—no one can know it, since it does not exist yet and depends on what we do today to prepare it and to prepare ourselves.

Something similar happens in the social dimension, in the relationship of individuals with others and with themselves. Here again necessary references (which are immutable and the same for everyone: heroes, saints, exemplary models from history and tradition) have been replaced by the contingent reference to the singularity of the individual, who recognizes him- or herself as unique and unrepeatable (different from the models, not conform to them). Originality, which had always been despised as deviance and arrogance—a sterile way to attract attention to oneself, contradicting custom and good usage[15]—becomes the cornerstone of the construction of identity: each of us wants to be defined and recognized on the basis of his or her independent perspective on the world, which is and wants to be different from every other one (Mortier 1982).[16] We are who we are not because there were no alternatives or because we strive to conform to predefined models. We are who we are because we formed ourselves in this way, but we could also be otherwise, as all other subjects as well. Social contingency is the correlate of the new autonomy and self-determination of the individual, who is defined on the basis of internal factors that are his or her own, not on the basis of external criteria, necessary and the same for everyone.

3. Fashion: Contingency as a principle

Imitation remains, but profoundly changes its form. Here is where fashion comes in, with all its power and improbability: what is imitated in the modern age are not *auctores* nor heroes, but the models of fashion, to which (as remarked by Simmel 1911) we refer not in order to be the same as them and as the others, but in order to be different—we use them as a background against which we express our specificity and uniqueness. The reference to time also remains, but as discontinuity: the only thing we can expect is that things will change, and that the future will bring about surprises—like fashion, which always changes and is defined by this. As Coco Chanel argued, fashion is here in order to get out of fashion.

Fashion relies on contingency, offers a form to manage it, and manifests thereby its absolute modernity. In Furetiére's *Dictionnaire* (1978) the definition of fashion is based precisely on temporal and spatial variability ("tout ce qui change selon les temps et les lieux"), which provides space for individual variability: everyone

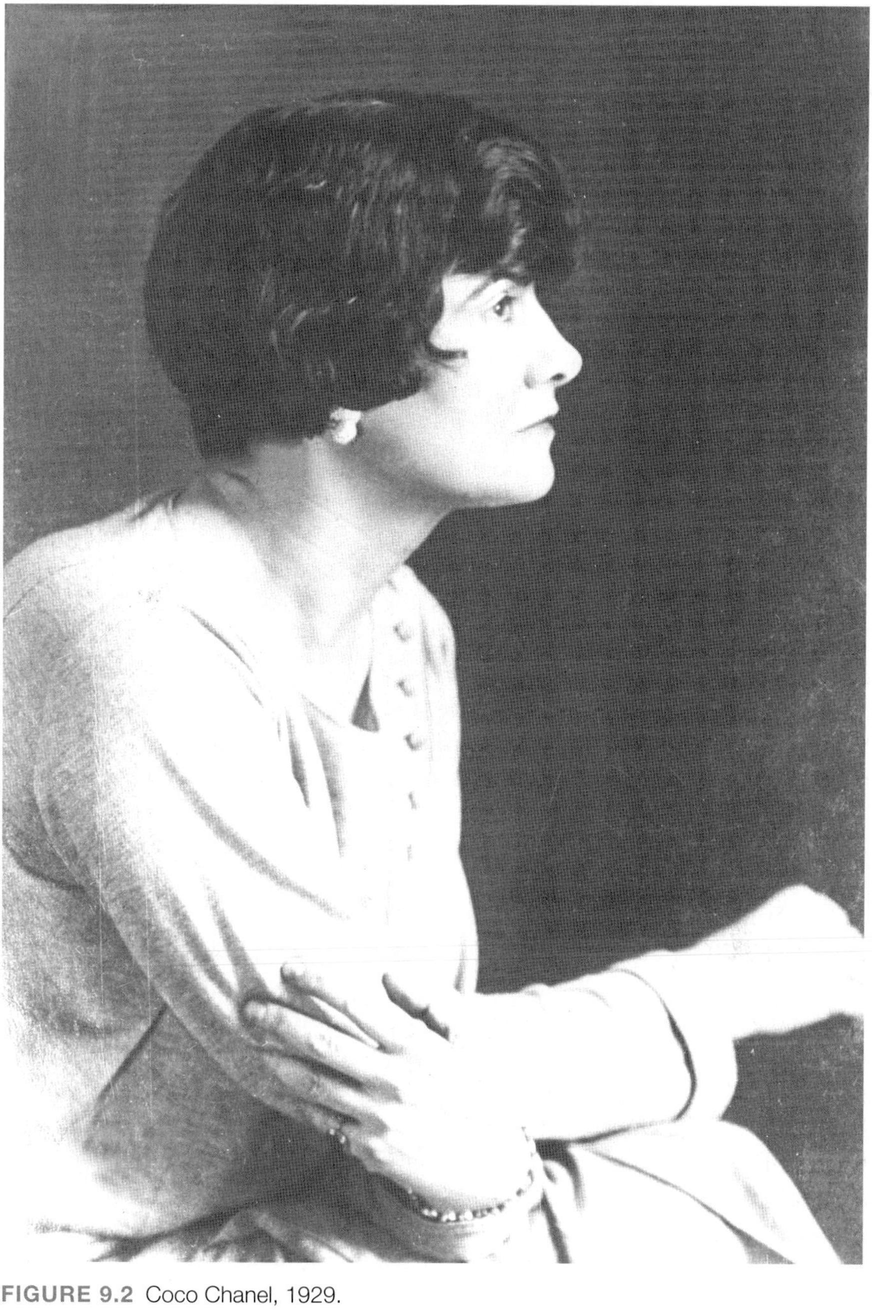

FIGURE 9.2 Coco Chanel, 1929.

interprets fashion in his or her own way, to express his or her originality and have it recognized by the others.

As the acknowledgment and exaltation of contingency, fashion arose, and could arise, only in modern times—as a kind of radicalization of their destabilizing trends, from the big moral and philosophical decisions to the minute issues of everyday life. But contingency is by its nature unstable and unpredictable—if approached directly, it causes confusion and disorientation: how do I decide what to do and to appreciate, if the "rule" is that everything could be otherwise, is different for everyone, and in any case will change with time? Fashion allows to have an orientation in this complexity, uses and operationalizes it. Fashion actually works—indeed, if we listen to the worried warnings of moralists from the seventeenth century, it works too well. Without realizing it and without caring too much, for a few centuries now we all use without difficulty contingent orientations whenever we look at fashion. Fashion changes, it could be different and we know it, but at any time it is reliable enough to show us how to dress and how to present ourselves. Fashion gives us indications without binding us and without calling into question the ultimate principles and the consistency of our criteria, because we know that it will change anyway.

Its very transience makes fashion a valuable tool in a world that needs to manage contingency, and can do it only with contingent tools. The fascinating side of fashion, especially in philosophical view, however, is that it not only makes modernity "work," but also shows a radical aspect of it, which often remains latent but is extremely revealing. The other side of the orientation to contingency is the inevitable existence of paradoxes, that are produced whenever a contingent criterion applies to itself and reflects on its conditions.[17] And fashion is actually an accumulation of paradoxes (Esposito 2004), both in the social and in the temporal sense—paradoxes that are nothing else than the reflection of its contingency.

We already mentioned it: fashion offers to the original individual (to all of us) models to imitate in order to express his or her uniqueness—not the moral models of tradition, but the deviant models of the genius and the original, who are followed as models because they follow no model. The modern form of imitation is a paradoxical imitation of those who do not imitate anyone, and for this reason are imitated. But the genius is not original only in the sense of being different and weird.[18] His or her originality must be recognized and appreciated by others—which is strictly impossible, if one requires that it is radically different from anything the others do and think. In this paradoxical imitation everyone strives to manifest his or her own originality, but this is the same ambition that drives everyone else, and everyone knows it. In his or her search for diversity, then, everyone is the same as everyone else. Nothing is as original as the desire to be original.

Fashion, moreover, changes every year and every season, showing that guidelines and criteria change with time. This we know by experience, which teaches us the discontinuity between the past and the present. From the past, according to Koselleck (1979), now we can only learn that we cannot learn anything from the past—but this, paradoxically, we can learn. In this volatility we have a stable reference, in the form of volatility itself: everything changes, but this we can expect, as we can expect that in each new season there will be a new fashion, different and deviant from what we like today. Fashion accomplishes a kind of "institutionalization of the ephemeral" (Lipovetsky 1987) in which continuous change becomes the only constant. In Baudelaire's terms, the secret of fashion is "extracting the eternal from the ephemeral" (Baudelaire 1964).

4. Use and practice of paradoxes

The fascinating side of fashion, in this view, is not only its paradoxical nature, but the fact that it is not a problem. This whole tangle of antinomies is not an obstacle for fashion, rather it is one of the most convincing elements of its strength and its (unmotivated, as Simmel showed) motivation. The paradoxes of fashion exist and multiply without blocking operations and without making them arbitrary. The centuries-old history of fashion offers many examples of transformation of paradoxes: the expectation of novelty, until novelty itself becomes repetitive and one looks for an effect of surprise in the rediscovery of tradition (vintage)—or provocation as a norm, with the effect that ostentatious normality becomes a form of deviance (Prada). Paradoxes produce continuously new paradoxes, which are the only way to keep the contingency and indeterminacy of the future open. But this by no means implies the dreaded consequence of arbitrariness and lack of criteria. Fashion works because it continues to provide an orientation, also and precisely because it operationalizes a network of paradoxes.

The problem of paradoxes, and the reason why they have always been dreaded,[19] was the fear of arbitrariness, which would make observation and also expectations impossible. If a system includes a paradox—it has always been said—it can include anything. It cannot exclude anything, and no longer provides any guarantee of reliability. But fashion, at any time, is able to discriminate very well what is "in" (very little) from everything that is not "in" (almost everything) and is very effectively excluded—all forms of heels, pants, jackets, colors, and materials are not "in" at that time, but also all lifestyles, holiday destinations, books, ways of speaking, and kinds of foods that do not meet the current trends. Its paradoxical nature in no way prevents fashion from selecting and distinguishing. It is a contingent selection, because everyone knows that it will change in the future and that all the elements now excluded will return "sooner or later" in a new form and with different value—therefore it is easier to follow it and to be influenced. The contingency of fashion does not make its exclusion of arbitrariness less effective.

Contingency and arbitrariness are not the same, and fashion shows it clearly. Fashion can actually exclude arbitrariness by exploiting contingency and producing a different form of validity. How can an orientation be valid if it is not stable and general? The rules of fashion do not apply despite their changing and not being valid for everyone—they apply precisely because of this.[20] The paradox is not resolved with a hierarchy of types or with a modal calculus—indeed it is not resolved at all, but neutralized and contextualized. In social practice, the "laws" of fashion operate clearly and highly effectively. That no one is able to formulate them (even if they would be very useful to firms, designers, and media) manifests indirectly the ungovernable nature of paradoxes, but does not make them any less valid. Fashion comes from below[21]—often from the street, from workers, from youth gangs. Designers and companies try to introduce trends, but they often must recognize that they are not accepted or are transformed by use, while unpredictable and uncontrolled fads become popular. Why are high-waisted pants still not trendy, after years of trying, while young people wear drop-crotch jeans? Why did Goggle glasses not become fashionable but silly bandz spread everywhere?

The only reason of fashion is the absence of reasons (Simmel's abstractness), i.e., the rejection of any necessity. The contingencies of fashion refer to one another and produce a set of criteria that are mutually binding and work in their very flexibility. The unique and idiosyncratic individual can follow fashion without sacrificing his or her originality (even if he or she does the same as everyone else, and looks at the same models) because fashion changes and everyone knows it. Before he or she, or the others, must confront the repetitiveness and uniformity of the search for originality (its paradox), fashion is already different and you must chase a different form. Stability through change effectively hides the paradox of originality, but is itself a paradox: change is stable and stability changes, in the constant oscillation between two opposite poles which is typical of paradoxes. But also in this case the paradox is subtracted from view by the practice of fashion: it is true that to orient to fashion is to expect surprises, but no one cares about it because everyone else does the same. Social conformity effectively neutralizes temporal inconsistency.

In a time like ours, of situated truths and anti-postmodern theories,[22] fashion provides a valuable link between theoretical reflection and social practice—a contingent practice of contingency that shows how paradoxes are not only inevitable, but must not necessarily be a problem. By now we know it: a paradox occurs whenever an observer who is part of the world reflects on him- or herself and on his or her relationship with the world—facing a condition in which he or she is at the same time a subject (as an observer) and an object (as an element of the world).[23] Taken abstractly, this is a typical paradox oscillating from one side of an opposition to the other one: the observer is a subject because he is an object because he is a subject. But this is the inevitable condition of all observers, and it makes little sense to label it as pathological—also because in social practice it happens continuously without any difficulty. Social life can be seen as a big apparatus for the management and neutralization of this paradox (and of other related ones).

Fashion, with its multiplication and use of paradoxes, is the evidence—showing, in all fields and with many examples, that modern society, which multiplied contingency, also produced orientations that are flexible enough to manage paradoxes and make use of them. The foundation of fashion is inevitably paradoxical, and if you look for them paradoxes multiply in all dimensions. Normally, however, fashion works without problems (actually it is often underestimated as something frivolous and superficial), offering to each of us (and to everyone else) the opportunity to develop our uniqueness, in the temporary stability of a time that regenerates in every present.

Notes

1 Cf. Godard de Donville 1978: 19 ff., with many examples and materials.

2 "Une chose folle et qui découvre bien notre petitesse, c'est l'assujettissement aux modes" (La Bruyère 1992a: XIII).

3 "Besser ist aber doch immer, ein Narr in der Mode als ein Narr außer der Mode zu sein" (Kant 1988: § 68).

4 "La curiosité n'est pas un goût pour ce qui est bon ou ce qui est beau, mais pour ce qui est rare, unique, pour ce qu'on a et ce que les autre n'ont point. Ce n'est pas un attachement à ce qui est parfait, mais à ce qui est couru, à ce qui est à la mode. Ce n'est pas un amusement, mais une passion" (La Bruyère 1992a : XIII [2]).

5 Simmel (1911: 30) speaks of abstractness (*Abstraktheit*) as one of the key features of fashion.

6 "Enfine, c'est la mode" (Madame de Sévigné 1955–7: letter dated January 3, 1689).

7 See Tarde 1921 (chap. 7). For Tarde fashion is not specific of modernity, but the alternation between stability-oriented "*âges de coutume*" and "*âges de mode*" oriented to innovations (and then back to costume) applies to all societies. Tarde recognizes, however, that the period of exposure to fashion which began with the Italian Renaissance is particularly long.

8 For example La Bruyère 1992b : XI, 147: "Les hommes n'ont point de caractères, ou s'il en ont, c'est celui de n'en avoir aucun qui soit suivi, qui ne se démente point, et où il soient reconnaissables."

9 Cf. Pascal 1992 : n. 58: "Condition de l'homme: inconstance, ennui, inquiétude"; and La Bruyère 1992b: XI, 6: "Un homme inégal [. . .] est à chaque moment ce qu'il n'était point, et il va être bientôt ce qu'il n'a jamais été: il se succède à lui-même."

10 Cf. Aristotle, *De Interpretatione*: 9 and 12–13. The problem of contingency arose for him notoriously especially in relation to the future, as in the treatment of *futuris contingentibus*. What do we know now of the truth conditions of a future event, as such unknowable? Aristotle's solution uses a kind of "provisional" indeterminacy that will be resolved when the course of time will give us the information needed to know what today is inaccessible to men.

11 According to which everything is possible that is not impossible, even if it never occurred.

12 Still in recent times: cf. Lewis and Langford 1932; Hughes and Cresswell 1968 (chap. 2).

13 A society which tends to describe itself in temporal form. The German word for "modernity" is *Neuzeit*: literally, "New Time."

14 "Il n'ya proprement que ce qui est nouveau qui plaise à nos yeux" (Grenaille 1642: 130).

15 Della Casa 1994: VII, 18; Faret 1630: 138 (Italian edition). Cf. also Gracián 1647, who recommends: "Do not exceed in showing your originality. [. . .] Displaying originality only serves to show off with a feature that moves alternately to laughter or to anger."

16 This implies, among other things, a restructuring of the combination between conformity and deviance. While in traditional societies deviance confirmed the rule (in negative but also in positive, as in the case of the hero), the aspiration to originality for everyone transforms deviance itself in a rule—the one with the highest level of conformity: we all must be original, i.e., different from the models. Cf. Esposito 2004 (chap. 4).

17 Logics knows it very well at least since Whitehead and Russell 1910–13: the combination of reflexivity and negation inevitably produces a paradoxical condition. Cf. Esposito 1990.

18 You must be original, but you must not be *an* original (Goblot 1967: 148).

19 Think again about Russell and Whitehead, but of course also about Frege.

20 One of the most disturbing features of fashion has always been its universality. You cannot escape its power, because the effort to be intentionally out of fashion requires a lot of attention and a lot of energy. Who does not want to follow fashion is still forced to refer to his instructions, even if in the negative. "Il y a autant de faiblesse à fuir la mode qu'a l'affecter" (La Bruyère 1992b: XIII, 11).

21 Contradicting every naive idea of trickle-down, from Garve 1792 to Simmel 1911.

22 See, among others, Latour 1991.

23 Luhmann's autology (1997: 16 ff.). Others speak of performativity: cf. Callon (1998); Callon et al. 2007; MacKenzie et al. 2007; MacKenzie 2006.

Bibliography

Aristotle (1980), *Categories and Propositions (De interpretatione)*, trans. with commentary and glossary by Hippocrates G. Apostle, Grinell (Iowa): Peripatetic Press

Baudelaire, C. (1964): "The Painter of Modern Life" (1863), in *The Painter of Modern Life and Other Essays*, trans. J. Mayne, London: Phaidon Press

Bruyère, J. de la (1992a), "Les Caractères de Théophraste" (1688), in *Moralistes du XVII*[e] *Siècle*, ed. by J. Lafond, 659–692, Paris: Laffont

Bruyère, J. de la (1992b), "Les Caractères ou les moeurs de ce siècle" (1688), in *Moralistes du XVII*[e] *Siècle*, ed. by J. Lafond, 693–968, Paris: Laffont

Callon, M., ed. (1998), *The Laws of the Market*, Oxford: Blackwell

Callon, M., Y. Millo and F. Muniesa, eds (2007), *Market Devices*, Oxford: Blackwell

Della Casa, G. (1994), *Galateo* (1558), Torino: Einaudi

Durkheim, E. (1893), *De la division du travail social*, Paris: Alcan
Eisenstein, E.L. (1979), *The Printing Press as an Agent of Change. Communications and Cultural Transformations in Early-Modern Europe*, Cambridge: Cambridge University Press
Esposito, E. (1990), "Paradoxien als Unterscheidungen von Unterscheidungen", in H.U. Gumbrecht and K.L. Pfeiffer (eds), *Paradoxien, Dissonanzen, Zusammenbrüche*, 35–57, Frankfurt a.M.: Suhrkamp
Esposito, E. (2004), *Die Verbindlichkeit des Vorübergehenden. Paradoxien der Mode*, Frankfurt a.M.: Suhrkamp
Esposito, E. (2013), "Wie viel Altes braucht das Neue?", in H.R. Fischer (ed.), *Wie kommt Neues in die Welt? Phantasie, Intuition und der Ursprung von Kreativität*, 133–45, Weilerswist: Velbrück Wissenschaft
Faret, N. (1630), *L'Honnête homme ou l'Art de plaire à la cour*, Paris: T. du Bray (Italian trans. *L'arte di piacere alla corte*, Bologna: 1662)
Fitelieu, M. de (1642), *La Contre-Mode*, Paris: Louys de Heuqueville
Furetiére, A. (1978), *Le dictionnaire universel* (1690), Paris: Le Robert
Garve, C. (1792), *Versuche über verschiedene Gegenstände aus der Moral, der Literatur und dem gesellschaftlichen Leben. I. Teil*, Korn: Breslau
Goblot, E. (1967), *La barriere et le niveau* (1925), Paris: PUF
Godard de Donville, L. (1978), *Signification de la mode sous Louis XIII*, Aix-en-Provence: Edisud
Gracián, B. (1647), *Oráculo Manual y arte de Prudencia*, in *Obras completas*, Book II, 185–304, Madrid: Biblioteca Castro
Graus, F. (1987), "Epochenbewußtsein im Spätmittelalter und Probleme der Periodisierung", in R. Herzog and R. Koselleck (eds), *Epochenschwelle und Epochenbewußtsein*, 131–52, München: Fink
Grenaille, F. de (1642), *La Mode, ou charactère de la Religion, de la Vie, de la Conversation, de la Solitude, des Compliments, des Habits et du Style du Temps*, Paris: Gasse
Hughes, G.E. and M.J. Cresswell (1968), *An Introduction to Modal Logic*, London: Methuen
Kant, I. (1988), *Anthropologie in pragmatischer Hinsicht* (1798), in *Werkausgabe*, vol. XII, Frankfurt a.M.: Suhrkamp
Koselleck, R. (1979), *Vergangene Zukunft. Zur Semantik geschichtlicher Zeiten*, Frankfurt a.M.: Suhrkamp
Latour, B. (1991), *Nous n'avons jamais été modernes*, Paris: La Découverte
Lewis, C.I. and C.H. Langford (1932), *Symbolic Logic*, New York: Dover
Lipovetsky, G. (1987), *L'empire de l'éphémère. La mode et son destin dans les sociétés modernes*, Paris: Gallimard
Luhmann, N. (1992), "Kontingenz als Eigenwert der modernen Gesellschaft", in *Beobachtungen der Moderne*, 93–128, Opladen: Westdeutscher Verlag
Luhmann, N. (1997), *Die Gesellschaft der Gesellschaft*, Frankfurt a.M.: Suhrkamp
MacKenzie, D. (2006), *An Engine, Not a Camera: How Financial Models Shape Markets*, Cambridge (MA): The MIT Press
MacKenzie, D., F. Muniesa and L. Siu, eds (2007), *Do Economists Make Markets?*, Princeton (NJ): Princeton University Press
Meier, C. (1980), *Die Entstehung des Politischen bei den Griechen*, Frankfurt a.M.: Suhrkamp
Montaigne, M. de (1991), *The Complete Essays* (1580–1588), trans. and ed. by M.A. Screech, London: Penguin Books

Mortier, R. (1982), *L'originalité. Une nouvelle catégorie esthétique au siècle des lumières*, Genève: Droz

Pascal, B. (1992), *Pensées* (1670), in *Moralistes du XVIIe Siècle*, ed. by J. Lafond, 321–604, Paris: Laffont

Quintilian (1969), *The institutio oratoria*, trans. H.E. Butler, Cambridge(MA)-London: Harvard University Press-Heinemann

Ritter, J. and K.F. Gründer, eds (1984), *Historisches Wörterbuch der Philosophie*, Basel-Stuttgart: Schwabe

Rochefoucauld, F. de la (1992), *Réflexions ou sentences et maximes morales* (1665), in *Moralistes du XVIIe Siècle*, ed. by J. Lafond, 134–93, Paris: Laffont

Sévigné, Madame de (1955–7), *Lettres* (1626–96), ed. by Geráld-Gailly, Paris: Gallimard

Simmel, G. (1911), "Die Mode" (1905), in *Philosophische Kultur. Gesammelte Essais*, Leipzig: Klinkhardt

Spörl, J. (1930), "Das Alte und das Neue im Mittelalter. Studien zum Problem des mittelalterlichen Fortschrittsbewußtseins", *Historisches Jahrbuch*, 50: 297–341 and 498–524

Tarde, G. (1921), *Les Lois de l'Imitation. Étude sociologique*, Paris: Alcan

Tertullian (2005), *De pallio*, with a commentary by V. Hunink, Amsterdam: Gieben

Valéry, P. (1948), *Tel quel 1: Chose Tues—Moralités—Littérature—Cahier B 1910*, Paris: Gallimard

Whitehead, A. North and B. Russell (1910–13), *Principia Mathematica*, 3 vols, Cambridge: Cambridge University Press

INDEX OF NAMES

Adorno, T.W., 32, 39 n, 87 n, 130
Aeschylus, 80, 87 n
Alain (Émile-Auguste Chartier), 29, 48
Alexander, F.M., 102
Alighieri, D., 119
Altman, R., 171 n
Ando, E., 91, 92, 93, 94, 97
Angelus Silesius, 166
Apuleius, 87 n
Arendt, H., 116
Aristotle, 82, 121, 134, 182, 187 n
Armani, G., 91, 110
Avanessian, A., 138

Bakhtin, M., 141
Ballard, L., 86
Balzac, H. de, 16
Barbey, d'Aurevilly, J.-A., 16
Barnard, M., 4, 34, 35
Barthes, R., 7, 8, 32, 134, 153, 155, 166, 167
Bataille, G., 139, 165
Baudelaire, C., 16, 160, 185
Baudrillard, J., 8, 32, 42 n, 159, 165, 166, 168, 171 n
Bauman, Z., 155
Beauvoir, S. de, 102
Becker, H., 56
Beer, G., 148 n
Bell, D., 13
Benjamin, W., 29, 32, 41 n, 144, 147, 162
Bertin, R., 19
Bierbrodt, J., 139
Blanks, T., 112
Blumer, H., 13
Böhme, G., 52
Bonfante, L., 87 n
Bourdieu, P., 32, 42 n, 57, 58, 59, 60, 102, 109, 115
Bown, N., 148 n
Brando, M., 86
Breward, C., 88 n
Brown, D., 111
Brubach, H., 112
Brummell, G.B. "Beau", 16
Brus, G., 130, 131
Bruyère, J. de la, 176, 187 n, 188 n
Burke, E., 139, 147
Burkert, W., 87 n
Busch, W., 142

Calefato, P., 160
Callon, M., 188 n
Carchia, G., 18
Carlyle, T., 16
Carroll, N., 113
Cartesio – see Descartes, R.
Cassirer, E., 3
Castiglione, B., 76
Chanel, 165, 182
Chloe, 114
Cicero, 86 n
Constantine (Roman Emperor), 75
Cresswell, M.J., 188 n

Danto, A.C., 8, 55, 56, 57, 111
Darwin, C., 7, 8, 65, 66, 68, 137, 138, 139, 140, 141, 142, 143, 144, 145, 146, 147, 148
Darwin, G.H., 65, 143, 144
Davis, F., 13

Della Casa, G., 188 n
DeLong, M.R., 9 n
Delsaut, Y., 32, 59
Descartes, R., 50, 154, 155, 160, 164, 169
Dickie, G., 56, 57
Diderot, D., 142
Diogenes, Laërtius, 86 n, 87 n
Dolce, D., 110
Douglas, M., 62
Durkheim, E., 176

Eberhard, W.G., 146
Eckman, M., 9 n
Eco, U., 169
Edwards, T., 9 n, 61
Eisenstein, E.L., 176
Ellis, P., 91, 92, 93, 105 n
Engels, F., 126
Entwistle, J., 34, 35, 39 n, 41 n
Erner, G., 164, 167, 171 n
Ernst, M., 47, 70
Esposito, E., 8, 39 n, 175, 180, 184, 188 n
Etcoff, N., 146
Euripides, 80, 87 n

Fabbri, P., 162, 171 n
Farennikova, A., 77, 78
Faret, N., 188 n
Fehrenbach, F., 138
Feldenkrais, M., 102
Ferry, L., 61
Figal, G., 41 n
Fink, E., 32, 33, 34, 35, 36, 37, 38, 41 n, 62
Fitelieu, M. de, 178
Flügel, J.C., 25
Foucault, M., 102
Franci, S., 58
Franko, B., 132
Frege, G., 134, 188 n
Freud, S., 133
Frohner, A., 130
Furetiére, A., 182

Gabbana, S., 110
Gadamer, H.-G., 33
Gagosian, L., 110
Gallagher, S., 34
Garve, C., 18, 19, 20, 28, 40 n, 188 n
Gautier, P.J.T., 16
Gecky, A., 9 n
Geertz, C., 154
Gehlen, A., 22
Gergen, K.J., 153
Girard, R., 160
Givhan, R., 112
Gladstone, B., 110
Goblot, E., 188 n
Godard de Donville, L., 178, 187 n
Goethe, J.W., 147
Gombrowicz, W., 170
González García, J.M., 162
Goodman, N., 8, 53, 54, 55, 58
Gould, C.G., 146
Gould, J.L., 146
Gracián, B., 176, 188 n
Graf, F., 80
Granata, F., 112
Graus, F., 180
Grenaille, F. de, 178, 188 n
Gründer, K.F., 176
Gucci, 110

Hadrian (Roman Emperor), 75
Hanson, K., 16, 39 n, 73, 87 n
Hartmann, E., 130
Harvey, J., 76
Hegel, G.W.F., 20, 25, 35, 38, 40 n, 67, 124, 125
Heidegger, M., 33, 41 n, 167
Heraclitus, 128
Herchcovitch, A., 115
Herder, J.G., 22
Hoffmann, E.T.A., 142
Hollander, A., 39 n, 48, 76, 80, 85, 87 n, 88 n
Horyn, C., 109, 112
Hughes, G.E., 188 n
Humboldt, A. von, 139
Husserl, E., 8, 33, 34, 134, 167, 171 n

Jacobs, M., 91, 114
James, W., 20, 21, 22, 28, 40 n
Johnson, K.P., 39 n, 40 n

Kafka, F., 130, 132, 133
Kant, I., 7, 12, 18, 20, 21, 28, 29, 40 n, 41 n, 61, 73, 87 n, 137, 138, 139, 140, 187 n
Karaminas, V., 9 n
Kawamura, Y., 13, 15, 16

Kelly, M., 39 n
Kennett, J., 9 n, 39 n, 59, 87 n
Klein, Y., 132
Kleinwächter, F., 25, 28
Koch, I., 130
König, R., 9 n, 13, 40 n, 52, 169
Koselleck, R., 182, 185
Kraus, K., 16

Lagerfeld, K., 165
Lande, R., 146
Lang, H., 110
Langford, C.H., 188 n
Latour, B., 188 n
Leddy, T., 56
Lehmann, U., 9 n, 41 n, 53
Leopardi, G., 16, 162, 165
Lewis, C.I., 188 n
Lieberman, P., 40 n
Lillethun, A., 16, 18
Lipovetsky, G., 8, 9 n, 18, 19, 32, 37, 40 n, 42 n, 50, 52, 73, 75, 78, 87 n, 108, 152, 153, 155, 157, 163, 169, 185
Lombardi, P., 127
Loos, A., 6, 16, 96, 97, 98, 99, 100, 105 n
Loschek, I., 9 n, 58
Lotze, H., 20, 21, 22, 40 n
Lowy, I., 133
Luchetti, L., 54
Luhmann, N., 156, 176, 181, 188 n
Lyotard, J.-F., 2

MacKenzie, D., 188 n
Maffesoli, M., 155, 163
Magris, C., 169
Mallarmé, S., 16, 109
Manso, P., 86
Marie Antoinette, 19
Marinetti, F.T., 160
Marino, S., 1, 4, 11
Marion, J.-L., 167
Marquard, O., 162
Martin, R., 39 n
Marx, K., 126
Matteucci, G., 1, 5, 18, 30, 39 n, 47, 60, 62
Mauss, M., 168
McDonnell, M., 87 n
McDowell, C., 112
McDowell, J., 40 n
McNeil, P., 112, 113
Meier, C., 180
Meinhold, R., 9 n, 28, 64
Melissus, 78
Menkes, S., 112
Menninghaus, W., 7, 65, 68, 137, 140, 142, 148
Merleau-Ponty, M., 34
Michaud, Y., 23, 41 n, 67
Michel, C., 6, 7, 119
Miller, S., 112, 113
Monneyron, F., 15
Montaigne, M. de, 180
Moreno-Márquez, C., 7, 151, 152, 153, 171 n
Morini, E., 19, 48
Moritz, K.P., 140
Morris, D., 147, 148 n
Mortier, R., 182
Muehl, O., 130
Müller-Sievers, H., 139
Murphy, J.P., 40 n

Nadar, F., 108
Nancy, J.-L., 170
Naukkarinen, O., 51
Negrin, L., 16, 39 n, 48
Neumann, M., 25
Nietzsche, F., 20, 22, 33, 37, 40 n, 69
Nitsch, H., 130, 131
Nooten, D. van, 114
Nunn, J., 87 n

Ockham, W. of, 127
Oesterle, G., 142
Owens, R., 114

Pappas, N., 5, 26, 36, 39 n, 78, 87 n
Parmenides, 78
Pascal, B., 176, 187 n
Pausanias, 87 n
Pearl Jam, 11
Pedroni, M., 59
Peirce, C.S., 21, 40 n
Perucchi, L., 31
Pfefferkorn, J., 41 n
Philip the Good, 76
Phoebe Philo, 115
Pico della Mirandola, 7, 153, 154, 168
Pinch, G., 87 n

Plato, 2, 78, 83, 85, 87 n, 94, 138, 153, 166
Plessner, H., 98
Poell, C.C., 6, 7, 119, 120, 121, 122, 124, 125, 126, 127, 128, 129, 130, 131, 132, 133, 134
Poiret, P., 19, 48, 108
Prada, 74, 185
Prinz, J., 77, 78
Purdy, D.L., 26, 28, 40 n, 41 n

Quintilian, 147, 178

R.E.M., 11
Rantala, M.J., 148 n
Renta, O. de la, 110
Riello, G., 12, 18
Rifkin, J., 159
Ritter, J., 176
Rocamora, A., 9 n
Rochefoucauld, F. de la, 179
Rousseau, J.-J., 73, 78
Russell, B., 188 n

Saito, Y., 51
Santayana, G., 73, 78
Sartre, J.-P., 165
Scanlon, T.F., 87 n
Scapp, R., 9 n, 39 n, 87 n
Scheler, M., 22
Schiaparelli, E., 49
Schnädelbach, H., 21
Schwarzkogler, R., 130
Seitz, B., 9 n, 39 n, 87 n
Sepp, H.R., 33
Serroy, J., 50
Sévigné, Madame de, 187 n
Shusterman, R., 5, 6, 91, 96, 105 n, 106 n
Simmel, G., 6, 8, 12, 13, 14, 15, 18, 20, 28, 29, 30, 31, 32, 36, 37, 39 n, 42 n, 61, 62, 65, 96, 97, 98, 100, 162, 163, 165, 171 n, 182, 185, 186, 187 n, 188 n
Simone, S., 119
Skinner, A., 148
Smelik, A., 9 n
Socrates, 3, 69, 73, 74, 83, 84, 86 n, 87 n
Spencer, H., 3, 23, 24, 25, 28, 39 n, 144
Spiegelberg, H., 33
Spook, P., 114
Spörl, J., 180
Squicciarino, N., 153
Stambaugh, J., 41 n
Sterne, L., 142
Strasser, I., 137
Straub, 88 n
Sullivan, J., 88 n
Sumner, W., 13
Svendsen, L., 2, 5, 6, 9 n, 18, 39 n, 73, 78, 87 n, 106 n, 107
Swetnam-Burland, M., 87 n

Tarde, G. de, 13, 87 n, 163, 187 n
Tertullian, 178
Thackeray, W.M., 16
Thom, R., 6, 120, 121
Thoreau, H.D., 73, 78, 79, 86
Thucydides, 87 n
Tieck, L., 142
Tönnies, F., 13
Tota, A., 54
Troy, N.J., 108

Valéry, P., 181
Veblen, T., 13, 28
Vinken, B., 38
Vischer, F.T., 25, 26, 27, 28, 41 n
Volonté, P., 59
Voss, J., 148 n

Wagner, J., 9 n
Warhol, A., 52
Washington, G., 87 n
Watson, C.A., 21
Wehinger, B., 39 n
Whitehead, A., 188 n
Wickler, W., 148 n
Wilde, O., 16
Wilson, E., 15, 38, 62, 63, 65
Wittgenstein, L., 8, 59, 60
Wolfendale, J., 9 n, 39 n, 59, 87 n
Wollheim, R., 59
Worth, C.F., 19, 108

Zahavi, D., 34
Zuckert, R., 139

INDEX OF SUBJECTS

aesthetics 4, 5, 6, 7, 8, 9 n, 18, 25, 37, 38, 39 n, 48, 50, 51, 52, 55, 56, 60, 61, 101, 119, 131, 132, 133, 137, 138, 139, 140, 141, 142, 144, 145, 146, 148, 181
- aesthetic, the 5, 39 n, 48, 50, 51, 53, 56, 58, 59, 60, 61, 66, 67, 69
- aesthetic aspect 111
- aesthetic attitude 50
- aesthetic challenge 69
- aesthetic character 38
- aesthetic characteristic 65
- aesthetic charm 37, 39 n
- aesthetic common sense 50, 61
- aesthetic concept 48, 50
- aesthetic conception 55, 56, 59
- aesthetic content 51, 56, 60
- aesthetic creativity 38
- aesthetic debate 53, 59, 60, 140
- aesthetic device 63
- aesthetic dimension 28, 38, 53, 57, 60, 61
- aesthetic domain 38, 47, 48, 66, 96
- aesthetic economy 52
- aesthetic element 38, 105 n
- aesthetic event 50
- aesthetic experience 51, 55, 59, 68
- aesthetic factors 5
- aesthetic failure 113
- aesthetic feature 68, 142
- aesthetic field 59, 67
- aesthetic function 38, 140
- aesthetic ideology 61
- aesthetic inquiry 2
- aesthetic institutions 58
- aesthetic level 24, 31
- aesthetic meaning 101, 134
- aesthetic means 38, 65
- aesthetic medium 38
- aesthetic object 50, 141
- aesthetic phenomenon 5, 47, 51
- aesthetic point of view 9 n
- aesthetic potentiality 38
- aesthetic practice 6, 50, 52, 66, 67, 68, 69, 107
- aesthetic predication 59
- aesthetic preference 108, 139, 142, 143, 147
- aesthetic problem 5, 18
- aesthetic process 39 n
- aesthetic qualities 55
- aesthetic realm 53
- aesthetic role 38, 63
- aesthetic root 61
- aesthetic significance 23, 68
- aesthetic standard 38, 115
- aesthetic subject 37
- aesthetic terms 38
- aesthetic theory 32
- aesthetic topic 36
- aesthetic value 97
- aesthetic world 66
- somaesthetics *ad vocem*

anthropology 22, 33, 66, 73, 87 n
- philosophical anthropology see "Philosophy"

anti-fashion 5, 8, 73, 76, 77, 80, 81, 82, 83, 85, 86, 87 n

arabesque 137, 140, 141, 142, 148

art 3, 6, 13, 16, 32, 39 n, 40 n, 48, 50, 51, 53, 54, 55, 58, 59, 61, 67, 70 n, 73, 101,

107, 108, 109, 110, 112, 116, 127, 148, 176, 181
applied arts 134
art creation 50, 101
art gallery 50, 56
art institutions 108
art of living 101
art scene 119
art theory 107, 111
artification 54
artist 6, 16, 96, 108, 110, 131, 133, 134
artistic career 91
artistic conception 48, 50, 56
artistic development 50
artistic dimension 55, 133
artistic language 55
artistic material 131
artistic movement 49
artistic object 69
artistic phenomenon 53
artistic practice 50, 51
artistic tradition 48
artistic value, status 19, 48, 56
artistry 48
arts of design 101
arts of sculpture 54, 91, 147, 148
artworld, world of art 49, 56, 57, 108, 112, 147
artwork, work of art 50, 54, 55, 65, 133, 134, 142
definition of art 56, 59
erotic arts 102, 103
fashion and/as art 39 n, 50, 51, 107, 108
fine arts 5, 8, 23, 29, 48, 50, 51, 53, 55, 57, 61, 65, 66, 67, 91, 112, 116
forms of art 31, 107, 108
martial arts 105
performing arts 55
philosophy of art 56
popular arts 53
visual arts 48, 107, 108

beauty 5, 25, 31, 37, 48, 68, 69, 70, 101, 102, 105 n, 114, 132, 137, 138, 139, 140, 141, 144, 145, 146, 147, 148
beautiful, the 19, 68, 137, 138, 139, 144, 168, 180
experience of beauty see "experience"
body 5, 7, 21, 22, 33, 34, 35, 39 n, 62, 63, 76, 78, 80, 82, 85, 86, 87 n, 88 n, 92, 93, 94, 95, 96, 98, 99, 100, 101, 102, 103, 104, 120, 121, 124, 127, 131, 132, 134, 138, 140, 141, 142, 145, 146, 147, 148, 154, 156, 160

caprice 137, 141, 142, 143, 144
catastrophe 120, 134 n, 135 n
catastrophic points 6, 120, 121, 125
comparison 6, 54, 59, 60, 66, 102, 107, 112, 113, 114
conformism 29, 36, 62, 64, 66, 86, 96
conformity 40 n, 96, 103, 186, 188 n
contextualisation 6, 53, 107, 112, 113, 114
contingency 8, 154, 155, 175, 176, 179, 180, 181, 182, 183, 184, 185, 186, 187
contingent conditions 28
contingent contents 155
contingent criterion 184
contingent orientation 184
contingent practice 186
contingent reference 181, 182
contingent selection 185
contingent state 180
contingent tools 184
critic, the 2, 48, 107, 109, 110, 111, 112, 114, 115, 116, 144
criticism 6, 25, 37, 107, 109, 110, 111, 112, 113, 114, 115, 116, 168, 169, 170
art criticism 22, 26, 107, 111, 113, 115
fashion criticism 6, 8, 107, 108, 109, 110, 111, 112, 115, 116, 117
independent criticism 116
literary criticism 32
negative criticism 6, 107, 109, 110
critique 7, 18, 41 n, 59, 102, 107, 111, 112, 113, 157, 169
critical approach 12
critical attitude 26
critical comment 39 n
critical comparison 59, 60
critical debate 134
critical discussion 91
critical explanation 4
critical observation 25
critical practice 115

critical review 111
critical scrutiny 114
critical stance 26, 64
critical standard 113
critical study 101
critical tools 116
critical treatment 113
critical vocabulary 112
critical writing 111
culture 4, 5, 8, 23, 25, 26, 30, 37, 40 n, 62, 73, 95, 99, 116, 137, 154, 155, 168, 169, 171 n
cultural activity 35
cultural analysis 102
cultural content 53, 55
cultural context 144
cultural development 66
cultural form 1, 13
cultural industry 36
cultural movement 8
cultural perspective 53
cultural practice 59, 138
cultural problem 48
cultural process 143
cultural product 23, 98
cultural question 47
cultural scene 52
cultural semantics 138, 142
cultural situation 51
cultural sphere 2
cultural studies 2, 3, 111
cultural system 5
cultural values 42 n, 101
cultural world 34, 98
global culture 52
pop culture 52, 53, 65
subculture 95, 97, 103
youth culture 97

description 6, 32, 77, 78, 82, 107, 112, 113, 114, 178
differentiation 12, 13, 14, 15, 20, 28, 29, 30, 36, 37, 64, 66, 98, 146, 176
diffusion 8, 13, 24, 31, 50, 56, 64, 112, 120, 176
dissemination 14, 51, 66, 176.
distinction 6, 14, 20, 23, 24, 27, 30, 36, 37, 42 n, 54, 58, 74, 75, 94, 96, 97, 103, 117, 126
ephemeral, the 5, 52, 65, 66, 68, 70, 134, 185
euphoria 151, 155, 165, 166, 167
evaluation 6, 24, 107, 109, 113, 114, 180
evolution 7, 11, 65, 66, 88 n, 91, 97, 122, 124, 141, 143, 144, 145, 176, 181
evolutionary biology 138, 140, 142, 144, 148
evolutionary break 146
evolutionary laws 23
evolutionary process 144
evolutionary race 143
evolutionary reasoning 147
evolutionary scale 146
evolutionary theory 7, 65, 66, 147
evolutionism 65, 68
exemplarity, exemplariness 6, 164, 165
experience 3, 5, 16, 20, 21, 28, 29, 30, 33, 34, 39 n, 41 n, 50, 56, 59, 61, 66, 69, 70, 75, 79, 91, 94, 99, 101, 102, 103, 104, 155, 160, 162, 165, 166, 167, 170, 176, 179, 184
aesthetic experience see "aesthetics"
experience of beauty 5, 68, 69
experience of clothing 3, 21, 22
experience of fashion 156

fashion *passim*
concept of fashion 12, 14, 15, 25, 27, 32, 68
cycles of fashion 76, 79, 179
empire of fashion 29, 37
enigma of fashion 62
essence of fashion 12, 31, 32, 37, 40 n, 78
experience of fashion see "experience"
fashion commentary 40 n
fashion company 92, 93, 94, 100
fashion designer 7, 19, 91, 99, 108
fashion economy 42 n
fashion event 50
fashion for fashion's sake 7, 8, 151, 153, 154, 155, 164, 167, 170
fashion industry 5, 75, 92, 97, 115, 156
fashion model 92
fashion phenomenon 7, 12, 14, 15, 23, 30, 36, 37, 39 n, 48, 53, 78, 165, 169
fashion/philosophy relationship 2, 3, 8, 16, 39 n
fashion practice 14, 56, 186

fashion reportage 6
fashion show 7, 8, 92, 157.
fashion studies 1, 2, 3, 4, 15, 18, 33
fashion system 134
fashion theory 1, 2, 4, 6, 12, 16, 32, 38 n, 48, 107, 111, 112.
fast fashion 7
field of fashion 58, 65, 104
nature of fashion 12, 15, 29, 40 n, 64, 97, 185
philosophy of Fashion see "philosophy"
power of fashion 62, 164, 170
rules of fashion 81
street fashion 7, 157, 159, 163
world of fashion 7, 12, 26, 39 n, 75, 107, 119
fit model 6, 92, 93, 94, 95, 96, 100, 105 n
fitting In 96
form of life 5, 59, 60

global civilization, culture, attitude 47, 52, 178
grotesque 131, 137, 140, 141, 148, 148 n

identity 5, 6, 8, 39 n, 60, 62, 65, 66, 69, 92, 95, 96, 97, 98, 100, 115, 120, 130, 155, 156, 163, 164, 182
imitation 7, 8, 11, 12, 13, 14, 19, 20, 23, 24, 25, 26, 27, 28, 29, 30, 31, 32, 36, 37, 40 n, 58, 68, 78, 79, 87 n, 97, 163, 180, 182, 184
drive to imitation 20, 35, 66
imitative activity 26
imitative features 51
imitative impulse 20, 26, 28, 78, 79
imitative pathology 79
imitative practice 14
imitative process 26
imitative relationship 13
individual, the 13, 24, 26, 27, 29, 47, 61, 63, 66, 96, 102, 163, 164, 171 n, 179, 182, 184
individualism 36, 64, 66, 96, 163
individuality 8, 24, 26, 36, 69, 96, 175
individualization 12, 20, 32
interpretation 2, 3, 4, 6, 7, 21, 24, 32, 33, 38, 39 n, 40 n, 55, 60, 81, 107, 113, 114, 117, 124, 134, 138, 140, 163, 176
interpretive act 55
interpretive approach 12
interpretive categories 62
interpretive framework 9 n, 53
interpretive lines 9 n
interpretive paradigm 26, 28

jeans 5, 80, 81, 86, 95, 98, 165, 167, 168, 186

modernity, modern age 1, 8, 15, 23, 24, 40 n, 62, 74, 76, 95, 154, 167, 168, 175, 176, 182, 184, 187 n, 188 n
modern ideals 37
modern institutions 74
modern life 16, 31, 40 n
modern self 16
modern semantics 8, 175
modern society, world 8, 24, 31, 39 n, 63, 74, 159, 175, 176, 180, 187
modern subject 52
modern theories 144

naked skin 7, 145, 146, 147, 148 n
novelty 6, 37, 97, 137, 139, 144, 160, 179, 180, 181, 185
nudity 5, 80, 81, 83, 85, 87 n, 152, 153, 160, 171 n

originality 8, 25, 26, 29, 36, 54, 62, 64, 114, 178, 179, 182, 184, 186, 188 n
ornament 7, 21, 23, 63, 137, 138, 139, 140, 141, 142, 144, 145, 146, 147, 148, 148 n

paradox 8, 65, 92, 94, 95, 96, 97, 98, 100, 133, 184, 185, 186, 187
phenomenology 21, 29
phenomenological analysis 121, 135 n
phenomenological hermeneutics 41 n
phenomenological movement 33
phenomenological philosophy 33, 41 n
phenomenologization 152, 157
philosophy 2, 3, 4, 8, 12, 13, 15, 16, 20, 22, 23, 28, 29, 30, 32, 33, 35, 38, 39 n, 48, 50, 51, 52, 56, 60, 73, 77, 78, 86 n, 87 n, 91, 101, 152, 154, 155, 168
philosophical account 4, 11, 33
philosophical analysis 2, 6
philosophical anthropology 22

philosophical approach 4, 12
philosophical attempt 32
philosophical circle 93
philosophical concept, conception 15, 21, 23, 130
philosophical content 16
philosophical debate 51
philosophical decision 184
philosophical discourse 5
philosophical enigma 62
philosophical inquiry 2, 34, 139
philosophical investigation 18, 32
philosophical paradigms 2
philosophical perspectives 1, 5, 7, 8, 29
philosophical point of view 37, 47, 184
philosophical problem 22
philosophical question 15, 16, 27, 73
philosophical reflection 4, 16, 60
philosophical research 2
philosophical study 37
philosophical survey 13
philosophical theorization, theory 14, 15, 100
philosophical thought 11
philosophical tradition 21, 144
philosophical treatment 18
philosophical understanding 151, 165
philosophical work 2, 3, 16, 18, 37
philosophical writing 95
philosophy of fashion, of dress 9 n, 12, 21, 22, 25, 32, 33, 37, 107, 116
postmodernity 2, 153
postmodern culture 170
postmodern society 156
postmodern subject 157
postmodern theories 186
postmodern thought 2
practice 4, 5, 6, 14, 20, 30, 39 n, 48, 50, 53, 56, 58, 59, 60, 61, 68, 69, 70, 80, 83, 87 n, 91, 101, 102, 103, 104, 105, 108, 113, 115, 138, 159, 164, 185, 186

seam 105 n, 121, 122, 123, 124, 125, 126, 127, 128, 131
sexual selection 7, 68, 140, 141, 142, 144, 145, 146, 147
sociology 3, 12, 23, 24, 38, 39 n, 42 n, 175, 176
somaesthetics 6, 91, 94, 100, 101, 102, 103, 104, 105, 105 n, 106 n
style 6, 7, 13, 19, 25, 26, 48, 54, 55, 58, 64, 67, 76, 82, 91, 92, 93, 95, 96, 97, 103, 105 n, 108, 144, 151, 152, 153, 154, 155, 156, 157, 159, 160, 162, 163, 164, 165, 166, 167, 169, 178, 185
suit 5, 80, 81, 85, 86, 88 n, 98, 99, 104, 114
symbol 54, 55, 62, 133
symbolic, the 133
symbolic articulation 53
symbolic content 38
symbolic dimension 28, 52, 108
symbolic function 169
symbolic level 24
symbolic role 38, 63
symbolic space 170
symbolic system 54, 58, 59, 62
symbolic transformation 168
symbolic value 37, 108
symbolism 132
synchronicity 134, 151, 152, 156, 157, 160, 167

taste 8, 19, 20, 25, 26, 28, 41 n, 48, 50, 58, 59, 60, 65, 68, 70, 95, 96, 103, 105 n, 108, 115, 137, 139, 140, 144, 145, 146, 160
articulation of taste 70
dimension of taste 51
domain of taste 47
education of taste 50
exercises of taste 59, 60, 61
fashion-taste 95, 105 n
logics of taste 51
practice of taste 56, 58, 59
preferences of taste 59, 62, 68
questions of taste 24
standard of taste 58, 61
tendencies of taste 60
transformations of taste 66
temporality 8, 160
trend 2, 58, 67, 68, 69, 97, 106, 109, 113, 116, 178, 184, 185, 186